Teaching the National ICT Strategy at Key Stage 3

A Practical Guide

Clare Furlonger
and Susan Haywood

 David Fulton Publishers

Introduction

There used to be a joke amongst teachers of ICT. It went something like this:

Q: What does the three-part lesson look like in ICT?

A: The kids log on. They get on with it. Then they log off.

It is, perhaps, understandable that ICT has come under the Qualifications and Curriculum Authority (QCA) and Department for Education and Skills (DfES) spotlight. The parody of an ICT lesson depicted above may be exaggerated, but concern about the standard of ICT in Key Stage 3 persists. Annual reports from Ofsted express ongoing concern about the standards in ICT generally, not just in Key Stage 3. In particular, Ofsted data makes unfavourable comparisons between standards in ICT and those in other subjects in primary education (Ofsted, 2002; main findings).

The most recent primary report states:

> The quality of teaching and pupils' achievements in information and communication technology (ICT) continue to improve, but there is more unsatisfactory work in ICT than in any other subject. (Ofsted, 2003)

In secondary education, non-compliance with statutory requirements for ICT remains a problem and progress in the use of ICT is described as "slow" (Ofsted, 2002: para 130).

Times are changing. The National Strategy for ICT has now introduced a framework for teaching ICT capability for Years 7, 8 and 9. The framework is part of the broader standards and target-setting agenda which covers literacy, numeracy and science as well as ICT. In Key Stage 2, national strategies in English and mathematics are now well established. The strategy for ICT in Key Stage 3 has been preceded by those for English, mathematics and science. Strategies for the foundation subjects accompany those for ICT.

Teachers of ICT in the early years of secondary school labour under particular difficulties, partly because standards of teaching in ICT in primary schools vary greatly. As a result, the levels of attainment of pupils entering Year 7 range widely compared with some other subjects. This makes issues of continuity and progression between phases particularly problematic. An additional factor relates to the great variation in children's experience of ICT outside school, and the influence of this on their general confidence and competence. This in turn exacerbates the variation in experience and attainment that pupils bring to the classroom. It would be valuable to audit pupils' prior experience of ICT in the contexts of school and home, as well as noting which schemes they have used, if any, before beginning to teach the first unit. This would enable the tailoring of content, and grouping of pupils and teaching approaches, as well as avoidance of repetition.

The issue of equal opportunities will also need to be considered. Auditing will indicate whether or not pupils have access to ICT at home, and schools will have their own policies or provision to ensure equality of opportunity as far as possible. However, even where pupils *do* have access to computers at home, there are still some issues that will need to be discussed by the teaching team, and teaching approaches or policies agreed. Theses could include:

- the length of time taken to download images on home computers and therefore what it is reasonable to expect of pupils when using images;
- whether or not pupils can store images and other large files at home or on the school network;
- whether floppy, zip or compact disks can be brought from home and used on the school network;
- the need to teach pupils about file formats, particularly graphics formats early on in the strategy (for example, Unit 7.1 requires them to collect images from the Internet).

Another difficulty is that the shortage of specialist teachers of ICT means that in Key Stage 3 the teaching of ICT often falls to non-specialists, who, apart from teaching their specialist curriculum area, also have to deal with the demands of ICT, a challenging and fast-changing subject. There is another complicating factor: ICT does not have its own natural context. In order to use the tools of ICT, the learner must have some content or a context to work with, and this is best drawn from other subjects across the curriculum. Using ICT effectively will certainly require knowledge, skills and understanding from other disciplines, such as:

- design skills and creativity for graphics, desktop publishing and presentation;
- mathematical knowledge and understanding for spreadsheets and data handling;
- scientific and technological understanding underpinning control systems, datalogging and remote sensing.

This is a significant challenge for teachers as well as for pupils.

Against this background, the introduction of materials to support ICT in Key Stage 3 will be welcomed by teachers in that phase. The framework and sample teaching units represent a huge body of resources, which exemplify the knowledge, skills and understanding that pupils should be developing. This is a very useful first stage in formulating approaches to the teaching of ICT in Key Stage 3. It is to be hoped that teachers follow the advice given in the guidance and make the materials their own, adapting them to their own situation and matching them to the needs of their own pupils. These professional judgements are important. The most creative teaching comes about when teachers, and teams of teachers share ideas and adapt materials for their own local circumstances.

About this book

This book is a practical guide to teaching the National Strategy for ICT at Key Stage 3. It is intended to support teachers beginning to implement the strategy and those seeking to develop the work beyond the initial implementation. It will also be of use to trainees and newly qualified teachers of ICT, as well as those non-specialists who may move into teaching some ICT in this phase.

It is a book that teachers are likely to "dip into", referring to the appropriate sections as they plan, review and develop their teaching of the units. At time of writing, the units for Years 7 and 8 have been published in detail, with Year 9 materials provided in a less detailed "case study" format. For each unit, the analysis and discussion consists of:

Learning objectives: a table showing the Key Stage 3 strategy framework objectives and National Curriculum references relating to the unit.

About this unit: a general description of the content of the unit.

Lesson by lesson: a more detailed examination of the unit's content.

Alternative approaches: a commentary on the unit and suggestions for other ways of tackling some of its content.

Each unit begins with a table showing the relevant learning of the unit, for example:

KS3 STRATEGY FRAMEWORK OBJECTIVES

Exchanging and sharing information

Fitness for purpose

- Use given criteria to evaluate the effectiveness of own and others' publications and presentations.

Refining and presenting information

- Plan and design the presentation of information in digital media, taking account of the purpose of the presentation and intended audience.
- Use ICT . . .

This is followed by a section entitled "About this unit", which provides a description drawing out the main aspects of the unit. The knowledge, skills and understanding required by pupils before beginning the unit are outlined, as well as the learning that will be developed. The subject knowledge needed by teachers is also identified, and organisational approaches are discussed.

A second table gives a breakdown of the suggested time allocations within each lesson, showing the balance between whole class teaching, pupil work (generally in pairs or groups) away from the computer, and pupil work at the computer. The bottom rows of the table give the overall timings and balance of time divisions in percentages. A typical table is shown below:

	Taught as a whole class	*Pupil work away from the computer*	*Pupil work at the computer*
Lesson 1	40 mins	20 mins	
Lesson 2	33 mins	5 mins	22 mins
Lesson 3	23 mins	2 mins	35 mins
Overall balance	**1 hr 36 mins** 53%	**27 mins** 15%	**57 mins** 32%

These time allocations are for guidance only and teachers are free to alter them, but nevertheless they give a good indication of the balance of teaching approaches suggested in the unit. Where appropriate, reference is made to units of work in the QCA Scheme of Work which relate to the ICT strategy being discussed.

This introduction is followed by "Lesson by lesson", a detailed look at the unit's content. Here the style of the book changes. The lesson summaries are accompanied by a commentary on the lesson content, presented in the form of "callouts" shown in tinted boxes alongside the appropriate paragraphs. The commentaries focus on various aspects of the lesson, including tasks and activities, presentation, timing, contexts and organisation. Comments that are brief and comprehensive are covered in the callout alongside the lesson discussion, but in some cases the issue is complex, and needs a fuller discussion. In these instances the comment in the callout is followed by a page reference to the concluding "Alternative approaches" or "Lesson commentaries" section, where the issues are considered further. An example of this format is shown below:

". . . In Lesson 7 pupils continue developing their web pages. In the lesson preparation section on the lesson notes it is suggested that sound files are copied into appropriate folders so that pupils can access them . . ."

This is the first mention of using sound files in the unit and you will have to decide whether or not to provide sound files or encourage pupils to develop their own. This is discussed on page 85. [7a]

In "Alternative approaches", as well as consideration of specific points arising from the lessons, there is also a general discussion of the unit and the broader issues that it raises. Here you will find suggestions for alternative contexts, cross-curricular links and changes that could be made to the activities in the unit as a whole.

How to use this book

Above all, this book sets out to be a practical guide for interpreting the ICT framework. The writers have looked at the framework in detail and have tried to summarise the information it contains in order to assist you in its implementation. Recently, the phrase "Reach and Teach" has come to describe materials intended to support teachers and cut down on the planning and preparation needed for effective classroom teaching. The ICT strategy is definitely *not* "Reach and Teach". Many of the units require extensive planning and preparation, from research to downloading and printing. This book is intended to offer support in making clear the preparation, development of subject knowledge and whole-school policy approaches that might be necessary in order to teach the units successfully. As you come to teach a unit, it is hoped that the analysis, description and alternative ideas suggested will help in this planning and preparation. One aspect that must not be overlooked is the time needed to download, print and prepare lesson notes, and teacher and pupil resources. In some units this is a substantial and time-consuming task. At the time of writing, some downloaded files have minor errors in filenames or printouts, so these should be checked carefully in advance.

Ideally, all the materials should be discussed by the teaching team, so that a common view of them and the way they will be used can be agreed. There are a number of aspects that need to be considered. For example, the team will need to agree where electronic resources will be stored on the network and where pupils' work will be saved. The filenames used for resources in the units, such as "8.1TFDa" or "Pupils Resource 5.xls", and the headings printed on paper resources are often cryptic and unhelpful. As a teaching team you could agree filenames that are meaningful for you, and rename files or change headings on resources accordingly. The work of downloading and photocopying materials, preparing wall displays of key vocabulary, and modifying or producing pupil resource materials can be shared by members of the team, or support staff where appropriate. The management and use of these resources will need to be agreed by the team.

Differentiation

One of the key issues which will need to be considered is that of differentiation. Some units include more challenging extension activities for high-achieving pupils, although generally there are no separate materials to support their independent work and these may have to be created by teachers themselves. Pupils working below usual expectations are not catered for so well. There are simplified resources in some units, but teachers will need to plan carefully and adapt the materials for such pupils, adopting a range of differentiation strategies.

Subject knowledge, generic knowledge and skills

At the beginning of each unit is a summary of the knowledge, skills and understanding required by pupils as they begin the unit and those it is intended to develop. The issue of subject knowledge in ICT teaching is a difficult one, and in recent years tension has emerged between stressing the subject knowledge involved in ICT and the alternative emphasis on the importance of ICT as a tool for learning. There is an additional question about what characterises "ICT subject knowledge". It is the belief of the authors of this book that ICT is both a subject and a tool for learning. Attempts to represent ICT either as an objective body of knowledge or merely as a tool diminish the role of this powerful technology to support learning. If ICT is seen exclusively or largely as a body of subject knowledge to be acquired, then its power as a medium to support learning is undervalued. If ICT is viewed as a tool, it is important that this is not trivialised, but that the full richness of the medium is recognised and understood by pupils.

To use ICT effectively, the learner needs knowledge and understanding as well as techniques. Knowing the techniques alone – which buttons to press – will not ensure the understanding and creativity to use ICT for problem-solving, to analyse, hypothesise and model, to communicate and present information effectively, to research, express ideas and so on. Ofsted has expressed similar concern about the current approach to the teaching of ICT in secondary schools:

> Although pace is a key factor in successful teaching, there are occasions when pupils are rushed through new work in particular applications. They follow instructions closely, often using work sheets, and achieve the desired end, but without a clear understanding of the underlying concepts. (Ofsted, 2003b: 3)

It is important that young learners have a sufficient grasp of ICT subject knowledge to use the medium effectively. They need to be able to apply the techniques they have learned to existing and new problems, flexibly, creatively and with understanding. This is vital if they are to become independent users of ICT, an outcome which is, perhaps, not well served by teacher-led and teacher-produced content. This runs the risk of not allowing pupils to have sufficient ownership of the context and therefore hindering their development into independent learners.

It is also important that pupils are not required to learn subject knowledge that is irrelevant to their needs, and that does not contribute to their ICT capability. There are some instances in the strategy of pupils being taught subject knowledge which, it could be argued, is not necessary and of having useful techniques demonstrated but not proceeding to use them. Genuine capability in ICT demands knowledge and skills. It also demands positive attitudes such as confidence and resourcefulness, the ability to take risks, to transfer learning and skills to new situations and challenges. Pupils will only develop these capacities if they have opportunities to use new techniques, to explore and experiment, and apply their learning to a variety of contexts both in ICT lessons and across the curriculum. This is a challenge facing teachers of ICT in Key Stage 3, as well as in all other phases.

Research into the use of ICT as a medium for learning increasingly focuses on the complexity and richness of the relationship between the learner (or learners) and the medium and the way in which their interaction supports learning. The Bibliography at the end of this book provides references for some recent research and writing on ICT and learning.

Terminology: graphs or charts

Sometimes, in the framework, different terms are used interchangeably to apply to the same notion. For example, the expressions "lower-attaining", "less confident" and "lower-achieving" are all used to describe pupils who are working at a level below the majority of the class.

In the lesson notes the terms "graph" and "chart" are also used interchangeably. This may be accurate and acceptable, but using both terms, without clarification, may cause confusion for pupils. In this book, the term "chart" is used throughout, as this is the term employed in the software used in the resources.

Lesson timing and classroom organisation

Generally, the units are organised so that teaching takes place as a whole class, in pairs or groups of four. Again, this is something that will need careful consideration. When pupils work in pairs and small groups on practical tasks it will be important to ensure that individuals have an opportunity to develop the techniques they need. There may not always be sufficient time for this development. It will be clear from the discussion of individual units that the authors have reservations about a number of suggested time allocations in the lesson plans. Where this is the case, details are given in the discussion of the unit. In general, the authors feel that insufficient time is given for practical activity throughout the units. The focus on active, well-paced teaching is to be welcomed, as this has not always been such a strong feature of teaching in ICT. However, there needs to be a balance between teaching and practical activity, exploration and experimentation by pupils. This is an aspect of the units that teachers may need to rethink. It is possible to extend the units with some additional lessons, and perhaps this time could be used to provide greater opportunity for practical work.

The way forward

The ICT strategy for Key Stage 3 will be reviewed and refined both by its authors and, more importantly, by the teachers who put it into practice in their classrooms. This book is intended to contribute to that ongoing process of reflection and evaluation that will bring about the future development of the ICT curriculum in this crucial stage of education.

Year 7 units

7.1 Using ICT In this unit of six lessons pupils design and create a presentation about themselves for their peers, incorporating a series of design elements. They adapt their presentation for an adult audience – the head of year.

7.2 Using data and information sources In the three lessons of this unit pupils search for, select and evaluate information. They access information on the Internet, identify its purpose and use it to answer specific questions. Questions to do with the reliability and accuracy of information are considered.

7.3 Making a leaflet In this unit of six lessons pupils plan and create a leaflet, taking account of a range of design considerations. The publication is about the subjects the pupils study at Key Stage 3, and they create it for an audience of Year 6 pupils.

7.4 Introduction to modelling and presenting numeric data In this unit of five lessons pupils use a spreadsheet as a modelling tool. They work with or extend spreadsheet models from different contexts, extending the models by creating formulae, adding variables, increasing the functionality of the spreadsheets, and using them to answer specific questions.

7.5 Data handling In this unit of six lessons pupils interrogate existing data and examine its source. They look at how to collect appropriate data through effective questionnaire design and consider how data can be displayed in charts. They also create a data structure, enter data, check it for errors and then interrogate it, drawing conclusions from their findings.

7.6 Controlling and monitoring This unit of five lessons develops knowledge and understanding of control and monitoring in everyday life. Pupils are introduced to flowchart conventions and use control software to create programs which use one or more variables. They are introduced to subroutines in control programs.

7.1 Using ICT

KS3 STRATEGY FRAMEWORK OBJECTIVES

Exchanging and sharing information

Fitness for purpose

- Use given criteria to evaluate the effectiveness of own and others' publications and presentations.

Refining and presenting information

- Plan and design the presentation of information in digital media, taking account of the purpose of the presentation and intended audience.
- Use ICT to draft and refine a presentation, including:
  – capturing still and moving images and sound (e.g., using a scanner, digital camera, microphone)
  – reorganising, developing and combining information, including text, images and sound
  – using the simple editing functions of common applications

About this unit

This unit teaches pupils to design and create a presentation for a specified audience of their peers on the subject of themselves. They consider the content and appearance of the presentation in terms of font styles, colours, animation, images and sounds, and some may record a sound commentary to accompany their presentation. The process of designing and creating a good presentation is modelled by the teacher through the use of Pat's Poor Presentation, a piece of work created by a fictitious Year 7 pupil which contains a range of poor-quality features. Each of the first four lessons in the unit considers a different component of the presentation – content, images, colour and fonts, and sound. In each, pupils critically consider the component in question and identify elements of good practice. They also have the opportunity to implement their new skills and understanding in their own individual presentations.

Pupils are given small inputs of specific subject knowledge about image types practical skills inputs relating to the use of:

- the outline function in a presentations package;
- the master slide in a presentations package;
- capturing images using a digital camera and scanner;
- simple editing of images using common tools;
- inserting images into their presentation.

Design-related skills and knowledge includes:

- the organisation of content;
- identification of suitable images;
- linking images with both design elements and text;
- organisation of different types of information in a slide;
- enhancing a presentation using appropriate sound.

The strategy advises that this introductory unit be taught first because it will develop pupils'

ICT capability and build on existing skills, knowledge and understanding in the subject. There is further comment on this point in Alternative approaches on page 15.

As in most later units, 7.1 involves a range of resources that require some thought and preparation before the lesson. It may be worth pulling together the resource requirements on a lesson by lesson basis in your advanced medium-term planning to ensure that all resources are available for all pupils. For example, in Lesson 3 the use of digital cameras and scanners will require a rota, and before Lesson 4 the teacher needs to check that the computer sound is functioning correctly.

A list of subject knowledge required by teachers is given at the start of the unit. It consists of a range of techniques and some generic design skills. These will be very familiar to teachers from any design-based subject, although they need to take account of the distinct nature of an electronic medium. While the subject knowledge requirements listed are accurate, they underestimate the need for prior experience and understanding in the area of sound and image manipulation. These are both suggested as areas to extend higher attainers, but the teacher would need to be confident of their own skills and understanding before they are able to accommodate this learning. This is explored further in the Alternative approaches.

The pupils work on this unit in pairs, although it is suggested that they each produce a presentation. If the recommended timings are followed, each partner will have only half an hour for development of their presentation. This will need careful organisation, depending on local circumstances, and some further suggestions are made in the Alternative approaches on page 16. It is expected that pupils will generally work at Levels 4 and 5, although more challenging tasks can be provided for high attainers.

It is anticipated that the unit will take six hour-long lessons. The suggested lesson time breaks down into an approximate ratio of three hours teacher-led exposition, discussion and demonstration; one hour paper- or discussion-based pupil activity; and two hours practical computer-based activity.

	Taught as a whole class	*Pupil work away from the computer*	*Pupil work at the computer*
Lesson 1	45 mins		15 mins
Lesson 2	30 mins	10 mins	20 mins
Lesson 3	20 mins	15 mins	25 mins
Lesson 4	30 mins	10 mins	20 mins
Lesson 5	30 mins	10 mins	20 mins
Lesson 6	20 mins	20 mins	20 mins
Overall balance	**2 hrs 55 mins** 49%	**1 hr 5 mins** 18%	**2 hrs** 33%

LESSON BY LESSON

Lesson 1: Selecting and organising content for a presentation

This lesson looks at the content of the slides as opposed to the overall design.

Starter: Identifying key content in a presentation

Pupils are introduced to a character called Pat through a demonstration of her personal presentation. They are asked to think about what the presentation tells them about Pat, and how they are still left wondering after the presentation.

Development: Considering the information in a presentation; and how the information should be organised in an initial design

Pupils discuss what the presentation said and didn't say about Pat, whether it was well sequenced and structured and whether the grammar and spelling were correct. They are asked how the presentation could be improved.

Pupils are told that by the end of the unit they will be able to produce an effective presentation, taking into account both content and design. There will be opportunities to learn the necessary software techniques during the unit.

> Is this so? There is very little practical independent hands-on time in which to master software techniques.

The pupils work in pairs to create their own individual presentation of six slides to introduce themselves to the rest of the class. The class is the audience and the purpose is to tell the class about themselves.

> There are no suggestions as to how to keep "non-working" partners occupied. "Myself" is a popular primary school topic, so you may wish to substitute an alternative. This is discussed further in Lesson commentaries on page 16. [1a]

Pupils are shown the outline mode, and using pupils' suggestions the teacher demonstrates entering headings, adding subheadings and promoting/demoting ideas. The file, containing a range of ideas for inclusion, is saved for pupil use.

> Many may have used the software to quite sophisticated levels. Check this, as you may consider allowing some pupils to use their preferred methods and develop their own ideas for content.

In creating their initial design, pupils decide how to group and organise their content and add their own ideas.

> The sequence of information is an important consideration here, although you may decide that when designing presentation slides, this is influenced by the size and quantity of text. This is discussed in Lesson 3. You could decide to consider them together.

Plenary and homework: Reviewing match of content to audience

Selected pupils show their ideas on the large screen, and the class evaluates the content, thinking about audience and purpose. For homework, pupils are asked to choose and collect photos and images from magazines and the Internet to enhance their presentation.

> You would need to think about how to organise this. If pupils are to collect images from the Internet, how will they store them for use when developing their presentation in school? A floppy disk would probably have insufficient capacity and may constitute a security risk for the school network.

Lesson 2: Selecting and using appropriate images

This lesson is about combining text and images, using the simple editing functions of common applications.

Starter: Images for a purpose

Pupils are divided into groups, each with a card showing two images based on the same subject but in a different style. For example, one image may be a less formal, cartoon depiction and the other may be a "real life" photograph. Pupils are asked to consider the images as a response to a question on the card. Feedback is via one group representative.

Development: Choosing images; and adding them to a presentation

The activity cards are displayed and pupils are asked for feedback leading to further discussion about the most appropriate image for a given situation. Pupils are to decide which images they are going to use, whether from a digital camera, scanned images or clip art. They are reminded to consider the relationship between the text and image and the purpose of the presentation.

They are shown how to insert images into their presentation and the difference between bit-mapped and vector images is explained.

> It is also important to mention the importance of retaining the proportions of vector graphics when resizing them (pressing control while resizing), as well as mentioning relative file size.

Pupils now acquire their images using a scanner and digital camera if possible. A set of questions, relating to consideration of audience and purpose, with which children should be familiar, are presented. Some pupils may go further and edit their images to fit their purpose more precisely.

Plenary and homework: Which images work well and why?

Pupils view Pat's Poor Presentation, Stage 2, showing her chosen images. They work in pairs to consider her choice and are asked to record their thoughts. Feedback is invited and recorded on the whiteboard.

> You might feel this discussion of appropriate images would be more useful before pupils acquire images for their presentations.

Pupils are asked to find three images that support a piece of text and explain how this is achieved.

Lesson 3: Selecting and using appropriate fonts and colours

This lesson examines the development of the presentation by considering the impact of colour and text-formatting techniques.

Starter: Appropriateness of text and colour in a presentation

Pupils are shown Pat's Poor Presentation, focusing on her use of colour. They are asked to record three good and three bad features of her use of colour and text style/display.

Development: Using different colours and text in a presentation; using text characteristics to convey meaning; and developing the presentation through fonts and colour

The slides are shown again and pupils invited to discuss the colour choices, text size and style in detail.

> You may want to deal with the size and amount of text in Lesson 1. There is further comment about the approach to the different elements of the presentation in Lesson commentaries on page 17. [3a]

Pupils are shown a supporting presentation, which includes discussion points relating to characteristics of text, fonts and colour, and asked to develop their presentations considering these points and their audience. Some good general guidelines for differentiation are suggested in terms of focusing lower attainers on the important questions.

Plenary and homework: Evaluating the effects of fonts and colour

Pupils are asked to jot down three guidelines they could give others about using fonts and colours in a presentation. Pairs are joined into fours to discuss this and brief feedback is given from groups, with justifications. For homework, pupils are asked to annotate printouts with any changes they would make to their presentations and give the reasons why.

> It may be better for pupils to get their peers to test their presentations and take account of their responses.

Lesson 4: Selecting and using appropriate sounds

In this lesson pupils consider and explore the function of sound in their overall design.

Starter: Different uses of sound in a presentation

Pupils are asked to watch and listen to a presentation thinking about the appropriateness of the sounds linked to the various images. Their contributions are summarised and extended to show how sound can be used effectively in a presentation.

Development: Using sound to create atmosphere; developing a presentation by inserting sound files; and evaluating the outcome

Pupils are asked to think about sounds they would use to match particular scenarios and then go on to consider the kind of sounds that may be appropriate in their presentations. A variety of sound files are discussed, which may be downloaded from the Internet, integrated into the animation features of the software, saved as sound files on a shared drive, or recorded by the pupils.

Pupils enhance their presentations with sound, constantly thinking about fitness for purpose. Differentiation can be used, giving some pupils the choice of the full range including recording their own sound files, whereas others may choose from a limited range. This is intended to reduce the use of inappropriate sounds.

The pupils work in pairs to review each other's presentations with a focus on use of sound. They are given a number of prompts to help them in their considerations.

Plenary and homework: Using sound effectively in a presentation

Pupils' ideas are gathered together and a model of good practice developed to guide them in their future work. For homework, they are asked to find three contrasting advertisements (preferably from television) and write a paragraph on each, considering their purpose and the use of sound.

Lesson 5: Modifying the style of a presentation for a different audience

In this lesson pupils consider the extent to which their presentations meet a set of rules for good presentations. They then consider how they can use the rules to adapt the design of their presentations for another audience.

Starter: Rules for a "perfect presentation"

Pupils are shown a "perfect presentation" developed for adults that follows specific rules. They are shown the rules and asked to consider whether the presentation has successfully adhered to them.

> Once some pupils have completed the adaptation exercise that follows, you may decide to use one of their presentations as an example here as opposed to another artificial "Pat" presentation.

Development: Comparing the outcome with the rules; applying consistent format in presentation software before adapting the presentation style for a different audience; and evaluating the outcome

Pupils consider their own presentations using the same rules as those in the starter example. As these are designed for an adult audience, they find that their presentations, designed for a younger audience, do not match them. Pupils are invited to identify the features in their designs that would appeal specifically to a younger audience. The pupils use the same rules to change the design of their presentations to meet the needs of an adult audience – the head of year.

> It is crucial that pupils use "Save as . . ." and save a second version by giving the new file a different name before they start this adaptation. You will need to check they all understand this requirement.

They are shown how to develop a consistent style using a tool such as the master slide and are made aware of design conventions when developing presentations.

> Some may have used the master page for their initial version as their preferred tool.

Pupils work in pairs to adapt the design of their own presentations for an adult audience following the suggested guidelines. Some good general guidelines for differentiation are mentioned here.

The ten-minute time allowance is not long for two individual pupils to adapt their designs.

Pairs evaluate each other's presentation against the guidelines used to create them and then discuss how far they have adhered to those rules.

Plenary and homework: Comparing the style of presentations for different audiences

Pupils compare their presentation for peers and their presentation for adults and decide which they prefer. They then go on to consider how features from one may be transferred to enhance the other. They are asked to contribute three pieces of information about themselves that the head of year would find useful and informative, and these are collected together. For homework, pupils annotate printouts of their newly designed presentations to indicate how they would change the information to meet the needs of their head of year.

While evaluation is a key element of this unit, you may feel you wish to combine some of the review opportunities. There is further discussion about this in Lesson commentaries on page 17. [5a]

Lesson 6: Modifying the content of a presentation for a different audience

The final lesson addresses the need to consider changes to the content when adapting presentations for a new audience.

Starter: Suggesting adaptations to a presentation

Pupils are asked to discuss suggestions emerging from the Lesson 5 homework task of changing the content of their presentations to meet the needs of a familiar adult audience, the head of year.

The objectives for the unit can still be met if you feel this conversion for another audience is not constructive at this time. See Lesson commentaries on page 17 for further comment. [6a]

Development: Adjusting the presentation content for an adult audience; and evaluating presentations against criteria

Pupils feed back on their ideas, leading to whole class discussion about possible new content that may be relevant for a head of year. This might include personal areas of strength and those for development, opinions about subjects, achievement in subjects, or any family connections in the school.

Pupils edit their presentations with a focus on changing content. The teacher supports individuals and asks for justifications of their choices. Pupils present their work to each other and they are given a resource to support their reviews (Pupil Resource 6b Evaluation sheet). This

It may be worth reorganising the evaluation sheet so that content and structure are considered before design.

prompts them to think about the appropriateness of the edited presentation for an adult audience and ask questions about design and appearance. Pupils are given ground rules to ensure they play the role of "critical friend" and are reminded that all of their comments should be justified and positive suggestions made for improvement.

Plenary and homework: Extending the presentation to a wider audience; and review of learning

Pupils have created two presentations for different audiences in school. The teacher suggests that a wider audience may be interested in their presentations and asks how this could be achieved. Pupils are shown the final version of Pat's Presentation and asked to comment on its suitability for other internal audiences and whether display on an intranet or website for a wider audience would be appropriate. It is suggested that pupils will find that it is not appropriate for anyone other than Pat's peers.

For homework, pupils are asked to review their learning in the unit and make brief notes to show their understanding of the need for a clear purpose and appreciation of their audience's needs when creating a presentation.

Alternative approaches

There are many key teaching points in this unit of work that will help develop pupils' knowledge and understanding of exchanging and sharing information in terms of refining and presenting information according to a specific need, and reviewing progress and outcomes.

As mentioned in the introduction to this unit, it is advised that this unit be taught first because it will develop pupils' ICT capability and build on existing skills, knowledge and understanding. It is not made explicit why this unit achieves this more than any other Year 7 unit, as, unlike the equivalent unit in the QCA scheme of work for Key Stage 3, the lesson notes do not stress the importance of pupils becoming familiar with the use of a network system. This may be because networks are now more familiar in primary schools than they were when the QCA scheme of work was written. The context used may be seen as relevant to a new start at secondary school, and the unit addresses a wide range of fundamental communication and design skills for exchanging and sharing information, but there appears to be nothing of major significance that checks or assesses pupil ability or prior knowledge any more than other Year 7 units. It is interesting to note that if pupils have followed the Key Stage 2 QCA scheme of work for ICT, they will have created a multimedia presentation at the end of Year 6. It is vital that in the initial year of secondary education, the curriculum addresses the considerable issue of pupils' previous knowledge and experience and makes the provision of an additional, fresh challenge for all pupils a priority. This will help to underpin the primary aim of the strategy – to raise standards at Key Stage 3.

From the start, you may question the time allocations for various tasks. Pairs work together, often sharing one computer, and are expected to produce their own personal presentation. The unit allows about an hour in total for each pupil to develop their presentation, but to draft, create and refine effective, quality presentations using text, images and sound requires time for considered thought and creative experimentation. There may also be a difficulty when the contributions of the pupils in the supporting role are undervalued or ignored, and they become bored and disenchanted. Many schools see one computer per pupil as the answer to this. However, there is no doubt that carefully planned collaborative work can be positive and productive, although this approach would usually relate to a joint outcome as opposed to individual pieces. Teachers may consider allowing pupils to work collaboratively to produce joint presentations. However, the teacher must be aware of the possible complications in terms of identifying individual contributions and the difficulties associated with accuracy of assessment.

It would certainly be necessary to plan pupil pairings carefully and ensure that protocols are discussed to ensure pupils understand their differing roles. This is important, both when pupils are developing and producing their own work, and when supporting their partner. Overall, it would seem that like-ability pairings might be most successful, with both pupils needing to acquire similar skills and techniques. If this pupil grouping is chosen, it is made easier if pairs of similar ability are located adjacent to each other to enable the teacher to be positioned where help is needed most. However, the unit notes suggest that those who are familiar with the presentation software and use of the scanner and digital camera can support less experienced users. This discontinuity of pairings may be too complicated, as pupils tend to prefer to work in a secure and constant partnership for the practical elements. The other difficulty with mixed-ability pairs is that one may be exploring a complex skill requiring more practical "hands on" time, while the other needs to concentrate on basic skills. This could lead to frustration for the lower attainer. Also, at times, higher attainers need additional support to push them further, for example in the areas of sound and image manipulation. This could also complicate the mixed-ability pairing scenario as the higher attainer's needs may be met through the provision of an instruction resource to facilitate independent work. An alternative is for pupils to work in friendship groups. This will be very acceptable to the pupils, but it will not necessarily lead to constructive collaboration, although friends may be able to assist each other with ideas for appropriate content.

Lesson commentaries

[1a] The suggested context for this unit: "Myself" is a familiar topic in primary schools, and pupils may have already undertaken activities in which they developed information about themselves for a stated audience and addressed some of the design issues considered here. This should be checked. Although they may now be working for a different audience, this may not be entirely satisfactory as identifying features about oneself for a like-minded peer group (some members of which will be well known to the authors) can be seen as too close to the individual, causing some pupils to have difficulty in disassociating themselves and approaching the task in an objective manner. Alternatively, it may be that other curriculum areas are using the "Myself" context and useful cross-curricular links could be made to enrich the activities.

At this initial stage of secondary education it is essential that pupils are faced with new, motivating, interesting and greater challenges. If it is decided that the "Myself" context is not suitable, this unit could be taught through a variety of relevant contexts and the framework objectives still achieved and even extended. A topic relating to another subject, perhaps in the Humanities, could be used, with possibilities including a focus on the locality to encompass the provision of historical and geographical information. This may encourage pupils to make connections across subject disciplines. The audience could include Year 6 pupils at their old school and as a second audience, local senior citizens or elderly relatives and family friends. Alternatively, a presentation relating to a whole school issue could be attempted. Some ideas might relate to litter, recycling or to the general "Care of our School", which would be very appropriate for Year 7 pupils at this time.

The Citizenship curriculum is also worth investigating for possible realistic contexts that may catch the attention of Year 7 pupils and enable them to investigate and identify suitable content which is essential for their development as independent users of ICT.

The approach to the unit could be radically altered to show pupils a different use of presentation software and enable them to show their creativity as they learn to use ICT. Pupils could choose a "mystery" personality, such as a famous sportsman or -woman, or a writer or fictional character, and then create a "Who Am I?" presentation. It could contain linear or non-linear slides (a possible source of differentiation) and provide a series of clues which build up to finally reveal the identity of the mystery person. Although considerations of content in terms of the organisation and sequence of the pieces of information would be paramount (this would be a positive aspect), design considerations would still be important. Elements such as images, colours, fonts and sounds would develop according to the impression of the mystery person the pupil wishes to portray. Pupils would have a clearly defined audience (their peers) and purpose, which may provide a strong motivational force. The ICT skills, knowledge and understanding relating to consideration of content, design, drafting and refining of a presentation, and use of criteria for evaluation, could all be taught as suggested in the unit and demonstrated effectively in the implementation of the presentation.

[3a] The process of design, implementation and evaluation against set criteria are key areas of this unit and should be retained in any alternative. However, some may feel that they wish to develop the content initially and then take a holistic approach to the remaining design. This would include the consideration of images, colour, fonts and perhaps sound, and their relationship with the content. These elements may be seen as having such a close relationship that it is not logical to separate them into discrete entities. Thus Lessons 2 to 4 could be combined to some extent, with more time being made available for pupils to apply and experiment with the ideas they have considered. They could also work creatively on linking the content and the design. This is in no way suggesting that pupils are given their task and left unchecked to create the presentation. One of the strengths of the strategy is that it encourages more questioning, discussion and exposition than is currently found in many ICT classrooms. Question and answer sessions are key. It is essential for teachers to plan their delivery strategy to ensure contributions from the full range of pupils and to check the perceptions of those who have difficulty with understanding concepts. The materials for the Teaching and Learning in the Foundation Subjects strand are also helpful in this area.

[5a] You may also wish to consider the number of opportunities for reviews and evaluations during the unit. While the development of an understanding of the importance and the process of both peer and self review is necessary, it will be revisited on many occasions during Key Stage 3. Homework, too, should be set only as an integrated and meaningful part of the whole process and fed back into the teaching and learning. Asking pupils to "write brief notes" about a fairly complex concept with no follow-up suggests a bolt-on, set only because homework is obligatory. A more useful final homework in the unit may be to put down some initial thoughts or to research in preparation for the next unit of work.

[6a] If time is at a premium, the redevelopment of the presentation for an alternative audience is not absolutely essential in this unit, and the omission of this activity would not prevent achievement of the framework objectives. It adds considerable time to the unit (two lessons), and you may feel that pupils will have more opportunity to develop their skills and understanding of presentation design if implementation is limited to one audience. You could then consider the requirements of a different audience through discussion, in order to check pupil awareness of alternative needs.

There is a need for one last word about teaching the techniques relating to presentation software. As already mentioned, the criteria for effective presentations are a key element in this unit, and ICT teachers must be confident and familiar with them. The use of specific views of PowerPoint, such as the outline mode, is not essential for a successful outcome to this unit and many less experienced teachers may feel more comfortable teaching their preferred method of slide development. This may be use of the outline mode, direct text input onto the slide or organising and designing text hierarchy and appearance in advance, using the Master page. Any of these are appropriate views to use. It is useful to explain to pupils that there are a range of features in PowerPoint to facilitate development of presentations, and they should experiment to find their preferred approach.

7.2 Using data and information sources

KS3 STRATEGY FRAMEWORK OBJECTIVES

Finding things out

Using data and information sources

- Understand that different forms of information – text, graphics, sound, numeric data and symbols – can be combined to create meaning and impact.
- Identify the purpose of an information source (e.g. to present facts or opinions, to advertise, publicise or entertain) and whether it is likely to be biased.
- Identify what information is relevant to a task.
- Understand how someone using an information source could be misled by missing or inaccurate information.

Searching and selecting

- Search a variety of sources for information relevant to a task (e.g. using indexes, search techniques, navigational structures and engines).
- Narrow down a search to achieve more relevant results.
- Assess the value of information from various sources to a particular task.
- Acknowledge sources of information used.

About this unit

This is a unit of three lessons in which pupils search for, select and evaluate information. They access information on the Internet, identifying its purpose and using it to answer specific questions set in the lessons. They begin by identifying sources of information and then go on to match information retrieval tasks to different purposes. Issues associated with surveys, such as sample size, and questionnaire design are explored, and in the final two lessons pupils use the Internet to answer specific questions. Questions to do with the reliability and accuracy of information are covered in the final lesson.

In order to complete the unit, pupils will need to be able to access a website, use a search engine and narrow down a search, although they are guided through this latter task by the teacher rather than working independently. Generic skills involve identifying correct information on a website. They will need knowledge of website address identifiers (.org, .com and so on) and to be able to make judgements about the quality and reliability of information contained in websites and other sources of information. These skills are similar to those taught in Unit 8.3.

Throughout the unit, pupils work either as whole class or in pairs. Of the three hours over which the unit is taught, the balance between the different aspects of the lessons is as follows:

	Taught as a whole class	*Pupil work away from the computer*	*Pupil work at the computer*
Lesson 1	40 mins	20 mins	
Lesson 2	33 mins	5 mins	22 mins
Lesson 3	23 mins	2 mins	35 mins
Overall balance	**1 hr 36 mins** 53%	**27 mins** 15%	**57 mins** 32%

The unit is aimed at pupils working at Levels 4 and 5, and the activities in the unit are generally appropriate for its content and level. However, the pupils may find some aspects of the module rather frustrating, as there is little consistency in the topics they are asked to research, and the information is not put to any use, except that of answering the specific question set. Some of the tasks could be refocused on a topic of interest to the pupils, a local issue, or a theme which can be revisited throughout.

The skills required by teachers in this unit are routine: the ability to make a relatively straightforward search using Google. When doing so, you are asked to narrow down the search, and though the lesson plan does not refer to using the advanced search option in Google, this is probably the most obvious means. In Lesson 2 it is suggested that you compare the results in a clustering search engine such as Vivisimo with those obtained in Google, which is a listing search engine. This is an interesting comparison, and it is important at this stage for pupils to learn to use a search engine efficiently. They need to find the search engine with which they are most comfortable and which therefore "works for them", as well as to compare different engines. In addition, it would be a mistake to imply that there are only two types of search engine as there are in fact several different approaches, and this is revisited in Unit 8.3.

LESSON BY LESSON

Lesson 1: Matching information to purpose

This lesson asks pupils to reflect on their previous experiences of finding information and engages them in a consideration of the sources and purposes of information. For example, a task comparing reports of an international cricket match between Australia and England would use information to discuss and present arguments from different viewpoints, while to produce a holiday brochure for a seaside town information would be used to persuade.

Starter: Identifying purposes of information

In the starter, pupils discuss their previous experience of finding information and relate it to their immediate surroundings and to their interests. The starter includes a matching task, relating to aims and the purposes of information.

The first task is a demanding exercise. This is discussed further in Lesson commentaries on page 23. [1a]

Development: Sample size and composition; choosing a sample; and phrasing questions

The lesson now goes on to a task which focuses on sample size and composition, and pupils consider survey information. This activity raises a number of important issues in an attractive way. Sample size, accuracy and validity are all addressed. The lesson then continues with a sequence of activities which require pupils to focus carefully on these issues. These are challenging but well-thought-out activities. "Choosing a sample" provides an opportunity for further consideration of some of the difficulties involved in surveys and questionnaires. The next part of the lesson, "Phrasing questions", goes on to consider the importance of refining questions so that they result in useful and reliable information.

Plenary and homework: Ensuring that all questions are answered

In the plenary, pupils decide which questions can be answered from the data they have, and identify any omissions.

The homework is a simple exercise in providing and structuring information.

The pupils do not use the computers at all during this lesson. You may want to include a practical, "hands-on" activity or move one of the activities from Lesson 2 into this lesson.

Lesson 2: Selecting sources and finding relevant information

Starter: Identifying relevant information

Lesson 2 begins with a discussion of the homework from the previous lesson and a paired activity to identify the information needed to complete a particular task. For example, pupils have to decide what information may be required to help the school canteen match the most popular meal choices to the menu for next week.

Development: Searching and selecting; and narrowing down a search

Pupils then move on to discuss information on the Internet, their use of it in primary school or at home, and the features that make a website attractive and useful.

You may find that it is difficult for the pupils to articulate this, especially if they do not have regular access to the Internet and are having to think back to their use of it in primary school. An alternative approach is suggested on page 24. **[2a]**

They then go on to look at the weather forecast for the day on the BBC website, and information about the Harry Potter books from the Amazon website. A few minutes are allowed for a discussion about the contrast between finding information in a book compared with a website. The idea of using a search engine to narrow down a search is then introduced, and the teacher demonstrates the use of quotation marks around a phrase to refine a search, looking for information about the Tower of London.

You might want to choose a local historic site, amenity or leisure facility to demonstrate this.

The latter part of the lesson involves the pupils in searching for information to answer three specific questions. They use Google to make these searches. Initially the teacher talks them through a search for the date of the last total eclipse of the moon in England by searching for moon, then adding England and then total eclipse. If they are using Google's simple search option to do this, they will need to be introduced to the notion of Boolean operators (in this case the + sign or AND). Some pupils may already be familiar with the advanced search option, which allows them to enter keywords into different fields such as "must contain" and "must not contain". Some pupils may find this easier than using Boolean operators, and this is the way that most users search for more specific information. This is revisited in Unit 8.3.

Working independently, pupils now complete two further searches, to find out whether dogs can be taken on the Bluebell Railway line in Sussex, and who won the marathon race in the Sydney Olympic Games. This latter task might cause some indignant questions in the class about the assumption that there was only one winner! In fact, the men's race was won by Abera of Ethiopia and the women's by Takahashi, the first Japanese woman ever to win an Olympic track or field event.

To make this exercise more relevant, you could consider asking questions that are more meaningful for the pupils, or something linked to the local event or amenity used for the first search.

Plenary and homework: Summary of learning

In the plenary, the teacher demonstrates the same search using Vivisimo, the clustering search engine. The homework asks pupils to list at least ten criteria they might use to decide on a holiday destination, based on the interests and needs of all the members of the family.

This task may be difficult for pupils, and it is discussed further in Lesson commentaries on page 24. **[2b]**

Lesson 3: Assessing the reliability of information

The final lesson of the sequence focuses on the accuracy and reliability of information.

Starter: Recognising that not all information is accurate

The starter is based on a Panorama "spaghetti harvest" story broadcast on 1 April 1957. You could also look out for local "April fool" spoofs published in your local press and use this material as an alternative.

Development: Recognising that missing or inaccurate information can succeed; and comparing information sources

The lesson continues with a whole class discussion and paired activity looking at a news story about a council planning meeting. The task involves looking at partial or incomplete accounts of the meeting, to illustrate how incomplete information can distort the accuracy of an account. This is intended to develop pupils' understanding of the need to recognise whether information is complete or incomplete.

> This is a useful activity, but you could think about lifting it into a more local context, to make it more "real". Some alternative approaches are suggested on page 24. **[3a]**

This activity is followed by a task which shows how easily electronic information can be deleted or amended so as to change its meaning. Pupils make minor changes to a piece of text to turn a description of Tyrannosaurus Rex into one of a dinosaur cartoon character.

Pupils then go on to compare information on a "reliable" website with some which they are told has come from a book. It does not add to the understanding developed in the previous activities, and may create the overall impression that websites are generally more reliable sources of information than books.

The second half of the lesson goes on to compare information from different sources in order to make judgements about its reliability. Pupils look again at information about the Tower of London, focusing on the URL identifier to make a judgement about the reliability of the site.

> The lesson plan seems to suggest that official equals reliable, and unofficial may equal unreliable, and this assumption needs further consideration. This is discussed on page 24. **[3b]**

This assumption that reliable equals official is reinforced on the printed proformas which are used for the evaluation tasks. The contexts for these are the Mary Rose warship, as well as Bristol and York as tourist destinations.

Plenary and homework: Recognising that reliability of information depends on its source

The final activity of the lesson involves pupils in making judgements about the accuracy of information based on its source. They have to evaluate the reliability of statements about the weather made by:

- a local farmer, yesterday;
- my grandmother, this morning;
- television weather forecast, this morning;
- a weekly newspaper, printed five days ago.

The implication is that both its source and how recently the information was provided are important when considering reliability, but this is not made explicit in the plan. It is a new context and a rather confusing activity, unconnected to anything else in the unit.

> Perhaps this aspect could be taught by reference back to the "Council meeting activity" earlier in the lesson.

The weather forecast activity is described as the plenary session, although it introduces new knowledge rather than consolidating the content of the three lessons.

Rather than complete three evaluations earlier in the lesson, you could consider cutting one or two of these. The time saved could then be used at the end of this lesson to recap on the main ideas introduced in the unit.

For homework, pupils are asked to list five criteria they would use to judge the relevance and reliability of a website when researching information for a report on a historical topic.

Alternative approaches

The activities in this unit will help pupils develop their understanding of using data and information sources. One of the major difficulties is that there is not a consistent context for the activities. Some of the contexts seem appropriate, such as that of a survey of young people's taste in music. Others are unlikely to be interesting, such as the activity in Lesson 2 in which pupils have to find out whether a dog can be taken on the Bluebell Railway in Sussex. Searching for information should ideally be for a specific purpose which is of use or of interest to the person doing the research. This provides the best opportunity for supporting pupils' understanding of the process and allowing them to make connections between the research skills and other areas of their learning. It is a real difficulty when the task is removed from a meaningful context.

Alternative contexts could offer the prospect of greater coherence, and also allow pupils to search for information and use it for a meaningful purpose. In the unit, they search for information only to answer the questions posed in the lesson, and these are not linked to any real need or purpose. Understanding how to find and use information in a meaningful context and for a particular purpose are important, if understanding and research skills are to be developed.

The unit covers some of the same content as is included in the QCA scheme of work Year 7 unit on information and presentation. The QCA tasks include a suggestion that pupils look at a topic from different viewpoints and using different sources of information. For example, they could look at an economic or environmental issue from the perspective of the government, industry, or an environmental pressure group. This is more likely to develop an understanding and critical awareness than accepting that official sources are reliable and others may not be.

In Lesson 1 you could consider identifying some contexts in discussion with pupils. While it may be impractical to allow each pair to pursue their own topic, you could agree a few contexts for the class as a whole which are of interest and likely to support pupils' learning in other subjects. For example, a controversial issue such as genetically modified foods, youth crime, the environment, smoking or foxhunting could be used to compare sources of information and make judgements about reliability and accuracy. Links could be made with Citizenship issues, or the unit could be related to topics being covered in History or Geography, if appropriate. The advantage of doing this is that the information gathered could be used by pupils for a real purpose, such as presenting an argument, case, or point of view on an issue of importance to them. The lack of such purposeful use of information is a key shortcoming of the unit.

Lesson commentaries

When considering the tasks in detail you may like to think about the following points.

[1a] In the first task it is important that pupils realise that sometimes information is to be used for more than one purpose. Before beginning the task pupils should understand that there are no "right" or "wrong" answers, and that there may be more than one information purpose involved in the suggested tasks. In the

example given of describing the process of flower pollination, information could be used both to explain or to instruct, depending on the audience. It is suggested that in writing a pamphlet to record the events of 5 November 1605, information is used to recount or retell events, but any such historical task may also include explaining, persuading and discussing.

There is no consistent theme for the three lessons of this unit, so this first lesson might be a good opportunity to begin to identify a number of issues or topics which might provide a consistent theme throughout.

[**2a**] It is likely that pupils will need some structured questions or criteria to help them identify the features that make a website useful and attractive. The criteria included in Pupil Resource 8 could be adapted for this purpose. You may need to direct them towards thinking about aspects such as: the quantity of text, quality and relevance of images, the balance of text and images, use of colour, navigation tools, site map, search facility and so on. They will be returning to this in Unit 8.2, when they create web pages, but it is still important for them to develop the skill of evaluating websites. You could select some suitable sites from http://www.theworstoftheweb.com/ and compare these with a site such as the BBC site, or a well-designed cultural, sport or leisure site which would be of interest to them.

[**2b**] Presumably, this task is designed to help pupils think about the sort of key words they might use in an Internet search, but this is not made clear in the lesson plan or picked up at the start of Lesson 3. It may be quite difficult for them to come up with as many as ten criteria, so you may have to simplify the task and make the link with Internet search strategies explicit.

[**3a**] It would be relatively easy to move this activity into a local context, which would make it more relevant. You could use the example given but use local place names. Alternatively, you could put it in the context of your community and its needs. This could be a real issue on which there are divided views in your community, or an invented one. For example, you could suggest that:

- the local council was considering an application to turn part of some play space into much-needed additional car parking for nearby shops;
- some parents had asked for their road to be made "no entry" at one end to stop motorists using it as a "rat run" and make it safer for children.

These activities would cover the same objectives as those suggested in the lesson plan.

[**3b**] This assumption that official equals reliable, and unofficial may equate to unreliable, is repeated in Unit 8.3. Perhaps rather than make such assumptions, pupils should be encouraged to develop a critical approach to information and draw a distinction between objective fact (for example: opening hours) and opinion (for example: a great day out).

It is also important to explain to pupils that information may be misrepresented on the Internet and that unreliable information can appear to come from an "official" source. This is discussed in detail in Unit 8.3 with reference to Holocaust denial sites. Having introduced the notion in this unit, you could illustrate it by asking pupils to search for information about, for example, the Loch Ness monster, or any topic about which conspiracy theories abound, such as the NASA moon landings, the identity of Jack the Ripper, or the causes of crop circles.

7.3 Making a leaflet

KS3 STRATEGY FRAMEWORK OBJECTIVES

Finding things out

Using data and information sources

- Understanding that different forms of information – text, graphics, sound, numeric data and symbols – can be combined to create meaning and impact.

Exchanging and sharing information

Fitness for purpose

- Recognise common forms and conventions used in communications and how these address audience needs.
- Apply understanding of common forms and conventions to own and others' ICT work.
- Use given criteria to evaluate the effectiveness of own and others' publications and presentations.

Refining and presenting information

- Plan and design the presentation of information in digital media, taking account of the purpose of the presentation and the intended audience.
- Use ICT to draft and refine a presentation, including:
  - capturing still and moving images and sound;
  - reorganising, developing and combining information, including text, images and sound, using the simple editing functions of common applications;
  - importing and exporting data and information in appropriate formats.

About this unit

In this unit, pupils plan and create a leaflet for Year 6 pupils, about subjects studied at Key Stage 3. They learn about design techniques for published documents, and consider the features of good design with an emphasis on different types of graphical images. Much of this teaching and learning relates to the concept of corporate image or house style and the use of logos to represent an idea or, in this case, a school subject department. There is also some teacher input relating to the features of useful and effective images. The pupils create an A4 subject information sheet about a subject they study. They then transfer the information to a leaflet for adults, capturing their own images which are appropriate for their message and audience. At the end of the unit, pupils have the opportunity to review what they have produced using criteria they have developed.

In Unit 7.1, pupils will already have encountered design skills relating to the use of fonts, colour and images. They will also have used a scanner and digital camera to capture images and have manipulated them using basic techniques. This is reinforced at the start of this unit. Pupils are then given practical inputs relating to techniques such as creation of frames for text and images, resizing, moving, layering and rotation of objects. As in Unit 7.1, the emphasis in this unit is on generic design skills related to the use of an electronic medium.

It would seem sensible for pupils to use a desktop publishing package such as Microsoft Publisher, or an integrated package such as Textease, as opposed to using a word-processing package. Many advocates of ICT as a creative tool would claim that an authentic desktop publishing package is a superior tool for the design and implementation of a leaflet containing multiple text and graphics objects. The alternative is a word-processing package, which will not have been designed with whole page layout in mind and is often more difficult to use successfully for the production of complex publications. Appropriate use of desktop publishing skills, such as consideration of page layout, alignment, rotation and layering of objects and graphics-based text tools such as Word Art, is an important element in the development of ICT capability. They may have been encountered by many pupils in primary school or at home, but there is always the opportunity to use them in more complex or sophisticated ways.

Teachers will need to have thought carefully about the skills, knowledge and understanding linked to the various elements of this unit. They must also be clear about the process of design and implementation for a defined purpose and audience. Just as this is not an obvious process for pupils, neither is it for adults with no design background. Considerable time may need to be spent in becoming a proficient user of desktop publishing software. Although it is relatively easy to pick up the basic techniques, it takes longer to learn to apply these skills to create an effective design; this is a key factor for the success of this unit. All teachers should have experienced the process of design and implementation and have produced a complex leaflet containing a variety of types of information organised for a purpose. It is not as easy as many people think! In addition, the theory relating to the different types of graphical images, while relatively simple to learn, would probably need to be provided by a specialist in order to develop real understanding.

Exact pupil groupings are not defined in the unit documentation, so it is important to plan for use of the computers. If there is one computer per pupil, they can develop individual leaflets, but if they are sharing computers, joint publications should be considered. However, this will require careful planning of assessment, for which pupils may have to monitor their individual contributions. It could be said that collaboration often produces better-quality outcomes than those of an individual working in isolation. If two pupils share a computer to produce individual outcomes, it can be very difficult for them to work in a constructive supporting role on each other's work over long periods. If there are not enough computers for each pupil, a parallel task may be required when the pupils are creating their logos in Lesson 3, as this involves intense personal engagement and would probably not be suitable for collaborative work.

It is anticipated that the unit will take six hour-long lessons and pupils are expected to reach Levels 4–5, although more talented and experienced pupils could go further. The suggested time schedule for the unit shows that substantially more time is spent on practical and developmental work at the computer than in some other units. This still may not be enough time, as this is fundamentally creative workand considerable time has to be spent developing and implementing for the highest quality outcomes to be realised.

	Taught as a whole class	*Pupil work away from the computer*	*Pupil work at the computer*
Lesson 1	30 mins	15 mins	15 mins
Lesson 2	10 mins	25 mins	25 mins
Lesson 3	30 mins	10 mins	20 mins
Lessons 4 and 5	45 mins	15 mins	60 mins
Lesson 6	15 mins	15 mins	30 mins
Overall balance	**2 hrs 10 mins** 36%	**1 hr 20 mins** 22%	**2 hrs 30 mins** 42%

LESSON BY LESSON

Lesson 1: Corporate image

This lesson provides the opportunity for pupils to revisit the notion of corporate image and consider how this is realised by maintaining consistent features in a regular publication.

Starter: What is a corporate image?

The lesson begins with a teacher-led discussion to identify similarities and differences, common themes and consistent design features in a range of leaflets on the theme of a fictitious town called Amstead. The idea of corporate image is discussed and pupils are asked to think of further examples.

Development: Planning another publication for same organisation; using software techniques to implement design; and creating a design

Through discussion, the teacher draws out which features the class thinks will and will not be in the following month's publication.

> This is a useful exercise but, if you can, you may wish to provide a series of professionally designed leaflets with more relevance to the pupils. There is further comment about this in Lesson commentaries on page 32. **[1a] and [2a]**

The teacher demonstrates the basic techniques of creating a new publication, including creation of frames, moving and resizing objects, importing text and graphics, layering and rotation of objects.

> This will take longer than the ten minutes allocated as it will need considerable exemplification. It should be noted that at the time of writing, the version of the documentation downloaded from the Internet in Word format has an error in the section about a time series chart. This should be ignored. See page 32. **[1b]**

Pupils create an August edition to complement the June and July versions and to show understanding of the consistent corporate image. They insert the logo and text provided.

> You may feel that the pupils have gained the necessary insight from the leaflets and feel there is little benefit in producing a publication that means nothing to them. It might be more positive for pupils to start developing something of their own.

Plenary and homework: Design brief for the task

Pupils consider the common elements in a series of school publications and reinforce the idea of a corporate image: logos, fonts, colour schemes, layout. They think about why a corporate image is important for the school.

Pupils are given a design brief for the unit. They will produce an A4 information leaflet for Year 6 pupils about a subject they will be studying in Year 7. They are given a list of features to incorporate in the leaflet. This includes the name of the school, photos of the school, the school logo, the name of the subject and text describing the subject (to be provided).

> This activity will not give the pupils any sense of autonomy. A successful leaflet represents the best of content, text size, style and organisation, use of colour, and choice of appropriate graphics combined in an interesting page layout, see page 32. **[1c] and [2b]**

For homework, pupils are to create a rough page layout consisting of blocks to represent the different items or objects. They are to suggest possible font styles and sizes for headings and text. They have to include the school logo.

You will need to emphasise that this is a rough draft, not a finished publication!

Lesson 2: Designing a leaflet

In this lesson pupils use existing publications to analyse design techniques They then implement their own draft leaflets and evaluate them against a set of criteria.

Starter: Elements of good design

The class discuss the Amstead leaflets to draw out ideas about elements of good design.

Again, it may be more constructive to find alternative examples from a local amenity such as a hotel chain, a tourist attraction or a concert venue, see page 32. [1a] **and** [2a]

Pupils consider their homework designs in the light of a series of criteria such as logo location and size, their use of space and colour, the balance of the elements on the page and whether everything lines up accurately. They make changes to their designs as appropriate.

It may be more useful to consider design features before pupils develop their designs! You may also feel that their sketches will not be sufficiently developed to carry out a thorough review using the criteria suggested.

Development: Transferring draft design layout to a computer; and using criteria to evaluate the leaflets

Pupils transfer their design to a computer using the techniques demonstrated the previous week.

They may not remember techniques such as importing text and graphics, and layering and rotation of objects, without some reinforcement or supporting instructions.

The resource files containing the text, logo and photograph are made available as well as a template for those who need it.

Again, the pupils are given limited creative freedom and insufficient time to complete the task proficiently, see page 32. [1c] **and** [2b]

In groups of four, the pupils judge the effectiveness of their leaflets using the familiar list of criteria and also considering dominant features and overall effectiveness.

It is unlikely they will have had time to print, but this would be necessary for effective evaluation. It may be better to set this activity as a homework so they can evaluate a hard copy version.

Plenary and homework: Evaluating leaflet design and logos

The teacher displays one good example produced by pupils to exemplify good design features. After a brief discussion about the design of well-known logos, pupils are asked to collect four more for homework and write briefly about why they are familiar and whether they are good-quality logos. A paper-based resource is distributed to support this work.

Lesson 3: Creating a logo

Consideration of the purpose of logos is the main theme for this lesson.

Starter: Considering different logos

In groups of four, the pupils consider the logos they collected for homework and comment on them, justifying their views.

Development: Considering why logos are used

The lesson continues with a review of corporate image and the design of familiar logos.

> Use more common examples that have a meaning for them. It is worth noting that the Becta logo has changed since development of this unit.

Pupils are asked to create a subject logo for their leaflet using a combination of a piece of vector-based clip art and graphics-based text such as Word Art.

> This is best suited to individual work, so it would be necessary to find an alternative task for the partners. Again there is not sufficient time for each pupil to produce high-quality outcomes.

Plenary and homework: Evaluating logos; and collecting images

Pupils are asked to review their own logos according to the design conventions discussed earlier. The teacher shows some of the pupils' logos and the class discuss the quality of the design features used. Pupils are asked to bring a piece of work relating to the subject they have chosen, to be scanned for inclusion on their leaflet.

Pupils collect leaflets incorporating images. They are to consider the content, the images and their purpose and identify any corporate features that have been used.

Lessons 4 and 5: Capturing images fit for the purpose

This series of activities concentrates on the acquisition, manipulation and role of images in leaflet design.

Starter: Why do we use images?

Pupils review a range of leaflets with a focus on images. They are asked to match the images in the leaflets with the reasons for inclusion listed on their resource handout.

> Some useful prompts are suggested, although perhaps the position and style of the images could also be noted.

Development: Using images in the subject leaflets

Now pupils return to consideration of their own creations: the subject leaflets. They have already used the school and their own subject logos, and they are now asked to contribute ideas about the sorts of images that would be appropriate. These may be photos of wall displays, classrooms, or pupils working. Pupils are then asked if the suggested images would be better displayed as scanned images or as photos.

Pupils are told that they will have three additional images – an image of the school stored on the shared area, a scanned image and an image captured with a digital camera which they will acquire.

Carousel of activities

Depending on the availability of resources, there are three activities that pupils carry out:

Manipulating images: pupils choose an image of the school and manipulate it using a graphics package. Some may add special effects if they can use the appropriate tools before adding it to their leaflet.

Most pupils would be able to manage this using simple tools such as those provided in MS Paint.

Using a digital camera to capture and manipulate images: pupils capture a suitable image, although the teacher is advised to provide a series of appropriate images if this is not feasible.

It would be a pity if pupils cannot capture their own choice of images. A set of instructions will probably be necessary.

Using a scanner to capture and manipulate images: pupils should be reminded that they will probably be saving a bit-mapped image and thus the image should be scanned at the required size as enlarging can distort images.

Saving as a .jpeg file will reduce file size.

Lesson 4 plenary: Using a scanner to capture images

It is suggested that this discussion can be used to reveal any problems encountered by pupils when using the scanner.

Any problems with the scanner, digital camera or placing of the images should be discussed, but perhaps this plenary could be used as a starter for the next lesson so the problems do not arise for subsequent users.

Lesson 5 starter: Improving images

It is suggested that the class is shown a range of images saved by pupils showing common problems such as blurred images, those with the subject too far away, over-cropped images and those in which the colour or shade contrast results in a photo that is too dark or too light. The class discuss the problems and possible solutions.

It is probably easier and more sensitive to create your own range of poor examples. Remember, pupil examples will be saved in their personal disk space unless you arrange transfer to a shared area.

Lesson 5 plenary and homework: Review of images and the production of the leaflet

Pupils are asked to think about their images and note the three most important things learned and share them with their partner. The class discuss any remaining technical problems or difficulties in using the software. For homework, pupils are asked to write a description of the process involved in producing the leaflets, including some thoughts about what they particularly like and what they would change.

Lesson 6: Creating a folded leaflet

This lesson focuses on the transfer of pupils' A4 designs to an alternative format.

Starter: Good design in a folded leaflet

Pupils are set the task of rearranging their subject leaflet into a folded leaflet for the department to give out on parents' evenings. Various formats are suggested.

> You may direct some pupils to simpler formats as a three-fold leaflet is quite complex. You must create one in advance using the same printer so you know what difficulties may be encountered.

Pupils are asked to plan out the leaflet on paper to indicate where the text and images will be placed. They are reminded to consider the principles of good design already used.

Development: Changing an A4 design to fit a different format; and creating a display of the final product

The teacher demonstrates how to move images and text from an A4 whole page layout into a folded sheet format. It is recommended that the teacher suggests some more advanced design ideas to the pupils using the three-fold format. The pupils carry out their revisions.

> The pupils have only 30 minutes for this task. Again, the opportunity to work independently and show real initiative is restricted, see page 33. **[6a] and [6b]**

Pupils create displays on large sheets of paper to include both their leaflets and their design ideas, as well as their written reviews. The displays can be annotated by hand to draw attention to particular details. The displays can be assessed by the departments in question.

> Again, not enough time is allocated to the production of a high-quality outcome.

Plenary and homework: Identifying elements of good design from printed material; and review of learning

Pupils work in groups of four to review and discuss the positive elements of each others' displays. They are reminded of the criteria and purpose of the leaflets and a prompt sheet could be provided for some.

> You will need to reinforce the need for them to be positive rather than negative and suggest ideas for improvement, adopting a "critical friend" approach, see page 33. **[6a] and [6b]**

Pupils are asked to review what they have learned and to make brief notes about the text and images they might include in a leaflet about the local area. They consider what changes could be made to the school's "corporate image".

> This is a brief encounter with yet another context. It may be useful to make some cross-curricular links, perhaps by asking pupils to think about tasks from other subjects for which they could use these new skills, see page 33. **[6c]**

Alternative approaches

This is a key unit in terms of developing knowledge and understanding of the design process and of the effective use of the features of DTP software. Although there are many valuable generic design skills being learned, the holistic experience of creating a leaflet is missing. This includes drafting and redrafting suitable text, developing an understanding of the subtle relationship between the content, the images, the colour, fonts and the overall layout. As there is only very limited opportunity in the units for pupils to develop their own content, it may be that teachers avoid the provision of text and images for the A4 information sheet and rearrange this unit to give pupils more responsibility for content and design decisions.

Teachers may be familiar with the parallel unit in the QCA scheme of work in which pupils work in groups to create a newspaper. It is interesting to note that in that unit, pupils have some responsibility for the development of textual content and, to enable this, links with topics studied in other subjects are suggested. Examples given include the weather, sport, or even production in another language. There is no reason why teachers should not combine the approaches suggested in the scheme of work with those of this unit. This would enable pupils to research and develop their own content while also meeting the strategy objectives.

Lesson commentaries

[1a] and [2a] The first lesson examines the idea of corporate images and pupils identify the consistent features of the series of Amstead publications. This is a very useful activity; in later years, examination coursework may require that pupils produce different versions of a regular publication incorporating such features. Alternatively, it may be felt that a series of simple but effective professionally designed leaflets would be better models than the Amstead examples, which lack artistic creativity. Any local amenity that produces regular leaflets could be a possible source. Examples might include concert venues, theatres, or sports clubs. Teachers may also decide that discussion of consistent features and corporate image is sufficient and the actual implementation of the cover of a future edition is not necessary. Pupils could then move on and spend more time considering design techniques to enhance their future creations.

Employing existing leaflets to model good design is a valuable activity. Although the examples may be more stimulating than the Amstead leaflets, it is important that they are appropriate, as pupils may want to be able to use some of the features they observe. It can be frustrating to see a special effect that a pupil has identified as relevant to their purpose proving to be completely inappropriate in terms of their skill level or the tools available in the particular package being used.

[1b] As has already been mentioned, it is quite easy to pick up the rudimentary techniques of using a DTP package, although in this unit the pupils have only a 10-minute demonstration to learn this range of skills. They then have a total of 25 minutes to create their initial leaflet and a further 25 minutes to adapt their information to a new audience (this excludes the time allowed for capturing and manipulating images). In addition, when pupils create their logo in Lesson 3 they are given 30 minutes in total, which also includes time for a lengthy teacher demonstration. As already indicated, it would be a difficult task to work on collaboratively; each pupil would have about 8 minutes maximum to create their logo. This is a useful activity, but teachers would need to think carefully about realistic time allocations to develop ideas.

[1c] and [2b] Ownership of the content could act as a motivating force, and if pupils develop just one publication, differentiation could be introduced to allow different groups of attainers to have responsibility for differing amounts of content. If they obtain existing subject information from publications written for an adult audience, they can still achieve the objective of refining information by reorganising and developing it for a Year 6 audience. Alternatively, as part of a differentiation strategy, pupils could choose their audience, some developing leaflets for Year 6 pupils and others focusing on a less familiar audience of visitors to a parents' evening.

[6a] and [6b] The pupils initially develop an A4 leaflet for Year 6 pupils and then transfer it to another format for an adult audience. This is not absolutely necessary for the achievement of the Strategy or National Curriculum objectives. The teacher may prefer to focus on each pupil producing a leaflet in one format, thus maximising time for creativity and outcomes of the highest quality. Some pupils will find the challenge of a high-quality A4 leaflet, designed and implemented for a purpose, appropriate, whereas some higher attainers would be able to move on to a more complex task, and take on the challenge of the three-fold format. The extra time could be spent on the design of the publication. This would include obtaining information from a variety of sources, reorganising and refining this to meet the needs of the audience, and choosing the range of font styles, colours and graphics. These are demanding but valuable skills which pupils generally find interesting and exciting. Time is allocated for thoughtful planning and, indeed, this is essential for a successful outcome, but design without sufficient time for implementation is frustrating and demotivating for pupils. This could also mean that the review and evaluation of the pupils' leaflets can be carried out at the end of the process after sufficient time has been spent implementing at least some aspects of the design. Reviews are also more helpful if undertaken by the proposed audience who, from their objective viewpoint, would be better equipped to identify any problems.

Looking at the use of logos is still relevant in this alternative scenario, as is the carousel of activities, giving time to capture images using the scanner and digital camera. The time allocations in the final lesson would be difficult to adhere to. Pupils are expected to transfer their information to a second format, create a display to show the development of their work and review the displays – all in one lesson. A final review is important, but the display charting development could be a substitution for the final homework. The resulting outcomes may well be used to make an interesting classroom display showing the development of design work.

[6c] There is also the option of using a completely different context for the leaflets, such as a local issue of interest to the pupils, or a cross-curricular context. Many relevant issues will have been discussed in subjects such as Geography, RE and Citizenship, and much of the research may already have been carried out in those lessons.

7.4 Introduction to modelling and presenting numeric data

KS3 STRATEGY FRAMEWORK OBJECTIVES

Developing ideas and making things happen

Models and modelling

- Use software to investigate and amend a simple model by:
  - formatting and labelling data appropriately (e.g. formatting cells to display currency);
  - entering rules or formulae and checking their appropriateness and accurate working;
  - explaining the rules governing a model;
  - predicting the effects of changing variables or rules.
- Test whether a simple model operates satisfactorily.

About this unit

In this unit of five lessons, pupils are taught to use a spreadsheet as a modelling tool. Although they are shown an example of a weather and wave model, both of which are animations, the examples they work with are all mathematical models. Generally they work with or extend spreadsheet models provided for them, rather than creating a spreadsheet to answer a specific question or explore a hypothesis. The strategy suggests that as long as the pupils have already covered Unit 7.1, this unit can be planned for any time during the year.

Prior to starting this unit, pupils require some knowledge of the techniques associated with spreadsheets and some understanding of spreadsheet use. They need some knowledge of the structure and elements which make up a spreadsheet (cells, rows, columns, labels, data, formulae, worksheet). Pupils should already have been introduced to spreadsheets during the last year or two years of primary school, and should have experience both of creating simple spreadsheets and exploring spreadsheet models.

In order to complete the unit, pupils have to be able to enter, amend, select, copy and format data in a spreadsheet. They need to format a spreadsheet, insert rows, and copy spreadsheet data into a word-processed document. They use a spreadsheet program to create a pie chart, using a chart wizard, and discuss what a pie chart represents. Generic skills and understanding include the ability to use simple formulae, format numbers as currency, grasp the meaning of the terms "model" and "rule", as well as the advantages and disadvantages of presenting data in written and numeric formats. As a demonstration, the teacher presents some data in several different chart formats, some of which are appropriate and some of which are not. It is left to the teacher to decide which formats to show. These formats are considered in a whole class discussion, but perhaps such an important idea needs greater consideration.

In addition to these skills and understanding, the teacher needs to be able to set print areas within spreadsheets and understand relative and absolute cell references. The conventions of absolute addressing are explained on page 12 of the sample teaching unit.

	Taught as a whole class	*Pupil work away from the computer*	*Pupil work at the computer*
Lesson 1	35 mins		25 mins
Lesson 2	45 mins		15 mins
Lesson 3	30 mins		30 mins
Lesson 4	15 mins		45 mins
Lesson 5	40 mins		20 mins
Overall balance	**2 hrs 45 mins** 55%		**2 hrs 15 mins** 45%

The pupils work as a whole class or in pairs throughout the unit. The balance of time in the lessons is as follows.

The unit is designed for pupils working at Levels 4 and 5, and the tasks reflect the expectations of these level descriptors. There is some extension work for those working at higher levels. Some aspects of the unit are problematic, including the lack of an opportunity for pupils to design and create a spreadsheet for a real purpose and the number of different contexts used during the unit.

LESSON BY LESSON

Lesson 1: Using a spreadsheet

In the first lesson of the unit, the pupils use a spreadsheet. Most of the time they work with spreadsheets that have been prepared for them, although they do produce one simple spreadsheet for themselves.

Starter: Problem-solving using a table and paper-based resource

The pupils' first task involves working on a paper-based spreadsheet, calculating the cost of feeding animals in a zoo. They are then shown the same data in a spreadsheet application by the teacher and they discuss the advantages of using a spreadsheet for the task.

Development: Using formulae; and creating a simple spreadsheet

The next part of the lesson is a PowerPoint presentation which the teacher shows to deliver some of the subject knowledge about spreadsheets.

> Arguably, this is not the best way to teach pupils how to use a spreadsheet. Reasons are given on page 39. [1a]

Next, the teacher demonstrates the advanced copy facility in Excel, using the days of the week.

> At this stage in the lesson this particular demonstration is not relevant and may cause confusion. This is discussed further on page 39. [1b]

Pupils then go on to create their own spreadsheet, based on a times table square.

> Pupils may already have covered this activity. Some alternative approaches are suggested on page 39. [1c]

Next, pupils work with a "football league" spreadsheet. It is suggested that those who manage the task quickly are shown how to use absolute referencing.

> Pupils would have to be very confident users of spreadsheets to understand the notion of absolute referencing and be able to apply it at this stage. You could consider leaving it until Unit 8.4, where it is covered in detail.

Plenary and homework: Advantages and disadvantages of using a spreadsheet

The lesson ends with a discussion of the advantages and disadvantages of using a spreadsheet. For homework pupils are asked to think of how they might use a spreadsheet themselves.

> The hard reality is that as 12-year-olds they almost certainly would not imagine using one, so it might be better to ask them to think about how someone else – a parent, youth club treasurer, shopkeeper or teacher – might use one.

Lesson 2: Modelling using a spreadsheet

This is likely to be a more coherent experience than Lesson 1, which used three different examples of spreadsheets, as some of the models used previously are revisited.

Starter: Problem-solving using a simple spreadsheet

This lesson builds on the work of the previous one, using the zoo animals spreadsheet to answer some "what if . . .?" questions.

Development: The idea of a model; and using and interrogating a model

The notion of a model is introduced briefly and the lesson plan suggests that the teacher shows one of two models on the Internet, both from the Met Office. The first is a weather chart and the second a model of ocean wave swell.

> These are problematic, both as examples of modelling and in terms of the length of time allowed. This is discussed in Lesson commentaries on page 40. [2a]

The lesson then considers how a model can be used to obtain information. The football league example is used for this part of the lesson. The terms "rule", "formula" and "variable" are explained, although these may need greater exemplification than is suggested in the lesson outline.

> The notion of a rule in this context could cause confusion and might be better introduced elsewhere. This is discussed on page 40. [2b]

The teacher is asked to decide next whether or not to introduce absolute referencing to all the class. Absolute referencing is covered in detail in Unit 8.4, so this can be omitted entirely if necessary. Pupils go on to a useful task where they have to answer some questions using the information in the spreadsheet.

The lesson now introduces another model, that of biscuit making. Again, the spreadsheet is provided and pupils discuss inputs and outputs, variables, formulae and unit costs. They go on to use this model to explore "what if . . .?" questions and interrogate it to answer specific questions. This revises, rather than develops, the knowledge covered in the previous tasks.

Plenary and homework: Advantages of using a model

The lesson ends with a discussion of the advantages and disadvantages of using a model. For homework, pupils are asked to identify the rules and variables for a number of examples drawn from the "football league" spreadsheet.

> It will be very important at this point to revise and check on pupils' understanding of the concepts of "rule" and "variable". If you decide to cover the idea of a rule in another context, make a note to check on their understanding of this later.

Lesson 3: Using a spreadsheet to build a model

This lesson introduces a new context, that of a school disco. In this lesson pupils develop a spreadsheet showing costs for a school disco to model possible options.

Starter: Identifying rules and variables

The notions of "rule" and "variable" are revised in a task in which pupils have to identify the properties of various cells in a disco spreadsheet model projected on the large screen.

Development: Using, developing and increasing the functionality of the model

Using the same spreadsheet, pupils are asked what they could calculate using the formulae it includes. The notions of profit and loss are discussed briefly and the teacher demonstrates how to format numbers as currency. They go on to use the model to answer questions and make predictions.

With this model as a starting point, and using paper-based support materials, pupils develop the model further. They are asked to open the disco spreadsheet (P3a) and use another resource (P3f) to develop it. Tasks include:

> Pupils may need some support with this activity. You might consider modelling at least the first part of it to them before they work independently.

- formatting data as currency;
- creating formulae;
- developing the model and increasing its functionality;
- interrogating the model to answer specific questions.

They continue to develop the functionality of the model by adding more variables.

Plenary and homework: Reviewing the model

The plenary poses additional questions and extends the model. For homework, the pupils have to identify further limitations of the model and suggest possible solutions.

> This is a difficult task for homework, and the teacher may need to set it up quite carefully, with examples, in the plenary.

Lesson 4: Refining and developing a model

In Lesson 4 the pupils add variables, based on different scenarios, to their disco model to increase its functionality. Tasks for the lesson include:

- inserting rows into the spreadsheet to include additional variables;
- recalculating costs.

Having amended their model, they are asked to predict the effects of their changes. They are encouraged to explain its weaknesses.

Starter: Ways of increasing income from an event

The lesson begins with a discussion of ways of increasing the income from an event. Notions such as profit and loss are revisited and that of a "loss leader" is introduced.

Development: Adding variables to the model

Pupils go on to add first one and then a second variable to their model: offering free drinks to people at the disco and printing posters to advertise the event.

Plenary and homework: Weaknesses of the model

The lesson ends with a discussion of the weaknesses of the model. For homework, pupils have to think of some ways in which their model could be improved and why the improvements would be effective.

You might want to consider working with an alternative model which could also be used in the next lesson. See page 40 for a further discussion of this. [4a]

Lesson 5: Ways of presenting data from a spreadsheet

In the final lesson of the series, the focus is on presenting data and the pupils create a report on the cost of organising the school sports day.

The context is puzzling. Pupils are asked to consider data from a school sports day, but the report required is not about sporting achievement, but about whether or not the event made a profit.

Starter: Presenting information for audience and purpose

Pupils evaluate a report on the costs of organising a school sports day, drawing out what it includes and what is omitted. A more effective presentation of the same information is then discussed.

Development: Using tables and charts to present information; and creating a report

The context of the lesson now changes. Pupils look at some data and charts about journeys to school, and the teacher explains a number of important terms:

- select a data range
- highlight
- chart title
- legend
- series
- values
- labels.

The teacher shows how this data could be used to produce different types of chart, some that present the data well and some that do not.

This part of the of the lesson focuses on important areas of subject knowledge, and you may find that you need to spend more time explaining it and give pupils an opportunity to create different charts themselves.

Pupils then look at two pie charts and discuss what they represent.

The context now reverts to that of the school disco, and in the final part of the lesson the pupils create a report on the school disco. The following tasks are included:

This is an important area of understanding, and overlaps with other elements of the strategy. This is discussed further on page 40. [5a]

- writing a brief report in a word processor;
- copying data from a spreadsheet into the word-processed document;

- using formatting effects to highlight important information;
- creating a chart and inserting it into their report (task for higher-attaining pupils).

Plenary and homework: Review of the modelling process

The lesson ends with a review of the modelling process and a comparison of the advantages and disadvantages of presenting data in numeric and written form. For homework, pupils consider how a spreadsheet model would be useful for organising a school trip.

Alternative approaches

This unit includes important areas of subject knowledge, both subject-specific, relating to the use and development of spreadsheets, and generic, linked to the presentation of data in the form of charts.

One limitation of the unit is the fact that although it is described as an introduction to modelling, the pupils meet only a limited range of models. The unit does not encourage them to make links in their learning between mathematical models and other models they might have encountered, such as simulations or adventure games. This issue is addressed in the final lesson of Unit 8.4, and you could bear this in mind when teaching this unit.

Another difficulty is that pupils have little experience in this unit of designing and creating their own spreadsheet. The only experience they have of creating their own spreadsheet may be a repetition of work undertaken in Year 6. Designing a spreadsheet for a real purpose is a demanding but a powerful opportunity to develop authentic understanding of the value of spreadsheets.

A final problem is associated with the number of contexts used. It would be difficult to keep to one context to develop all of the aspects of the work, but this unit moves between seven different contexts (times table, zoo animals, football league, biscuit making, school disco, journeys to school and school sports day). Some of these are touched on briefly, some are returned to more than once, but the overall feeling is of a rather fragmented approach.

It might be possible to use one of the more substantial contexts, such as the school disco (or the school play example suggested below), to support a greater part of the work of the unit. Pupils could begin by designing their own spreadsheet, in pairs, so that they have experience of this, before using the spreadsheet provided.

Lesson commentaries

[1a] A PowerPoint presentation is not the best way to teach about a dynamic, interactive application such as a spreadsheet. You could consider incorporating these teaching points into your demonstration of the zoo animals spreadsheet earlier in the lesson. This would enable you to demonstrate the features of the spreadsheet that pupils will need to use and understand.

[1b] Although demonstrating the copying function by using the days of the week is impressive and may prompt admiration from pupils, it might be better to show this tool using the numbers they will need, starting with 1–2–3 to set the pattern. You could then show the advanced copy with days of the week, months of the year, dates and so on, later. At this stage in the lesson it is not relevant and may cause confusion.

[1c] This is an activity suggested in the QCA scheme of work for Year 6, so pupils may already have covered it. However, it is really important that pupils have an opportunity to create a spreadsheet, and not

just use spreadsheets provided for them, so it is probably not a good idea simply to omit the task. You may like to use one of the following contexts as an alternative:

- a football league table similar to the example given but based on the pupil's own favourite team (and its rivals) which can then be used for the tasks in Lesson 2;
- a spreadsheet based on the sales for the last three or four CDs released by some popular singers or groups;
- a spreadsheet based on pocket money.

[2a] Only five minutes is allowed in the lesson plan both for the discussion of the notion of a model and for viewing the online models. The idea of a model is a complex one, and may need further explanation. There are also significant areas of subject knowledge introduced in this brief part of the lesson, such as model outcomes, input and output, variables and the use of models in commerce and manufacturing.

When explaining the idea of a model, care will be needed. The notion of a spreadsheet as a model is complex and may be difficult for pupils. Making the connection between the visual model of the weather and the wave with the more abstract idea of the spreadsheet is also challenging. It might be better to show a number of different spreadsheet models and discuss the way that mathematical models are used in commerce, industry and services. For example, the data showing rates of interest on personal loans which appear in magazine and newspaper advertisements could be presented as a spreadsheet model, or a simple production process could be modelled.

[2b] The notion of a rule introduced in this context might cause confusion. The definition of a rule given in the lesson plan is "how different quantities can be combined or manipulated to find new quantity". For pupils, the football context might suggest that rules are practical sporting or games applications rather than mathematical or program constructs. It might be better to introduce this in the context of one of the other spreadsheets in the unit.

[4a] You could consider using an alternative model, such as that for the costs of staging a school play. This would allow pupils to complete similar activities, introducing variables and recalculating costs. The advantage is that they could use the same spreadsheet in Lesson 5, thus increasing the coherence of the lessons.

[5a] Understanding charts is very important generic subject knowledge for pupils. It is likely that they will need to revisit the information presented in this part of the lesson, and use it in creating charts of their own, to ensure that the knowledge is secure. This topic also occurs in Units 7.5, 8.1 and 8.4. You could decide to focus teaching in one of those units instead of here, or teach this as a separate lesson so that the knowledge can be applied by pupils wherever it is needed. If you think your pupils may struggle to understand this, it is probably best left until later. Whatever approach you adopt, it is vital that all pupils create some charts of their own as well as watching a demonstration of the process by the teacher. In the lesson plan it is suggested only as an additional differentiated activity when pupils have completed other tasks.

7.5 Data handling

KS3 STRATEGY FRAMEWORK OBJECTIVES

Finding things out

Using data and information sources

- Identify the purpose of an information source and whether it is likely to be biased.
- Identify what information is relevant to a task.
- Understand how someone using an information source could be misled by missing or inaccurate information.

Searching and selecting

- Narrow down a search to achieve more relevant results.

Organising and investigating

- In an investigation:
  - design and use an appropriate data handling structure to answer questions and draw conclusions;
  - design a questionnaire or data collection sheet to provide relevant data;
  - check data efficiently for errors;
  - investigate relationships between variables;
  - use software to represent data in simple graphs, charts or tables, justifying the choice of representation;
  - derive new information from data;
  - check whether conclusions are plausible;
  - review and amend the structure and its data to answer further questions.

About this unit

This unit consists of six lessons in which pupils interrogate existing data and learn to question its reliability and possible bias by an examination of the data source. They spend some time generating hypotheses and then look at the ways in which questions can be designed to ensure they acquire the necessary data. They consider the ways that data can be displayed through charts, and how this can also be used as a method of error detection. Time is spent looking at and designing their own data structures, into which they enter data. They then interrogate those data to find evidence to prove their hypotheses. At the end of the unit they consider how their investigation could have been improved and what additional data would need to be collected in order to generate more appropriate results.

Many pupils will have already experienced some aspects of data handling in Key Stage 2. This may have included interrogating an existing data file or creating a class database. If they have undertaken Unit 7.4, they will also have encountered some methods of chart creation.

The unit recommends establishing what pupils will have experienced in Mathematics lessons linked to the Data Handling Attainment Target so that their learning in ICT can represent continuity and progression from this. It is also worth considering links with other subjects. For example, the detection of bias is an important skill in the study of historical documents, so any existing experience the pupils have in this area should be taken into account. In addition, one of the data contexts is related to journeys to school, so it may be worth checking to see if Geography or Citizenship could provide a cross-curricular link here.

Teachers need to be confident in the relevant ICT subject knowledge in terms of the principles of designing database structure, efficient data collection, interrogation methods and approaches to the display of data. In order to acquire the associated software skills, it is essential that teachers work through the entire data handling cycle in preparation for this unit. They need to be prepared to offer support at all stages and must be completely secure in their knowledge of the way different elements interrelate.

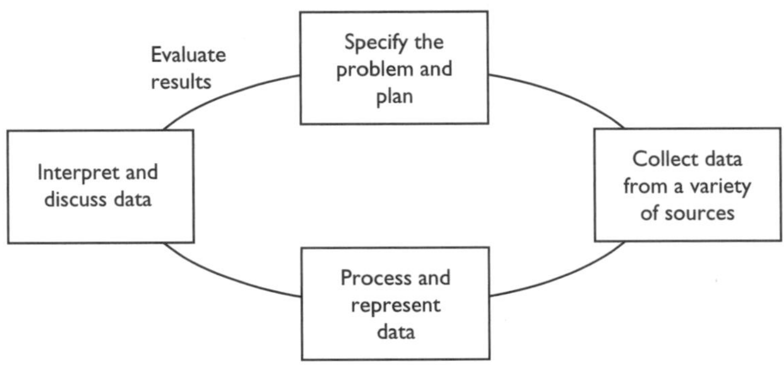

The data handling cycle

Pupils generally work in pairs in this unit. It is recommended that these are similar-ability groupings and they need to be organised in advance. Again, the resources need to be considered carefully, and possibly pruned to cut down on printing costs, and arrangements made to organise availability of the electronic resources.

It is anticipated that the unit will take six hour-long lessons. The table opposite shows the suggested breakdown of lesson time on the basis of teacher-led whole class teaching, pupil work away from the computer and practical, computer-based activity. Nearly 60 per cent of time is spent in teacher-led, whole class activities, just over 20 per cent on paired collaboration away from the computer, and the same on practical, computer-based work. If pupils are to develop a thorough understanding of the data-handling cycle in its entirety, they need to work through all stages from start to finish and spend some time on the practical problem solving elements. In a series of lessons lasting six hours, although the taught element and teacher support is absolutely crucial, the amount of computer-based work representing autonomous problem solving is minimal. The question has to be raised as to how far this unit prepares pupils to work independently on data handling investigations.

	Taught as a whole class	*Pupil work away from the computer*	*Pupil work at the computer*
Lesson 1	40 mins	10 mins	10 mins
Lesson 2	45 mins	15 mins	
Lesson 3	50 mins	10 mins	
Lesson 4	25 mins	25 mins	10 mins
Lesson 5	20 mins		40 mins
Lesson 6	25 mins	15 mins	20 mins
Overall balance	**3 hrs 25 mins** 57%	**1 hr 15 mins** 21%	**1 hr 20 mins** 22%

LESSON BY LESSON

Lesson 1: Evaluating and interrogating an existing data set

Starter: Checking pupils' knowledge and understanding

In this lesson pupils learn how to question the reliability and bias of data, and how to use graphs and percentages to derive new information from a collection of data.

There is no mention of the difference between data and information, so you can only assume that the terms are interchangeable in this unit.

Pupils briefly discuss their previous use of databases.

As this lesson is based on numerical data held in a spreadsheet, this discussion could be postponed until Lesson 3 when knowledge of data structure is addressed.

Development: Considering an existing data set; interrogating existing data; and generating charts

Pupils are shown a table of data about visits to the UK by overseas residents and the fields/categories are identified, understanding of the shortened form of numbers is checked and ideas for the miscellaneous field discussed.

This discussion of fields and categories could also be postponed until Lesson 3, and an alternative data set relating to a more relevant context for the pupils could be substituted here.

In pairs, the pupils discuss a card with a question about the accuracy, relevance and possible bias of the data.

Make sure they know "I can't tell" is a reasonable answer, as these questions are difficult to answer without establishing a background context. The source of data is revealed as the government.

It is important that you do not give the impression that pupils need have no reservations about data from an "official" government site.

Pupils answer a series of questions about the data using manual searching methods. It is suggested that the last questions are used as extension work.

This work is not discussed, so make sure you monitor the pupils working in order that you can see who has problems. The last three questions may need some prompts, so it may be useful to discuss them briefly, see page 51. [**1a**]

The teacher then demonstrates how to create a chart to show the number of business visits every year and uses the opportunity to demonstrate that some chart formats are better suited to communicating this data.

You need to consider whether this demonstration is appropriate here. It may be worth waiting until next lesson, as the pupils will not reinforce the knowledge through application until then. Chart formats are also considered in Unit 7.4. See Lesson commentaries, page 52, for further comment on this point. [**1b**]

Plenary and homework: Considering everyday uses of graphical data; and considering the clarity of information represented graphically

The teacher elicits and records pupils' suggestions of different types of data that may be represented in a chart, and where they might find them. The accuracy and bias of their sources is considered.

Again, it is important not to assume official statistics are necessarily totally reliable. It is also important to think about relevant contexts. Some of the suggestions are satisfactory, but do pupils study charts of house prices or government reports in the newspapers?

Pupils are reminded that they have considered how important it is to check the reliability of data. They have also begun to think about how charts can be used to display data in different ways in order to give new information.

If new information has been generated, it is important that pupils are aware of this fact, so it could be made more explicit than suggested in the lesson plan.

For homework, pupils collect some charts from electronic and non-electronic sources and assess how clearly they communicate the information.

Perhaps they could consider accuracy and reliability as well.

Lesson 2: Presenting information in different formats to test hypotheses

Starter: Review of previous learning

Learning in the previous lesson is revisited and the homework findings relating to effective charts are incorporated into the discussion. In this lesson pupils will consider what information can be derived from the data used last lesson about to visits to the UK. This lesson will involve pupils in making and testing a hypothesis based on the visits data. They then present their data in different ways to derive new information and test their hypothesis more easily.

> Again, you should consider the need for an interesting and relevant context to enable pupils to participate fully in proposing a hypothesis which is meaningful to them, and which they have a desire to test and prove.

Development: Proposing and testing hypotheses; and using percentages to derive new information

Possible hypotheses are discussed and suggested by the teacher and a demonstration is shown relating to the creation of charts to display relevant information to confirm or disprove the theory. Pupils propose their hypothesis and embark on testing it by the use of appropriate charts.

The teacher then raises the question of the limitations of displaying simple numeric values and suggests that using percentages to show the changes as a proportion of the whole is more effective. Pupils then re-test their hypothesis using percentage figures.

It is suggested that the teacher identifies pupils who are likely to have difficulties and supports them during these activities.

> It is likely that a significant number of pupils will need help here. It may be that you propose a very simple hypothesis for the lower attainers and provide them with some structured support so that they do not demand your full attention, see page 52. [2a]

Plenary and homework: Presenting conclusions; and collecting data

Pupils discuss what they did in the lesson and the results of using both numerical values and percentages for proportional values.

> To use these 15 minutes well, and consider all ideas, you could organise group discussions between those who considered the same hypothesis followed by feedback to the whole class.

For homework, pupils are provided with a simple form and asked to collect data about travel to primary and secondary school for the next lesson. A historical perspective is implied by asking them to talk to people from the previous two generations.

Lesson 3: Designing a questionnaire to collect data

Starter: Introducing questions to be answered

This lesson is about capturing the correct data for the purpose in appropriate and efficient ways. Pupils are to consider a hypothesis, think about the data they will require to answer their question, and then design a questionnaire to collect it accurately and efficiently. The data handling cycle is used to reinforce the process:

- specify the problem and plan;
- collect data from a variety of sources;
- process and represent the data;
- interpret and discuss data – evaluate.

The question "Does a pupil's age affect their method of travel to school?" is provided and pupils are asked to think of a related hypothesis to work on.

It may be useful to set the scene here and make the context more meaningful, see page 52. [3a]

Development: Considering what data are required; framing the questions for a questionnaire; and considering answers to questions on a questionnaire

Pupils are asked to consider what they want to know and what kinds of questions will be asked of the data. A list of necessary data types (items of information) such as "age of pupil" is drawn up and their purpose considered.

The lesson plan suggests you collate a list of data types. This is an unusual use of the term and may lead to confusion as it is also used later when considering data structure. It may be better to stick to asking what specific items of information are needed.

The lesson then moves on to address the development of effective questions, and pupils are invited to suggest possible questions that can be asked to collect the required data.

It may be useful to collect some questionnaires and distribute them among the pupils to give them ideas of the ways in which questions can be asked, see page 52. [**3b**]

The Teacher Resource 3 is a very useful document. It presents an example of a data structure showing questions, possible responses and data types. It offers the potential for some interesting discussion about categories of transport or ways of recording more complex journeys using, for example, more than one method of transport.

It may be useful to introduce the notion of data or field length here, which could include the idea of shortening answers such as male and female to M and F, see page 52. [3c]

Plenary and homework: Comparing local and national data; and collecting data

In this final few minutes the class look at another set of data relating to a national survey of trips to school.

This is likely to be of more personal interest to pupils than the visits to the UK data. They will understand the context and possibly find it easier to carry out those initial tasks in Lessons 1 and 2.

The class considers the survey data and what it tells them about their question: whether a pupil's age affects their method of travel to school. The homework findings about pupils' personal circumstances are collated and the current data compared with those of the previous generations. These are then considered alongside the national data and the question of reliability is raised.

Although this appears to be a useful discussion, it is important that it is given sufficient time to tease out the detail and to ensure that all pupils have some understanding of the analysis, see page 52. [3d]

The homework involves the collection of more data to help find out if local transport provision meets the needs of young people in the area. Pupils are asked to record all of their journeys in terms of day, purpose, distance, method of transport and reason for choice.

You may consider that yet another set of data for another investigation is overcomplicating this unit. Some pupils find the discipline of data collection difficult and it is likely that some will be falsified. This is an important point as it is vital that pupils see this as a worthwhile and relevant exercise.

Lesson 4: Creating a questionnaire and designing a data handling file structure to answer a key question

Starter: Designing a questionnaire

This lesson starts with an appraisal of what has been learned in the last lesson and then pupils create their own questionnaire, design their data-handling structure and input and interrogate their data.

Usually the data handling structure would inform the design of the questionnaire, so should be considered before data collection takes place.

A question is presented: "Is there adequate public transport to meet the needs of young people in this community?" Pupils are reminded that questions must be designed carefully to obtain the required information. They are asked to consider potential questions for their questionnaires. To help them, they are shown some examples, which are then discussed in terms of their precision and the kinds of answers they may elicit.

Development: Completing a questionnaire

Pupils work in pairs to develop their questions, supported and prompted by the teacher. The results are discussed and ways of refining the questions, by the use of coded categories, is considered.

The lesson plan suggests entering A–D as groups of different methods of transport. This would be difficult for anyone else to understand and could be substituted by the use of a word describing each group. For example, "bus" could be used to describe bus or coach; this would be explained on the questionnaire, see page 52. [4a]

The pre-prepared questionnaire is distributed, and each pupil completes it based on the data about journeys they collected for homework.

The Teacher Resource 6 template is not a realistic questionnaire, so you may feel it is worth designing your own, see page 52. [4b]

Plenary and homework: Designing and creating a data handling file structure; and evaluating individual database designs

Pupils are given 15 minutes to create and print their data file structure. They consider responses to the questions and abbreviations.

The design of the data structure is a crucial concept and cannot be completed satisfactorily in 15 minutes. There is no advice as to how the structure is created in Excel, see page 53. [4c]

Pupils evaluate their data structures for homework using a helpful resource which presents a series of valuable considerations relating to the essential features of an efficient data structure.

This resource, or at least the points it addresses, would have been useful before the design stage. It is often difficult to assess one's own design, so getting someone else to complete the questionnaire as part of an evaluation allows some valuable immediate feedback on the design.

Preparation for Lesson 5: It is recommended that a copy of each completed questionnaire is made available for each pair of pupils to give each individual sufficient experience of data entry.

This could mean an enormous number of copies, particularly if you want each class to use their own data, which is recommended for valid results. It may be easier to copy, say, a set for each four pairs of pupils and organise a carousel so each pair has a quarter of the set and passes them on to the next pair as they complete entry, see page 53. [4d]

Lesson 5: Entering, checking and testing data

Starter: Checking data for errors

The pupils will spend a significant part of this lesson entering data, but the initial activity is focused on checking data for errors before they commence data input. A file of data containing heights, ages and hair colour is displayed, and pupils are asked to spot the deliberate data errors it contains. Their findings are discussed.

A valuable activity, but if the file is similar to the one they are creating, pupils may make more positive connections. It may be an idea to get a copy of one of the first files created, introduce deliberate errors and use this with subsequent classes, see page 53. [5a]

Development: Entering and testing data; creating charts and graphs for initial data analysis; sorting data; and using selective searching

The completed questionnaires are distributed for entry into the structures defined and implemented in the previous lesson.

The design of the data structure and the questionnaire should interlink and complement each other. This prompts the question as to how the one questionnaire designed by the teacher has managed to meet the needs of the assorted data structures designed by pupils, see page 53. [5b]

Pupils work in pairs, with one reading the entries from the questionnaires and the other entering the data. It is suggested the pupils change roles half way through and when they have finished check their data for errors.

It is essential that you insist on the change of roles. Monitor progress carefully.

The teacher demonstrates the creation of a chart from the data used in the checking activity at the start of the lesson to accentuate the errors. Pupils then create charts to try to spot their own errors. Teacher Resource 8, containing a further data file, is used to demonstrate sorting and searching methods.

Microsoft Excel is probably not the best tool for complex searches using more than one condition. Again, it would probably be more appropriate to demonstrate using one of the files created earlier that lesson.

Pupils then go on to interrogate their own data and are reminded of the original question as queries should be linked to it.

You would probably need to discuss appropriate queries at more length with most pupils, see page 53. [5c]

Plenary and homework: Recognising the need to collect extra data to draw conclusions; and improving data collection to avoid pitfalls

The class shares their findings. The teacher draws out the realisation that they are unlikely to get what they need from their data and would have to collect further data to provide really positive evidence for conclusions.

It is worth recording these conclusions as the pupils consider them again next lesson.

For homework, pupils are asked to make notes about the difficulties of designing efficient questionnaires.

An alternative may be to develop a "Top Tips for Designing Questionnaires" sheet for a specific audience, as it may help pupils focus on what is required.

Lesson 6: Drawing conclusions and selecting data to support them

Starter: Ways of checking the plausibility of conclusions

The lesson starts with an activity in which some pupils hold up response cards designed to help the others understand the notion of checking the plausibility of data.

It would be advisable to insist that the pupils hold up cards only when indicated by you, to ensure you get an accurate picture of individual judgements. It may also be useful to question specific pupils about their decisions. Should this activity be extended to consider reliability and bias too?

Development: Drawing conclusions; providing evidence to support conclusions; and checking for plausibility

Pupils consider the plausibility of the conclusions reached during the previous lesson.

This is quite a long time after the event. Having spent 25 minutes discussing them last lesson, this seems a generous time allocation for revisiting the issue.

The pupils go on to produce an outline report presenting their conclusions, supported with evidence from their data files.

It may be useful to give at least some pupils a template, as they may have difficulty with this. You need to remind them to relate it to the initial question.

Plenary and homework: Relating conclusions to original questions; and extending the investigation or preparing for the next unit

This part of the lesson is a whole class activity to feed back findings and examine the evidence used to support conclusions. The homework asks pupils to either prepare for the next unit or describe how they would extend their study in terms of additional information requirements.

The second suggestion could be incorporated into the development of the lesson, when pupils consider their conclusions, and it would be easy to take the next step to identify the additional requirements they might include in any extension of the investigation.

Alternative approaches

This unit addresses a range of generic thinking skills, including logic, categorisation, observation, analysis and evaluation, and applies them to an electronic tool. The use of this tool necessitates additional skills, knowledge and understanding that could be described as ICT subject knowledge. In order to really understand the different elements that comprise the data handling cycle, it would be preferable for pupils to be familiar with and fully involved in the subject matter as they move through the sequence of steps from start to finish. This suggests the need for knowledge of the context and implies that it should be a familiar problem which has influence and meaning in their lives. In this unit pupils work with a number of different data sets and they do not have a meaningful, consistent context with which they can engage.

The other major concern is the lack of continuity shown in the approach to the series of steps in the data handling cycle. This unit approaches each element independently and does not appear to link them to make the whole. Starting with a detached investigation into figures about overseas visitors to the UK, pupils move on to the difficult task of developing hypotheses. This is made more problematic by the lack of explicit background information. They then proceed to derive new information by creating charts presenting the data. While the topic may be relevant to many pupils, the discrete approach used, devoid of any extra contextual background, means that the exercise exists purely to develop a set of skills in isolation. Much of this initial work relates to the latter part of the data-handling process, usually carried out only when active and intense engagement has been ongoing for some time, and the problem refined to the point at which outcomes of an authentic nature are possible.

Pupils then collect some interesting data for homework relating to their journeys to school. It appears they are now looking at data relating to a relevant context, about which they may realistically be able to make predictions and hypotheses based on their experience. There is useful work on designing appropriate questions, but then the data set changes again to a consideration of a national travel survey about trips to school. Here we have some pertinent data which surely could have formed the basis for the whole unit. However, the unit then switches again, this time to the question of public transport and the needs of the young people in the community. This is then the topic for the development of questions and the data structures. However, it is interesting to note that although the questionnaire is designed by the teacher, it has to match the data structures designed by the pupils.

There are many excellent teaching points in the lessons, but the sequence could be re-organised and the sessions reinterpreted around one familiar topic. All of the skills, knowledge and understanding could be taught through a meaningful context, possibly relating to journeys to school and/or public transport for young people in a specific area. Pupils could collect data from school members and carry out a full data handling exercise with real outcomes, for a genuine audience. These more familiar investigations could help pupils generate hypotheses, identify data requirements, design questions, collect authentic data and design a data structure. This would lead naturally to the later stages of data input, data interrogation, and finally development of a report on findings with evidence presented in a range of ways. Pupils will have undertaken a major investigation, involving them in valuable learning, decision making and independent problem solving. It is worth looking at the related unit in the QCA scheme of work, as that takes a different approach. There is further comment about this below.

The other issue relates to the software tool used for this unit. The preferred software is Excel, but you may feel that this will serve to confuse pupils when faced later on with data handling tasks that do not lend themselves to development through use of a spreadsheet package. The use of a database at this level is no more difficult, and possibly provides an easier interface for the whole concept of data handling, including for the development of a data structure and for appropriate data interrogation. It is the grasp of these concepts that provides the real challenge in this unit, and many might feel that a database provides the best medium for this learning. It would also provide a useful progression to the use of databases later in Key Stage 3 or for course work in Key Stage 4. Pupils may have undertaken the Key Stage 2 QCA scheme of work unit "Introduction to databases", so they may well have some familiarity with the complexities of data structures and interrogation. If teachers do not wish to use Microsoft Access for this unit, other simpler packages are perfectly adequate for the suggested tasks. Alternatives include Pinpoint, in which the approach to the development of the questionnaire sets up a helpful progression to the use of more sophisticated packages later on. It provides a structure for a variety of field types, including Boolean and key word fields, and makes pupils think carefully about the design of their questionnaire. In addition, the new Junior Viewpoint is worth considering, and even Information Workshop, generally used at Key Stage 2, could be employed here. Any of these packages provide a sound approach to the interrogation of data and generation of charts, although the Information Workshop chart generation component has less functionality.

The equivalent unit in the QCA scheme of work for Key Stage 3 also recommends the use of a database package. In addition, the process of the collection, structure, interrogation and analysis of data is based on a continuous theme which has direct relevance for the pupils. Although there are many useful additional teaching points suggested in this strategy unit, an amalgamation of these and the best features of the scheme of work unit could be considered.

Lesson commentaries

[1a] While it is important for pupils to understand that particular charts show information more clearly and certain types of data can only be shown by specific chart types, they also need to apply this knowledge to underpin and secure their understanding. Ideally, the reinforcement would follow on from the discussion, rather than in the following lesson, which means suspension of the completion of the learning process. The difficulty with approaching learning related to charts piecemeal through a number of units is that sometimes it does not fit naturally and is ultimately less co-ordinated. As has already been suggested, the Mathematical and ICT skills, knowledge, and understanding relating to the creation and use of charts is so fundamental that some kind of stand-alone unit could be considered. This could develop a coherent body of knowledge and embed the learning, which could then be reinforced during subsequent modules

where appropriate. In addition, the creation of charts usually takes place in the analysis and presentation stage towards the end of the data handling cycle, so it would seem sensible to address it in its logical place. There is overlap on this issue with Units 7.2, 8.1 and 8.3, so this needs to be considered in the light of all four units.

[**1b**] There is a teacher demonstration of chart creation in Unit 7.4 and in Lessons 1 and 5 in this unit. The concern is that on all occasions the teacher creates the charts and the pupils do not get the opportunity to reinforce this understanding by making decisions or problem solving in order to create their own. You may question how this approach provides progression for pupils.

[**2a**] As discussed at the start of this section, there is probably a limited number of possible hypotheses that can be generated from this data set due to the restricted contextual information given to the pupils. You may find that a number of pairs work on the same hypotheses. It may be useful to balance the size of groups working on one idea and after the task allow a discussion, followed by feedback to the whole class.

[**3a**] As the previous homework was about collecting school journey data, this may be the opportunity to expand on the context, as pupils may have some interesting contributions to make and the scenario will become more relevant to them. This, in turn, will make the identification of required information easier and perhaps give an insight as to the kinds of questions that should be asked. To create an effective questionnaire, the author needs to have a complete grasp of the topic in question, enabling them to clarify requirements and work towards developing effective ways of obtaining the right data.

[**3b**] The design of questionnaires is absolutely key, and frequently, even at GCSE, if it has not been explicitly addressed, pupils will fail to apply the accepted methods of defining questions. It may be useful to extend this activity and include an evaluation of questionnaires and consideration of some simple guidelines for developing precise questions. This will give pupils the opportunity to identify those questions which, through poor design, will not collect the required data.

[**3c**] As questionnaire design and data structure are inextricably linked, you may consider it useful to introduce the notion of data or field length here. The unit addresses this later, at the end of Lesson 4, although if the preferred software is Excel, you may feel this teaching point is extraneous.

[**3d**] You will find that for proper learning to take place, these nine questions cannot be discussed in five minutes. This is very valuable discussion, and it is important that it is given sufficient time to tease out the detail and to ensure that all pupils have some understanding of the issues in question. It may be valid to change the whole approach here. Earlier in the lesson you discussed questionnaires and the idea of data structures influencing the format of questions. It may be worth continuing with this and leave the consideration of the national survey until the following lesson. Alternatively, if you used this data instead of the visits to the UK data as an introduction to the unit, this discussion could be very useful during Lessons 1 or 2. Whatever you decide, this addresses very pertinent issues which give useful pointers for when the "real" data handling task is undertaken.

[**4a**] It is considered sound practice to abbreviate data entries or provide a list of key word alternatives. However, it is also necessary to ensure, if possible, that these abbreviations are clear to a user who has not been involved in the design of the file structure. Judgements have to be made to balance clarity and efficiency. However, calling a broad category of transport "A" means that the definition would have to be checked at each point of use, whereas it is easy to remember that the word "bus" stands for any motorised road transport carrying a number of people.

[**4b**] There is no example questionnaire provided and this is unhelpful to a non-specialist. It seems a pity

that the pupils have spent a considerable time designing their questions and looking at questionnaire design, but they do not have the opportunity to design or use their own. This is a problem because, to get enough records for a viable database, pupils have to collect the same items of information. It may be that you decide to allow them to design their questionnaires and develop complementary data structures, but when it comes to data entry you adopt the "Blue Peter" style and provide them with a structure and data that have been prepared earlier. While not perfect, it gives pupils the opportunity to experience the key steps in the data handling cycle without spending weeks inputting records.

[4c] It is important that pupils document their data structure to show understanding of field types and lengths and to show that each field has a distinct purpose. This creation of an efficient data structure is a crucial concept and cannot be completed satisfactorily in 15 minutes. There is also the question of whether it is actually necessary for a data file to be created using spreadsheet software, as it would be an obligatory element in the process of using a database package.

[4d] It is true that pupils need experience of inputting data into a prepared structure, but how much? You may consider asking each pupil to survey five people, create five records each, and then integrate their files into one file for interrogation. Of course, you would need to organise the time to do this.

[5a] Again, this is the issue of familiar contexts adding interest and enabling coherent understanding. It is also worth noting that data integrity can be tested and errors identified by a series of queries for extreme data.

[5b] As already mentioned, in terms of the data handling cycle, the design of the data structure will have already taken place in advance of the questionnaire design, as the two need to interlink and complement each other. The question of the necessity for pupils to tackle each step of the data handling cycle in a logical sequence is addressed earlier in this section.

[5c] It would be important for pupils to discuss their queries with you so that you can ensure they are on the right track. "Garbage in, garbage out" comes to mind and brings us back to the necessity for an efficient data structure, designed so that the correct information is collected and which, in turn, enables effective retrieval.

7.6 Controlling and monitoring

KS3 STRATEGY FRAMEWORK OBJECTIVES

Developing ideas and making things happen

Analysing and automating processes

- Represent simple processes as diagrams, showing:
  - how a task can be broken down into smaller ones;
  - the sequence of operations, and any conditions or decisions that affect it;
  - the initial information needed.

Control and monitoring

- Implement a system to carry out a simple control task, including some that involve sensed physical data, by:
  - compiling sets of instructions, identifying those which can be grouped to form procedures or loops;
  - testing and refining the instructions.

About this unit

This unit introduces and develops aspects of control and monitoring. It consists of five lessons which focus on control in everyday life, the practical techniques as well as the knowledge and understanding involved in control.

The unit introduces some important new knowledge, such as flowchart conventions, which may or may not have been met in other subjects. If this has not been covered, say, in Design and Technology, then pupils may need much more reinforcement and opportunities to explore and use this new knowledge if they are to retain it.

In the documentation it states that prior to starting the unit pupils need to be able to program a floor turtle; write, test and modify sequences of commands; and link output devices together. They may have had experience of doing this when using Logo and control equipment in primary school. To complete the unit they will need to understand and be able to use procedures and subprocedures. Generic subject knowledge needed for the unit includes an understanding of what switches and sensors are, and the different types. Pupils will also need to create simple and more complex flowcharts with loops, as well as to understand the notion of a system.

The pupils are taught as a whole class, in pairs or small groups, or as individuals. This unit introduces individual work for the first time, although it is not clear why, as this approach differs from the shared approach used throughout other units. In fact, collaboration is better suited to work in control so that pupils can discuss their ideas with others, as this is an important aspect of the problem solving approach. Throughout the unit they use mimic or simulation software rather than control equipment, and you may want to think about providing actual control equipment at least for the introductory tasks if at all possible.

This is a unit of five lessons. The balance of teaching and activity in the unit is shown in the table that follows. This indicates the suggested breakdown of teacher-led whole class teaching, individual, paired or small group work away from the computer, and practical, computer-based activity. Approximately 65 per cent of the time is spent in teacher-led, whole class activities, with 15 per cent spent on collaborative tasks away from the computer, and 20 per cent on practical, computer-based work. It is important that pupils are taught the principles underpinning control and monitoring. However, it is questionable whether sufficient time is allowed for practical tasks to enable the development of a good understanding of what is essentially a problem solving process.

	Taught as a whole class	*Pupil work away from the computer*	*Pupil work at the computer*
Lesson 1	50 mins	10 mins	
Lesson 2	43 mins	12 mins	5 mins
Lesson 3	30 mins	15 mins	15 mins
Lesson 4	42 mins	3 mins	15 mins
Lesson 5	31 mins	3–4 mins	25 mins
Overall balance	**3 hrs 16 mins** 65%	**44 mins** 15%	**1 hr** 20%

One key resource issue for this module is the provision of control equipment: buffer boxes, and input and output devices such as switches, lights and buzzers. Some of the teaching points included in lessons need practical resources for demonstration, or for pupils to use. For example, in Lesson 3 they are introduced to the idea of sensing light levels. Some pupils may need at least to see a light sensor working and registering light levels if they are to grasp the idea of a sensor.

The contexts for the activities are different sorts of lights: traffic lights, a lighthouse and flashing lights. The contexts are all appropriate for the activities, although you may find that pupils have already met these in Years 5 or 6. There may be other contexts linked to work in Design and Technology or Science that you can use instead.

The skills needed by the teacher are fairly straightforward control programming techniques. You will need to be able to set up control equipment, and program software to write control sequences which include decisions, loops and procedures. Non-specialists will need to research these thoroughly before starting to teach the unit. The teacher will also need to be able to look at control programs written by pupils and debug them, if necessary, in order to support pupils' thinking and help them to see errors.

The unit is designed for pupils working at Levels 4 and 5, and generally the units meet the expectations of these levels, although pupils' experience of sensing physical data and monitoring and measuring external events is limited in the unit.

LESSON BY LESSON

Lesson 1: Understanding control in everyday life

Starter: Checking pupils' knowledge and understanding

The lesson starts with a brief discussion intended to elicit pupils' prior experience and understanding of control.

Development: Everyday control; traffic lights, using instructions to control events, and improving sequences

The first lesson continues with a video showing the sequence of traffic lights, which the pupils analyse. Having made notes on the sequence of the lights, the pupils then discuss the sequence and decide what further commands are needed to control the traffic flow. They then watch a video clip of the traffic controlled by the opposite set of lights and use cards to sequence the system of lights used to control a two-way flow of traffic. A whole class discussion follows on how sequences can be modified and improved. The lesson ends with a discussion of the advantages of using ICT to control traffic lights. This lesson provides a structured approach which will support pupils' learning.

The examples of control given are limited and do not inform pupils about the extensive use of control technology. See page 62 for a discussion of this. [1a]

If pupils have already programmed traffic lights in Key Stage 2 (which is a distinct possibility), you may be able to revise this briefly and move on to sequencing two sets of lights.

Plenary and homework: Merits of using ICT to control events; and comparing manual and automated road crossings

In the plenary session pupils discuss the usefulness of ICT to control events. The homework asks children to compare a school crossing patrol with a pelican crossing.

An alternative task might be to ask them to identify control systems in use in their home, school, shops or leisure venues.

Lesson 2: Using flowchart symbols and writing instructions

Starter: Sequencing instructions

The lesson begins with pupils sequencing instructions to make a cup of coffee.

Development: Flowchart symbols; writing efficient instructions; and using software to control events

In the next part of the lesson a major topic is introduced: the idea that sequences of instructions can be summarised in flowcharts, and that there are conventions for expressing different types of instructions.

Some very demanding ideas are covered in this part of the lesson and these may need to be explored in greater detail. This is discussed on page 62. **[2a]**

One of the slides in the PowerPoint resource introduces these flowchart conventions:

This is also important knowledge, which may need further development if pupils are to be able to use it with understanding.

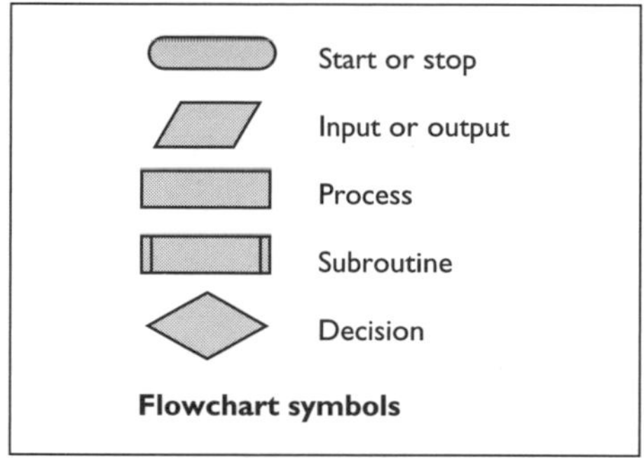

Flowchart symbols

Pupils go on to create a sequence of commands to make toast, using the following flowchart planning sheet:

Our own words	Control words (very precise)	Flowchart symbol

Pupils complete the first column, expressing the sequence of commands in "our own words". The teacher then demonstrates how these commands can be translated, first into more precise "control words" and then flowchart symbols. Pupils complete their own flowchart plan on making toast. The teacher then demonstrates a flowchart showing a traffic light sequence, which pupils load and examine.

The teaching points linked with the demonstration of the flowchart are important, but there may be little to be gained by the pupils loading and running the teacher's flowchart, so this part of the lesson could be omitted.

Plenary and homework: Matching instructions to actions; and creating a flowchart

The lesson ends with a discussion of the function of the decision command and how the coffee-making flowchart can be extended. The homework asks pupils to create another flowchart for buying a bar of chocolate from a vending machine.

This is an attractive example of a simple flowchart which can be extended. You could think about using it as an additional example for pupils to create during the lesson.

Lesson 3: Using a sensor as a switch in a control model

Lesson 3 introduces more new and important knowledge: the nature and functioning of sensors.

Starter: Using a webcam to sense and log movement

The introductory activity uses a webcam to observe pupils' movements as they enter the room.

In some ways this seems an attractive activity, which will capture pupils' interest. However, a webcam is not generally used as a movement sensor. This is explored in greater detail on page 63. [3a]

Development: Loops; and using software to control events

In the next part of the lesson, the notions of decisions and loops in a flowchart are introduced. Pupils examine a decision diagram and then construct their own.

The decision diagram task is rather confusing and could be difficult for pupils. Details are given in Lesson commentaries on page 64. [3b]

The next task requires the pupils to complete a decision diagram based on a question of their own:

Depending on the question they ask, the second task might also be rather confusing. For examples of this, see page 64. [3c]

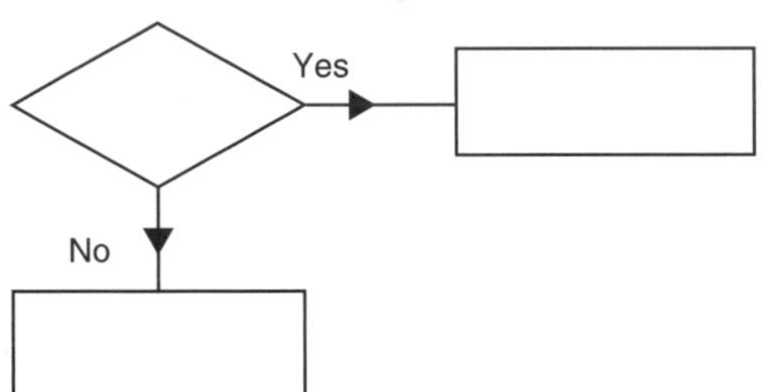

The lesson continues with a PowerPoint presentation, showing a flowchart which represents a system for monitoring light levels. The light levels are sensed, and if they are below 50 a light is switched on. If light levels remain above 50, the system beeps and goes back to checking the light levels.

Showing this sequence as a set of slides, without running it through a control program, is unlikely to help pupils understand what is happening. At this stage they have not even seen a light sensor, nor had any discussion about how light sensors operate or what the value in the flowchart (50) represents.

The final slide shows a similar flowchart with two loops and an unconventional layout, with lines crossing over one another:

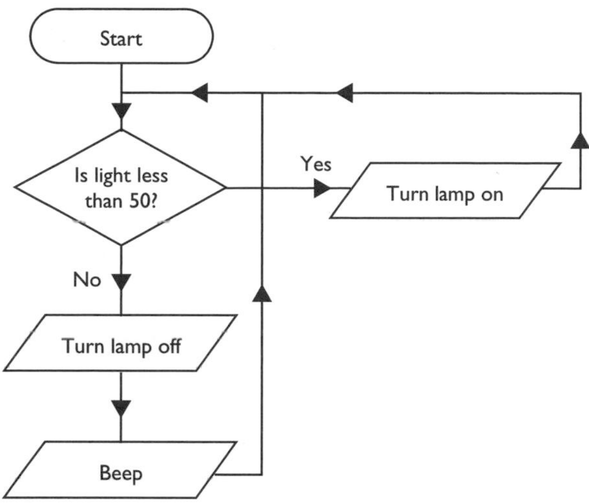

Flowchart with loop

You could consider omitting this and just show the orthodox presentation, as the unconventional layout adds little to the knowledge pupils need at this stage.

To develop the lesson you set up a control box and software to test this flowchart. The commands used earlier in the lesson, such as "turn lamp on" and "is light less than 50?", are now expressed using technical terminology, such as "turn output 1 on" and "is val <50?".

It is very important that you fully explain this change to the pupils and explain the reasons why commands are expressed in this way.

Pupils then go on to create their own flowchart like the one shown below. This should include a loop to monitor input from a digital device, such as a doorbell push, and to produce an output when it is on:

The lesson plan does not suggest a context or purpose for this, but it might be better to give pupils a few possible starting points. Some ideas for this are given on page 64. [3d]

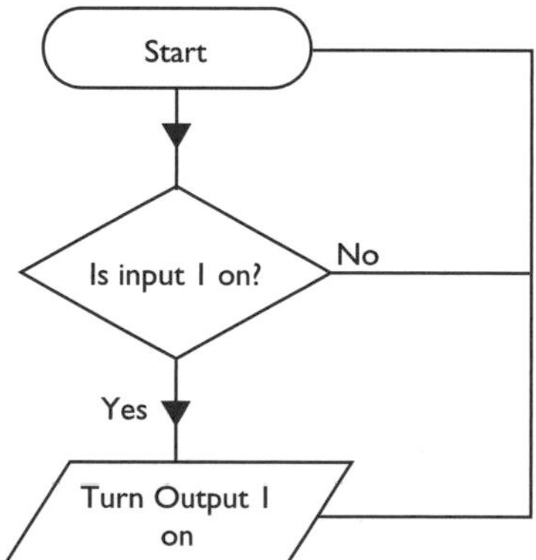

Plenary and homework: How a loop can improve the efficiency of a system; and control systems that use a loop

The lesson ends with a discussion of the use of such systems in reality. For their homework pupils have to think of three systems that use loops and create a flowchart for one of them.

Lesson 4: Creating and testing control models

Starter: Linking flowcharts to systems

Pupils begin by matching three flowcharts to different scenarios, which is useful revision of the work to date. These are common examples: a burglar alarm, an automatic door and a street light.

You could also follow up on pupils' homework and discuss any examples they have suggested.

Development: More complex systems; using more than one variable; and monitoring two variables at once

As the lesson continues the focus is on monitoring temperature, and pupils have to imagine a scenario in which an electric heater and a cooling fan are used to control the temperature in a room. They have to complete the following decision table with "on", "off" or "do nothing" as the options:

It will be really important here to explore the difference between "off" and "do nothing" before pupils complete the task.

Room temperature	Electric fire	Cooling fan
Too cold		
Just right		
Too hot		

The teacher then demonstrates the creation of a flowchart based on this scenario using the control software. The term "Val 1" is now being used as a measure of temperature, and this will need to be explained. The electric fire and cooling fan are labelled outputs 5 and 7 respectively, with no reason given, so you may want to refer to them as outputs 0 and 1, or 1 and 2.

The lesson plan does not suggest that you allow pupils to step through the example you have shown and create a flowchart of their own, but this might be a useful exercise, before they move on. For example, you could demonstrate the "electric fire" sequence and ask them to work out the "cooling fan" flowchart.

The next task requires pupils to create a flowchart which monitors two variables at once. This is a challenging task, particularly given the very limited "hands on" and practical problem solving opportunities they have been given to date.

The lesson plan suggests that pupils work individually or in pairs. Without doubt, this is best approached as a shared activity. Fifteen minutes have been allowed for this task, but you may find it takes longer for them to plan, test and refine their flowchart to solve the problem set.

Plenary and homework: Advantages of using a computer for control; and controlling greenhouse conditions

The lesson ends with a discussion of the advantages of using a computer for control and the homework requires pupils to apply what they have learned to another scenario. They are asked to list the physical conditions a gardener might want to control and create a flowchart for controlling one of them.

Lesson 5: Creating an efficient system to monitor an event

Starter: Identifying the characteristics of a model

The final lesson begins with pupils identifying the characteristics of a model, using a zebra crossing, lighthouse, street light and emergency flashing light as examples.

Development: Developing the model; and using procedures to build a program

The next part of the lesson introduces the notion of procedures or subroutines. The pupils may have met the idea of a procedure in Logo, and the term "PROC" is used in the first example they are given, a procedure for cleaning shoes. If they have met the term before in Logo, you will need to make a connection between that understanding and the idea of a subroutine in control. If they have not met this before the notion of a procedure or subroutine will need careful explanation.

The context then moves to that of a person with impaired hearing and the way that ICT could be of use to them in the home. Pupils are asked to adapt their flowcharts to cause a light to flash when a doorbell is pressed. There is also a differentiated activity, involving the writing of a subroutine called "Fast" to make a light flash briefly. This subroutine is then called up within the main flowchart.

This demands a high level of understanding and experience in the use of subroutines and will probably need a lot of explanation. You might find it better to leave subroutines until pupils revisit control in Unit 9.1.

Plenary and homework: Understanding a system; and using control in different environments

The lesson ends with a summary of what the unit has covered. For homework pupils have to consider:

- how their system could be altered to make it suitable for someone with a visual impairment;
- other ways that control systems could be used by people with hearing difficulties;
- how the system could be changed to help a disabled person get into and move around a building.

The first two tasks are fairly straightforward developments from work covered in the lesson. You might consider omitting the third task, in which the disability is not specified, making it rather vague.

Alternative approaches

The major difficulty with this unit is that pupils have relatively few opportunities to explore, hypothesise, plan, test and refine the control flowcharts they develop. Control is essentially a problem solving process. Without this direct, practical opportunity it will be difficult for pupils to gain the knowledge and understanding that the unit aspires to. More time for practical activity is essential. In the unit there is relatively little opportunity for pupils to go through the programming–testing–debugging process independently, with work at the computer and away from it. In addition, some important subject knowledge is introduced but there is very little opportunity for exploration, or application, by the pupils. Included in this are the following:

- flowchart conventions;
- procedures, routines and subroutines;
- the term "system", which is used but not fully explained.

Some of the tasks in the unit are based on controlling traffic lights. As this is commonly used as an introductory activity in control technology, it is likely that the pupils will have already done this in Key Stage 2. If this is the case you may want to omit some of the early tasks in Lesson 1, or revise them briefly, and move on to sequencing two sets of lights. Almost all of the activities in the unit are based on the context of controlling some form of light. This is a very limited view of control, and pupils will need a much more varied experience, both practically and in the examples presented to them, if their understanding is to be developed. It might be possible to link this work in control with topics being covered in Design and Technology, which is the natural context for this work.

While the use of mimics in packages such as Flowol, which simulate control systems, reduces the resource demands and makes the management of the lesson more straightforward, it would be useful to have equipment available for pupils to use, perhaps on a rota basis. This is particularly important when the lesson introduces new subject knowledge, such as the operation and function of different sensors. One of the possible difficulties with this unit is ensuring that there is progression, but not repetition, from the work that may have been covered by the pupils in their final years in primary school.

The unit uses flowchart conventions to construct the control programs. Again, depending on the pupils' experience of control, this may be an issue for you to consider. They may have already met these conventions if they have used similar software before. Alternatively, they may have used control software that employs different conventions, such as Lego Dacta or Coco. Having elicited pupils' prior experience, you may need to provide additional demonstrations or change the first lesson to help them make connections between what they are learning now and their previous experience of control.

Lesson commentaries

[1a] Although the lesson is described as "Understanding control in everyday life", in fact there is discussion only of traffic lights. In order for the pupils to appreciate the widespread use of control technology, you may want to initiate a broader discussion and draw out the experience of control in their everyday lives. You could make reference to the use of control systems in domestic appliances in homes (such as microwave ovens, video recorders, CD players, and so on), as well as in schools, factories, shops and offices: automatic doors, burglar alarms, optical character readers, photocopiers, automated production lines and many other systems.

[2a] Both the idea of a flowchart, which pupils may not have met before, and the conventions associated with flowchart design involve key ideas that pupils need to learn. It is likely that you will have to spend longer than the suggested ten minutes explaining these ideas and give pupils further opportunities to explore and apply these principles.

In addition, the first flowchart they see has a decision loop within it (whether or not to add milk). Instead, you could start with a simple flowchart, based on the coffee-making sequencing task already completed, before introducing the idea of a decision and loop.

Making coffee

- Boil water
- Drink coffee
- Take kettle from cupboard
- Fill kettle

Put the instructions in the right order.

Identify instructions that are missing.

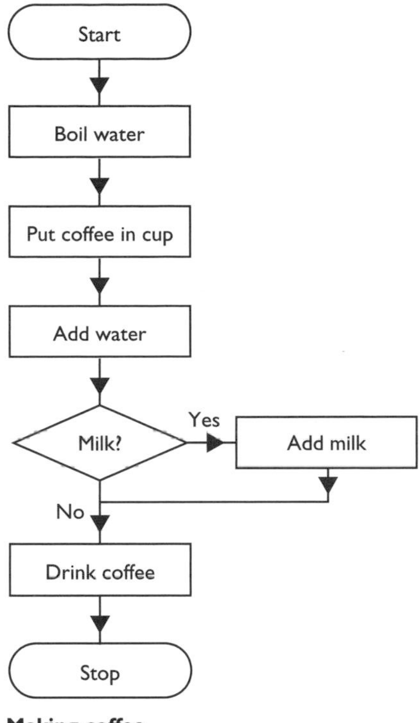

Making coffee

The "Watching TV" flowchart is also problematic. Following the decision statement "Is programme interesting?", there are two possibilities: "Yes, watch programme", or "No, switch off TV". In reality, there is another possible and more likely output, "No, change channel", which creates another loop. Depending on your pupils' understanding, you could use this as a teaching point, or omit this slide.

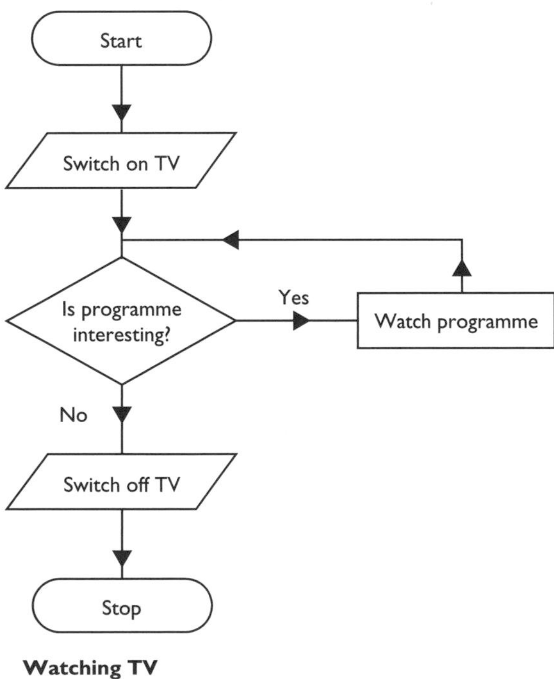

Watching TV

The difficulties with this exercise illustrate the need for very clear examples and the need for good preparation before using them with pupils.

[3a] In this example, the camera is only operating as a sensor because it is connected to movement-sensing software. It is extremely important that pupils understand this distinction between the camera alone (which is not a sensor, as such) and the camera plus software. This is problematic and not the most

easily understood example of a sensor. An additional difficulty is that the other examples of movement sensing suggested for discussion – a burglar alarm, a cat flap, or an automatic door – do not, in fact, use cameras. Because of these concerns you may wish to consider whether this activity is appropriate.

[**3b**] The decision diagram task is rather confusing and could be difficult for pupils. This is the example the pupils are given:

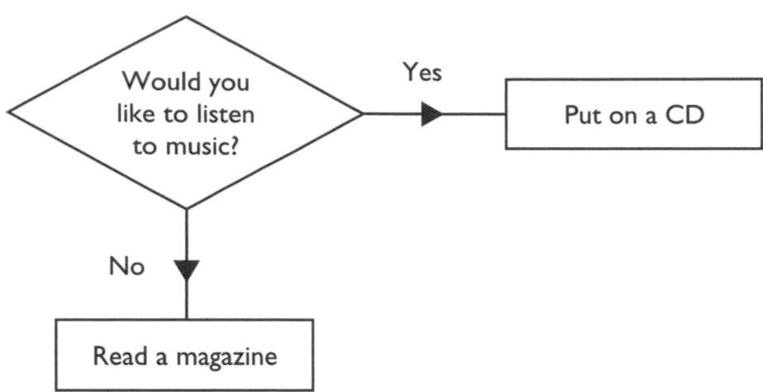

The problem here is that the loop has already been introduced as a way of checking whether the state of the existing situation has changed. For example, has a burglar approached the door, has the cat approached the cat flap or has a person walked up to the supermarket door? In those examples, the "yes" choice would result in an action (or output) and the "no" option would lead to no action but loop back to a point before the decision in the flowchart. The example given, therefore, is rather confusing for the knowledge being developed. This sequence would be better shown as:

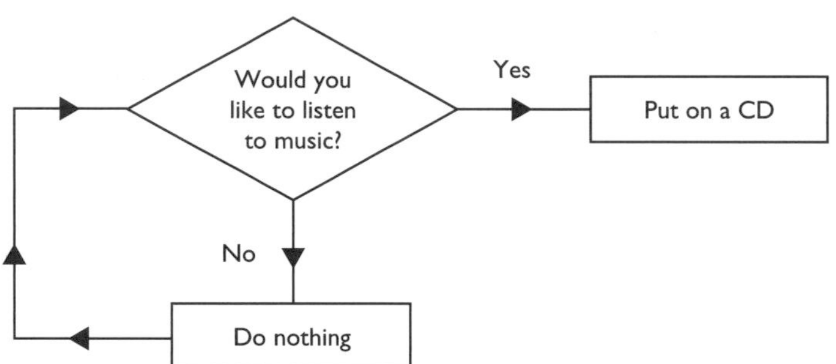

[**3c**] The question used by the pupils is crucial here, and could cause confusion. For example, the question "Are you hungry?" could lead to "yes, make a sandwich", but the "no" choice would lead to no action, rather than to another output or choice. You could either make this an explicit teaching point or suggest some examples of the type of question they should choose. A suitable question might be: "Have I got long enough to get to the leisure centre?" The "yes" outcome could then be "walk there" and the "no" outcome, "take the bus".

[**3d**] The following are possible suggestions or "hints" for pupils trying to think of systems that use loops:

- A system using a movement sensor to switch off classroom lights when the room is empty, to conserve energy.
- A light sensor which ensures that street lamps are switched on as dusk falls.
- A burglar alarm system which sets off an alarm because the temperature has fallen suddenly when the window is broken by an intruder.a

Year 8 units

8.1 Public information systems This is a unit of five lessons in which pupils obtain climate information from the Internet and import this into a spreadsheet using a web query to provide an information system for a travel agent. The process of gathering and displaying the information is automated to make it more efficient.

8.2 Publishing on the web In this unit of eight lessons, pupils design and create a website to provide a visitor with information about the school. They use HTML, a word processor and then web-authoring software to create a linked series of web pages. The unit aims to develop pupils' understanding of the ways in which different web browsers display web pages and the importance of taking account of this when creating websites.

8.3 Information: reliability, validity and bias In this unit of four lessons, pupils consider the validity of electronic sources of information. They retrieve information using key words and evaluate the performance of a range of search engines. They search for information for a specific purpose. Pupils have been introduced to these ideas in Unit 7.2.

8.4 Modelling This is a unit of five lessons in which pupils develop their understanding of the concepts of modelling and presenting numeric information. They investigate and improve an existing model through the acquisition of a number of spreadsheet techniques. Pupils have been introduced to these ideas in Unit 7.4.

8.5 An ICT system: integrating applications to find solutions This unit of nine lessons brings together a range of skills, knowledge and understanding developed by pupils through a number of units in Years 7 and 8. Pupils carry out a feasibility study of a fund-raising project for a local charity. It is proposed that pupils grow bedding plants from seedlings to maturity and then sell them to the public, making a profit for the charity in the process. The unit requires pupils to model the financial aspects of the operation, develop an appropriate control system, carry out data handling in relation to customer details and create publicity materials for the project.

8.1 Public information systems

KS3 STRATEGY FRAMEWORK OBJECTIVES

Finding things out

Organising and investigating

- In an investigation:
  - use software options and formats to store and present electronic material efficiently;
  - explore and interpret collected data in order to draw conclusions.

Exchanging and sharing information

Fitness for purpose

- Recognise how different media and presentation techniques convey similar content in ways that have different impacts.

Refining and presenting information

- Plan and design presentations and publications, showing how account has been taken of:
  - audience expectations and needs;
  - the ICT and media facilities available.

Developing ideas and making things happen

Analysing and automating processes

- Automate simple processes by:
  - creating templates;
  - creating simple software routines.

About this unit

This is a unit of five lessons in which pupils first discuss the use of sensors and then obtain climate information from the Internet. They then import this into a spreadsheet so that it can be used by a travel agent to inform customers about the weather they can expect at a particular holiday destination. The process of gathering and displaying the information is automated to make it more efficient. The unit also emphasises the input–process–output structure of the system, where the input is the Internet-based climate data and the processing and output are undertaken using the spreadsheet.

While this is an interesting activity and will contribute to important understanding of automated information systems, you may find that you do not need the full five hours allowed for the unit. Alternatively, you may decide to spend some of the time available looking again at the use of sensors, as so far the focus has been almost entirely on sensing light (in Unit 7.6). You could always give further opportunities for pupils to create and interpret charts.

In order to start the unit, pupils will need to be able to access information from the Internet, as well as to edit, insert, delete, move, copy and paste text and images. During the first lesson they are taken through the process of creating a chart step-by-step, and they create charts of their own. They may need additional experience of creating charts as well as further discussion of chart types if they are to understand this fully and be able to create appropriate charts independently. They will need knowledge of the units of measurement used by weather stations and to be able to interpret weather data.

The generic knowledge developed in this unit relates mainly to presenting and interpreting data. The ICT subject knowledge focuses on the creation and formatting of information presented as text, charts and images. Pupils will also learn how to present data in a spreadsheet and rename worksheets. They will develop understanding of the ways in which information can be accessed automatically and be dynamically linked between different spreadsheet worksheets or ICT applications. By the end of the unit they will be able to set up a web query to download data automatically and to create dynamic links to update this information in the spreadsheet.

The unit is organised into individual, pair, and whole class work. The suggested breakdown of teacher-led whole class teaching, individual, paired or small group work away from the computer and practical, computer-based activity is as follows.

	Taught as a whole class	*Pupil work away from the computer*	*Pupil work at the computer*
Lesson 1	35 mins	10 mins	15 mins
Lesson 2	40 mins		20 mins
Lesson 3	40 mins	5 mins	15 mins
Lesson 4	30 mins	5 mins	25 mins
Lesson 5	35 mins		25 mins
Overall balance	**3 hrs** 60%	**20 mins** 7%	**1 hr 40 mins** 33%

Approximately 60 per cent of the time is spent in teacher-led, whole class activities, with 40 per cent spent on collaborative tasks, most of it at the computer. This is a more even balance of taught time and pupil activity than is suggested for many other units, but you may still feel that more time spent on practical activity, to support understanding, would improve the experience for pupils.

The unit is designed for pupils working at Level 5 and relates to the requirement of that level description that pupils "use ICT to structure, refine and present information in different forms and styles for specific purposes and audiences". There is some differentiation for pupils working at a higher level. There are no differentiated tasks suggested for pupils working at Level 4, although in a section headed "Further development" on page 38 of the sample teaching unit suggestions are made for ways in which pupils can be given additional experience of using the new techniques introduced in this unit.

To teach the unit, as well as the knowledge and techniques above, the teacher will need understanding of different types of charts, including radar charts, as well as the formats in which raw data can be imported, as CSV (comma separated values), tab-delimited or length-delimited files. The "noise" data file, used in Lesson 1, is provided in three formats, .sid, .csv and as an Excel spreadsheet. The teacher will need to decide which format to apply and be familiar with its use. As pupils are going to use the spreadsheet to process their own data, it might be a good idea to use this format in the introduction.

Teachers printing the charts (81T3e, 81T3f, 81T5e) for their own notes will need to check the print options to obtain a landscape printout.

LESSON BY LESSON

Lesson 1: Revising datalogging, sensors and data representation

Starter: Revising sensors

As pupils enter the room and during the first activity, the sound is logged using a sound sensor. The first activity for the pupils is a worksheet intended to revise the work on sensors undertaken in Unit 7.6.

Pupils may have some difficulty here. This activity is discussed in Lesson commentaries, page 72. [**1a**]

Development: Interpreting data from a datalogger; revising graphing software; and displaying data graphically

Pupils go on to interpret the chart of the sound data that has been collected. The data is then exported to a shared area, and the process of charting it as a time series chart (line chart) is demonstrated by the teacher. As the teacher demonstrates how to create the chart, pupils are asked to explain which option to take, and why.

The lesson notes state that the teacher should ensure that pupils understand that this is the appropriate chart type to use. This is vital understanding. You may need to show some inappropriate chart types, too, to ensure that this understanding is secure.

Pupils go on to create a time series chart of their own.

The lesson notes suggest providing support materials, but both the suggested strategies are problematic. This is discussed in Lesson commentaries, page 72. [**1b**]

Plenary and homework: Reviewing how information is displayed; and more work on sensors

The lesson ends with a review of how the data were collected and displayed.

In the lesson only passing reference is made to some key issues relating to the presentation of data, such as the use of colour, fonts, changing the axes on charts and so on. These are really important teaching points and will need further discussion in the lesson.

For homework, the pupils have to answer specific and more open questions about sensors.

The more open questions are rather vague and pupils may need some preparation if they are to tackle them successfully.

Lesson 2: Using and displaying live data

Starter: Considering data from a remote source

The second lesson begins with a whole class discussion of live data from a remote source displayed in real time. The suggested source is a weather station in Lancashire. Pupils make notes to answer questions displayed on a whiteboard or flipchart. A discussion follows on the difficulties of interpreting these data and ways in which this information could be made easier to understand.

Development: Importing the data file into a spreadsheet; and selecting and displaying it graphically

Pupils go on to import some data into a spreadsheet, having seen a demonstration of how this is done. The lesson notes suggest that you may have to modify the instructions to suit the format of the data file if it differs from the given format, which is a fixed-width text file.

> Any changes that are needed will have to be planned and organised in advance.

The notion of a public information system is introduced as pupils look at the weather website. The teacher is advised to explain that the website gathers data from sensors in the weather station, selects and processes the data and then displays them in different ways.

> You might like to make a link between the input–process–output of control systems, which pupils met in Unit 7.6.

In this activity the pupils are instructed to display the data as a line chart.

> You may need to revise pupils' understanding of why this chart format is suitable for these data. You could show the weather station data in several formats and discuss the suitability of the different types.

Plenary and homework: Reviewing how information is displayed

A discussion of why different forms of data are presented in different ways concludes the lesson, and for homework the pupils have to find examples of how different types of information are displayed.

> You might like to give an example of each type on the worksheet to get them started.

Lesson 3: Planning and creating a simple public information system

This lesson moves on to looking at the forms of information needed by different users and creating a basic information system for a particular purpose.

Starter: Identifying information needs of different users

Pupils first complete a worksheet which asks what information is needed by various groups, such as farmers, hospital administrators and air traffic controllers. This is completed in pairs and then discussed with the whole class.

Development: Planning and creating a basic ICT-based information system for a specific audience

Pupils then go on to look at a website which shows general weather information as well as specific forecasts for particular groups, such as racing drivers.

They now begin to plan their own information system, which a travel agent might use to determine the weather conditions at a holiday destination, York.

> Other possible contexts for this task are discussed on page 72. [3a]

They go on to create a spreadsheet workbook with three worksheets, linked to the input–process–output model, and they cut and paste data from the website into the first worksheet. They then have to transfer the data into the second worksheet representing the process, using dynamic links.

> Some pupils may need help to understand dynamic linking, as well as with the techniques for creating dynamic links. See page 72. [3b]

Plenary and homework: Checking understanding of displaying data

Having planned their own system, in the plenary the pupils return to evaluating a chart (resource 8.1T3f) by suggesting improvements to an exemplar line chart showing temperature data. For homework, they evaluate and complete charts showing weather information.

Lesson 4: Automating processes in a simple public information system

Having designed their basic information system, pupils now move on to automating the input of information.

Starter: Illustrating automation in a spreadsheet

Pupils revise their understanding of dynamic linking by working out what will happen on the "process" and "output" worksheets when the data on the "input" page change.

Development: Using a web query to create an information system; and consolidating understanding of automated processes

The teacher now demonstrates the way that a web query can be used to import data into a spreadsheet automatically. The dynamic links ensure that this changed data is reflected in the process and output (chart) aspects of the spreadsheet.

> It is suggested that pupils are given access to a PowerPoint presentation (8.1T4a webquery.ppt) to support this activity. Again, printed material may be better for this purpose, and easier for pupils than moving between the two applications.

Having set up the web query they are shown how to change the URL in order to collect data for a different location.

Plenary and homework: Checking understanding of the web query

The plenary emphasises the input–process–output structure of the system and this is developed in the homework task.

> The system is referred to as having this structure throughout the unit. It may not be entirely accurate as a description, and this is discussed on page 72. [4a]

Lesson 5: Meeting the needs of the user

The final lesson of the unit is used mainly to review and develop the information systems pupils have created.

Starter: Evaluation of the system

The system developed in the previous lesson is shown in a PowerPoint presentation, set to run as a continuous display of the three worksheets. Pupils evaluate their systems and decide what they would like to change. This is discussed with the whole class.

Development: Modifying the system to suit the user and make it easier to use

Using a spreadsheet-based sample system (8.1T5b) with a live Internet connection, the teacher now shows how the system can be changed to allow data from different locations to be processed and displayed by the information system. This is done by changing the URL of a web query and linking it to a cell in the first (input) worksheet of the system. The user can now input the name of a location to download specific weather data for that place.

Pupils go on to refine their own systems by making these changes. They also make improvements to their system through the appropriate use of formatting, providing on-screen instructions, changing chart scales and so on.

> The lesson notes suggest that you provide help sheets or guidelines to support this task, and these will probably be needed. The teacher will have to prepare these in advance.

Plenary and homework: Reviewing the system

The plenary provides an overall review and discusses the use of public information systems in transport, sporting events and so on. For homework, pupils are asked to reflect on the advantages and disadvantages of automated processes and suggest two other automated processes.

> There is an additional resource, 81T5e, included in the unit, which is not referred to in the lesson notes. You might wish to show it to pupils to illustrate how the use of colour can enhance or hinder communication.

Alternative approaches

In this unit the term "graph" is used to describe the graphic display of data, but the software application used by the pupils may refer to these as charts. It is important that pupils understand that the terms can be used interchangeably, and they carry the same meaning.

The main issue you may want to consider when teaching this unit is that of context. The specific context of York may not be particularly relevant for pupils, and you might like to consider alternatives which may be more motivating. Perhaps they could create an information system for an outdoor pursuits centre used by the school or by its feeder junior schools. It could be based on a number of locations that pupils would like to visit on holiday. Alternatively, there may be opportunities to make links between this unit and work in other subjects, such as a study of a particular geographical location.

There are a number of important topics which are included and which could be given greater emphasis. For example, it is vital that pupils have a good understanding of chart styles and the selection of styles which are appropriate to the data and the needs of the audience. In order to really understand these important aspects, they need experience of a range of charts, good and bad.

One effective way of doing this is to make a collection of charts from different sources and for different purposes. Newspapers and magazines often use charts to illustrate articles or advertisements. Sometimes these are inaccurate or misleading, particularly in the case of financial services. Often, three-dimensional formats are used to make the chart look more interesting, at the expense of readability. Often, charts such as pie charts are printed without values or percentages, making them difficult to interpret. These would be good examples to show pupils.

Being able to select appropriate chart style, create, and interpret charts is an important generic skill and aspect of understanding. Units 7.4 and 8.4 also address this. You may decide to take one or more lessons for this aspect of the work and teach it discretely, so that it will support work in all these units.

Lesson commentaries

[**1a**] The sensors shown include a temperature probe, which pupils may not have encountered, unless it has been covered in Science. They might find it difficult to identify the sensors used in a music keyboard or computer keyboard, and their effects.

This is planned as paired work. You could also approach it as a whole class discussion if you wish. If you think your pupils might have difficulty identifying the sensors, or have limited experience of the use of sensors in Science or Design Technology and might not easily make connections between this activity and the work in Unit 7.6, then it is vital to set up some sensors for them to see working.

[**1b**] The lesson notes suggest that pupils who need help are given access to a PowerPoint presentation (8.1P1g helpfile.ppt). This will require them to switch between the PowerPoint presentation and the spreadsheet, something that less confident pupils may find difficult.

The alternative suggestion is that they are given the PowerPoint presentation as a printed handout, but the printout is difficult to read and such a resource is not ideal as support material for a staged process. It might be preferable to provide structured instructional support materials on paper.

[**3a**] Although it is suggested that you record the weather in a specific city, York, the context for this activity could be any location that interests the pupils. You could select weather data from, for example, a local destination, a polar weather station, a location which experiences extremes of temperature, holiday destinations pupils have visited, or a sporting or concert venue.

[**3b**] The resources in the unit include a PowerPoint presentation designed to show pupils how to create dynamic links between applications. If pupils have not previously met the notion of dynamic linking, this may need further explanation. As an example you could remind them of the dynamic link between data in a spreadsheet and the chart displayed alongside it. You could then copy the chart (dynamically linked) into a word-processed document and then show the way that changes to the original data are reflected in the chart presented in the word-processed document.

[**4a**] The system is described as being an "input–process–output" model. However, the process stage is somewhat limited, as the information is selected or filtered rather than being processed in the way that information is processed in a control system. You might want to discuss this distinction with pupils or omit the reference to this structure.

8.2 Publishing on the web

KS3 STRATEGY FRAMEWORK OBJECTIVES

Exchanging and sharing information

Fitness for purpose

- Understand that an effective presentation or publication will address audience expectations and needs.
- Devise criteria to evaluate the effectiveness of own and others' publications and presentations, and use the criteria to make refinements.

Refining and presenting information

- Plan and design presentations and publications, showing how account has been taken of:
  – audience expectations and needs;
  – the ICT and media facilities available;
- Use a range of ICT tools efficiently to combine, refine and present information by:
  – extracting, combining and modifying relevant information for specific purposes;
  – structuring a publication or presentation.

Communicating

- Understand some of the technical issues involved in efficient electronic communications.
- Use ICT effectively to adapt material for publication to wider or remote audiences.

Developing ideas and making things happen

Analysing and automating processes

- Automate simple processes by creating simple software routines.
- Consider the benefits and drawbacks of using ICT to automate processes.
- Represent simple design specifications as diagrams.

About this unit

This is a unit of eight lessons in which pupils design and create a website to provide a visitor with information about the school. They work in groups of four to create a linked series of web pages. The unit uses the web-authoring program Microsoft FrontPage, although it is suggested that pupils first create a web page using HTML (HyperText mark-up language) and then a word processor such as Microsoft Word. As well as developing the techniques of web authoring, the unit aims to develop pupils' understanding of the ways in which different web browsers display web pages and the importance of taking account of this when creating websites.

Prior to starting the unit, pupils will need to be able to use a word processor to create and present information. They will also need an understanding of file structure, the properties of different graphics formats, and be able to use an Internet browser and a search engine. Some knowledge of copyright restrictions is needed, as well as generic skills and understanding relating to techniques in design. The unit makes reference to the need for pupils to have prior experience of "storyboard" techniques in publication design. Pupils may also have met this term as a technique for structuring narrative in English, so if it is introduced as a design term this potential confusion will need to be clarified.

This unit demands a high level of subject knowledge and technical understanding compared with previous units, assuming that these have been covered sequentially. With that in mind, the teacher may decide to leave this unit until later in Year 8. If the teacher's subject knowledge is insecure in these areas, the unit suggests that reference is made to an online dictionary (such as http://wombat.doc.ic.ac.uk/foldoc/). While this will provide definitions of terms, non-specialists may need to refer to other sources to develop a real grasp of the subject knowledge, sufficient to teach the unit with confidence, answer pupils' questions and engage with pupils, some of whom may themselves have a high level of subject knowledge in this area. Teachers will also need an understanding of HTML, broadband communications and transmission rates. They will need to be able to create and use style sheets in a web authoring program and use a graphics animation package with a web function. In preparation for the unit the teacher will also need to create folders on the school's intranet for pupils to store their work, and check that they have the permission they need to access the web-authoring software and store their web pages on the intranet. The resources in the unit focus on the use of Microsoft Front Page. If the school uses different web-authoring software, then the teacher will have to produce alternative versions of the support and teaching materials.

The unit aims to cover work at Level 5. Pupils work as a whole class, in pairs or in small groups. For the first time they are expected to work on ICT-based tasks in groups of four, and you will need to consider how you can ensure that all of the pupils in the group will have access to the computer and will develop the skills and understanding that the unit is intended to teach. In Lesson 7 this unit also introduces the idea of pupils as peer tutors. If you wish to have pupils support their peers in this way, you could introduce this way of working gradually throughout the unit. The balance of activities throughout the unit is as follows.

	Taught as a whole class	*Pupil work away from the computer*	*Pupil work at the computer*
Lesson 1	40 mins	5 mins	15 mins
Lesson 2	35 mins	10 mins	15 mins
Lesson 3	40 mins	20 mins	
Lesson 4	45 mins	5 mins	10 mins
Lesson 5	15 mins	15 mins	30 mins
Lesson 6	15 mins	45 mins	
Lesson 7	15 mins	5 mins	40 mins
Lesson 8	12 mins	8 mins	40 mins
Overall balance	**3 hrs 37 mins** 45%	**1 hr 53 mins** 24%	**2 hrs 30 mins** 31%

It is vital that sufficient attention is given to the planning, design and evaluation aspects of this work, but web publishing is also an activity in which practical realisation of the design is extremely important. It seems likely that the lack of time for practical work at the computer will be a shortcoming of the unit and prove frustrating for pupils, particularly as some of the computer-based tasks are undertaken in groups of four.

As with other units, it is suggested that pupils have access to PowerPoint presentations as support materials during some lessons. Here too, pupils might be better supported with printed materials, rather than by having to switch between two applications, especially as this would also mean moving between two views in PowerPoint itself (the slide show view to see the support material and the working view to switch to the web-authoring application).

There are a number of issues relating to time management in the unit. Specific aspects are covered in the more detailed consideration of each lesson that follows.

LESSON BY LESSON

Lesson 1: Comparing methods of producing web pages

Starter: Reviewing Year 7 learning

The unit begins by revising the work done in Unit 7.2 using data and information sources. There is a discussion of the notions of accuracy, validity, relevance and ease of use, based on pupils' recall of previous work. This discussion is referenced to a web page from the BBC website displayed in the classroom.

Here, as in Unit 8.3, the idea of reliability is equated with "official" and unreliability with "unofficial", which may not help pupils develop critical awareness of web-based material. Other approaches to website evaluation are discussed on page 83. [1a]

Development: Introducing HTML; and creating a simple web page

The lesson continues with a discussion of the aims of the unit, and the teacher then introduces web-authoring techniques through the use of HTML. Fifteen minutes is allowed for teaching basic HTML techniques and the same length of time for pupils to replicate the page that the teacher has created using a step-by-step handout. The web page has hyperlinks to three search engines, Yahoo, Excite and Google. The HTML code and the resulting web page are shown below:

This is a problematic activity and its value is questionable here. It is discussed in Lesson commentaries on page 83. [1b]

```
<html>
<head>
<title>Information on search engines</title>
</head>
<body>
<h1>Search engines</h1>
<a href="http://www.yahoo.com">Yahoo</a><br>
<a href="http://www.excite.co.uk">Excite</a><br>
<a href="http://www.google.fr">Google</a><br>
</body>
</html>
```

Search engines

Yahoo
Excite
Google

Plenary and homework: Planning extra features; and the home page of a website

The lesson ends with a whole class discussion of the criteria for evaluating websites, and pupils suggest ways in which the page they have created could be improved. For homework, they have to consider what information should be on the school website home page, and plan a home page of their own.

Lesson 2: Planning the website structure

The notes for this lesson include a considerable amount of information about electronic communications, and you may need to research this further before the lesson to be secure when teaching it. When discussing this with pupils it will be very important for them to realise the implications of these technical specifications for website design, particularly aspects such as download times for graphics and other large files.

Starter: Relationship between audience and purpose

The lesson begins with a discussion of the different purposes of websites: to inform, entertain, advertise, persuade and so on. Pupils evaluate a children's website (www.bbc.co.uk/cbeebies) to establish its audience, purpose and special features.

It is not clear why this particular website alone has been chosen, and the information is not used at this point. This is discussed on page 83. **[2a]**

Development: Using MS Word to create a web page; and comparing methods

They go on to create the same "search engine" web page as that produced in the previous lesson, this time using a word processor. Some of the techniques taught in this part of the lesson, such as inserting hyperlinks and the use of styles to apply consistent formatting throughout a document, are useful for a range of applications. However, it is important that pupils fully understand the limitations of web pages produced using a word processor.

Having created the page, there is a whole class discussion about the different methods by which they were created. An important part of this discussion is a comparison of the file sizes of the same web page created in HTML and in a word processor.

This task could be altered or omitted, and this is discussed on page 84. **[2b]**

Plenary and homework: Looking forward to the task for remaining lessons; and evaluating the use of a word processor to create a web page

The plenary session sets the scene for the creation of pupils' own web pages, allocates pupils to groups and assigns areas or themes for the pages to each group. The homework asks pupils to consider the advantages and disadvantages of using a word processor to create a website.

Lesson 3: Planning the website structure

Lesson 3 includes a great deal of new information for pupils and also a significant task, the design of the website using website schema, for which only 15 minutes is allowed.

Starter: Considering audience needs

The lesson begins by considering different formats for presenting information on a website, looking at various screen resolutions and text-only and non-visual browsers.

> The website used for this demonstration is the Becta site, which is not particularly relevant to pupils.

These different formats are related to the needs of the users, and it is stressed that the website being designed by pupils will need to meet the needs of its audience: parents and pupils.

> They may also need help to make the connections, in a practical sense, between this principle and the previous website formats they have looked at.

Development: Outlining the structure; identifying routes through the information; and file and folder structure

The lesson moves on to look at website schema. Again, this is new information, not connected with what has come before it. The PowerPoint presentation shows two views of the same information, one set out using website schema and one showing a hierarchical folder structure:

> This is a complex notion and pupils may find it difficult. It could be argued that pupils do not need to understand the distinction at this stage, so you could choose to omit the comparison, and only discuss the website schema.

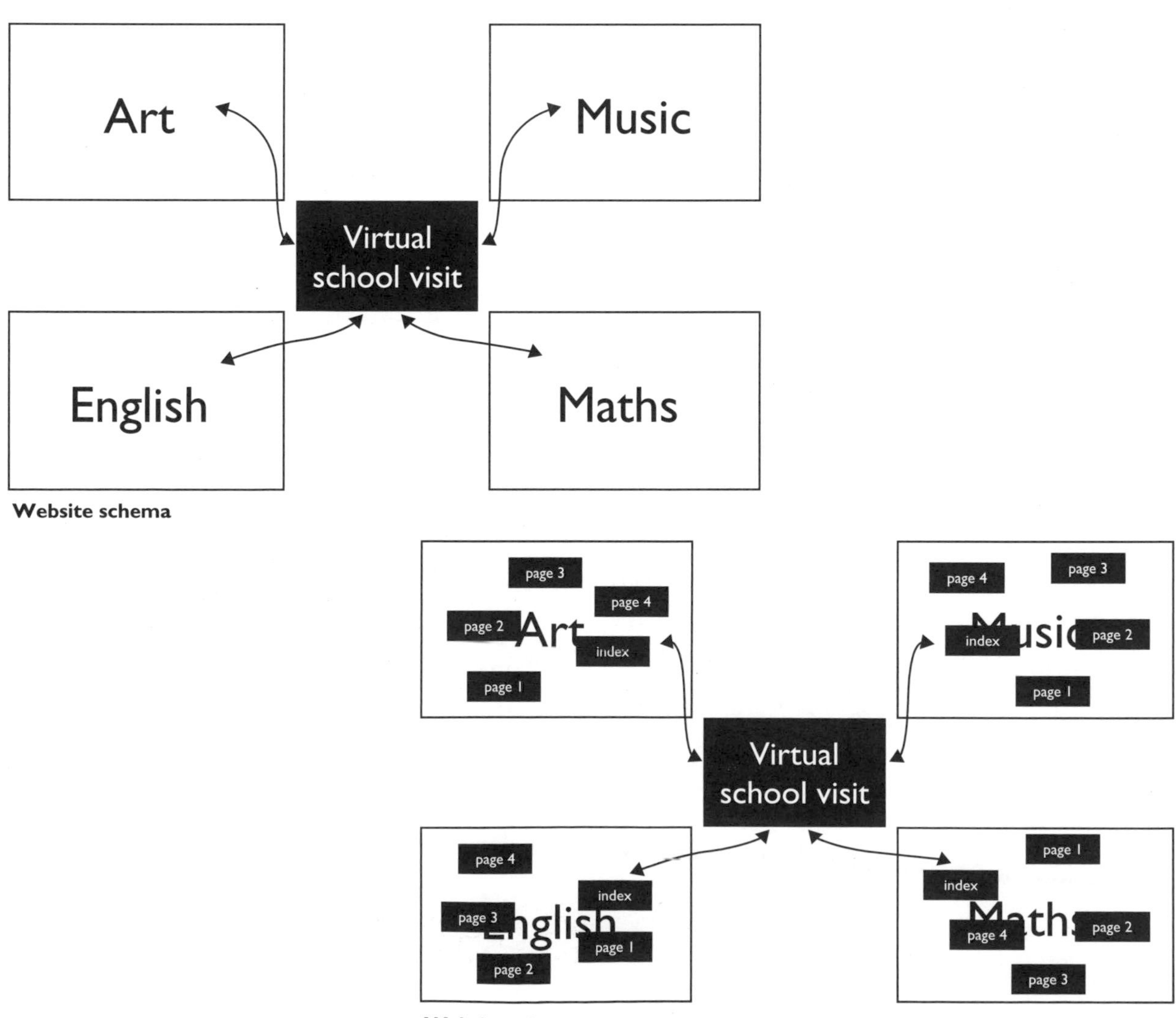

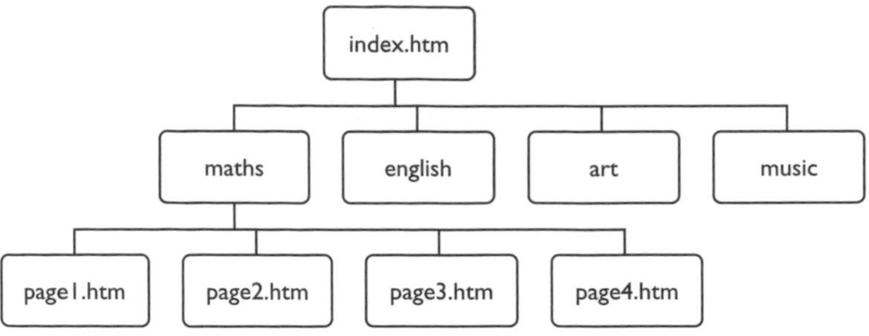

A hierarchical folder and file structure

In groups of four, pupils go on to plan their section of the proposed website, using sheets of A3 paper and yellow sticky notes. The focus is on routes through the pages, and having planned the structure pupils are asked to then reconsider their plan bearing in mind the needs of at least two different visitors.

> Only 15 minutes is allocated to this entire task, and you may find that, in fact, it takes much longer for pupils to achieve a satisfactory outcome.

Having planned it in this way they sketch the plan on paper. In the next part of the lesson they relate their plan to the hierarchical file structure.

> This may not be the best time to cover this. See page 84 for a discussion of this. [3a]

Plenary and homework: Reviewing the website plan; and researching users' needs and interests

The lesson ends with a review of pupils' plans to draw out good features. For homework, pupils compare the needs of adults visiting the school website with their own views.

> In fact pupils only establish the needs of their own adult family members and this limitation should be explored.

Lesson 4: Introducing web page creation, structure and appearance

Lesson 4 includes a great deal of new information and techniques. It is the first experience pupils have of creating a web page using web-authoring software. They look first at possible page layouts, watch a demonstration of web page creation and then complete their own. They go on to consider the use of style sheets and consider the advantages of using style sheets in the plenary session.

> Important aspects of the web creation process are covered in this lesson and there are some significant issues to do with timing, which are discussed on page 84. [4a]

Starter: Thinking about page layouts

The first activity focuses on the use of different page layouts, and suggested layouts are provided in the introductory PowerPoint presentation and as a paper-based resource. Only one of the suggested layouts follows the convention of placing the outline or map of the content or navigation tools on the left of the screen and content on the right.

> You could adopt a more active and, arguably, more effective approach to developing this knowledge and understanding. See page 84 for details. [**4b**]

Development: Demonstrating web page creation software; and style sheets

The teacher then demonstrates the web creation software, and pupils go on to create their own web page. The technique of using tables to organise information on a web page is introduced. The page includes text and a logo.

> There are significant issues connected with teaching points and practical management here, which are discussed on page 84. [**4c**]

The final section of the lesson focuses on the use of style sheets, which can be shown as a live demonstration, or as PowerPoint slides. Pupils then go on to apply a style sheet to their own page by inserting the HTML code for the appropriate style sheet between the <head> and </head> tags on the HTML view of their web page.

> If you have decided to omit the work on HTML, you will have to show pupils the HTML view of their page and provide a brief explanation of it here.

Plenary and homework: Advantages of style sheets; and finding images

The advantages of style sheets are discussed in the plenary, and the homework requires pupils to find at least two images which could be used to enhance their web pages.

Lesson 5: Designing and creating a front page for a section

Lesson 5 develops pupils' understanding of website design and develops the techniques of website creation.

Starter: Evaluating web pages

At the start of the lesson pupils return to website evaluation, this time to consider visual aspects such as fonts and font size, the effectiveness of images and the balance between text and images, as well as the use of white space.

> This is important knowledge and understanding, which is discussed further on page 85. [**5a**]

Development: Designing and creating the front page

Pupils then go on to plan their front page on paper in groups of four, bearing in mind the design that they developed in the previous lesson. The lesson suggests that they have 10 minutes to design and then 30 minutes to create their front page. Links with other pages are considered at this point. As the group of four continue to create the page it is suggested that they could also:

- take digital photographs;
- scan images.

Pupils working on this in groups of four has implications for class management. The lesson notes suggest the following strategies:

- the group could split into two pairs, each of which create a web page; they then discuss these and combine the best features from both into an agreed web page;
- one pair of the group produce the images and one the text.

These are key decisions and some of the implications are outlined on page 85. **[5b]**

Plenary and homework: Evaluating the pages produced; and suggesting improvements

In the plenary of the lesson pupils evaluate their pages, particularly in relation to the needs and interests of the users. For homework, they think about the ways in which their page can be improved.

The notion of audience has been referred to throughout this unit. However, pupils have had little opportunity to investigate the needs of the presumed audience, and this is something you may need to consider when planning the context for the unit. Alternative contexts are discussed later on page 82.

Lesson 6: Designing web pages

In Lesson 6 pupils go on to develop their web pages.

Starter: Considering the purposes of websites

Pupils begin by considering the various purposes of websites: to inform, educate, illustrate, advertise or entertain. Working in pairs, they look at nine website pages shown in Pupil Resource 8, a PowerPoint presentation. They decide on the purpose of each and evaluate the use of images, recording their ideas on a worksheet. Based on this activity, they evaluate their own page.

In the lesson notes only 10 minutes are allowed for this task and the whole class discussion which follows, and this is almost certainly insufficient time.

Development: Planning and designing pages for the section

Pupils then continue to design the remaining pages of their section of the website.

Plenary and homework: Sharing examples; and drafting the text for a page

In the plenary session pupils share their work and the resource implications of their designs are considered. For homework, they draft the text for one of their pages.

Lesson 7: Creating more web pages

In Lesson 7 pupils continue developing their web pages. In the lesson preparation section on the lesson notes, it is suggested that sound files are copied into appropriate folders so that pupils can access them.

> This is the first mention of using sound files in the unit and you will have to decide whether or not to provide sound files or encourage pupils to develop their own. This is discussed on page 85. [**7a**]

Starter: Reviewing home pages and the use of links

Pupils begin by looking at the home pages of the BBC and the Department for Education and Skills websites to evaluate and develop understanding of the use of hyperlinks. They are then asked to apply this knowledge to their own websites.

> Although these sites use hyperlinks effectively, the DfES site in particular may not be of interest to pupils. An additional difficulty is that these sites are intended for two different audiences, a general one for the BBC site and a specialist education audience for the DfES. Other sites may be more appropriate.

Development: Creating the pages

Pupils go on to create the web pages that they planned in Lesson 6.

Plenary and homework: Sharing examples; and reviewing the pages

Some of the pages created by pupils are reviewed in the plenary. For homework, it is suggested that each print out their web page, take it away and annotate it with improvements or additions.

> This could be difficult to manage, and some possible approaches are suggested on page 85. [**7b**]

Lesson 8: Completing and evaluating the project

In Lesson 8 the web pages are completed and evaluated by pupils.

Starter: Revising definitions of key vocabulary

The lesson begins with pupils working in their groups of four revising definitions of key vocabulary, with a card sort activity. Early finishers are given an extension activity making notes on more difficult technical terms. These more difficult terms are then revised with the whole class.

> These are important areas of subject knowledge for the pupils, some of which are referred to only briefly early in the unit. If you find that pupils do not have an adequate grasp of the terms you will need to allocate additional time to this. See page 85. [**8a**]

Development: Completing the pages; and creating the website

Pupils then go on to complete their web pages and evaluate them using given criteria. They link the first page of their own section to the home page for the whole site. Pupils will need to know where this page is stored and how to link to it. Each group then shares their work with the rest of the class.

No advice is given about how to merge the pupils' pages, so you will need to plan ahead for this. Only 20 minutes is allowed for looking at the whole website, made up of all the work produced by all the groups. Perhaps you could consider other possibilities for publishing their work, such as those suggested below.

Plenary and homework: Evaluating the unit; and setting personal targets

The lesson ends with a very brief discussion in groups, lasting two to three minutes, of how effectively pupils felt they had worked together.

The ability to work collaboratively is vital, particularly in ICT. If pupils are to value this collaboration and recognise the importance of being able to work effectively with others, then you should allow time for a more meaningful discussion with useful outcomes for the pupils.

Alternative approaches

There are a number of issues associated with this unit, the main ones being those of context and audience, which are connected. The context suggested is that of creating website pages for a "virtual" visitor to the school. The visitor is not specified. It could be a parent, pupil, or governor. In reality these three visitors represent different audiences, and this is exemplified by many published school websites which have separate sections for these groups of people, each with a different style. An added difficulty is that with one small exception (finding out about their parents' views) pupils do not undertake any research to establish the needs of these three groups. This notion of a needs analysis, whether formal or informal, is an important aspect of a number of ICT-based tasks, including data handling (databases and spreadsheets) and some publishing and communications applications (web authoring, desktop publishing, word processing and presentation).

Pupils may ask how their web pages are going to be used when they are completed. It is likely that the school already has a website, which diminishes the purposefulness of the task for the pupils. In reality, the web pages the pupils are creating already exist and as a result their pages serve no real purpose. It might be possible to shift the emphasis while retaining the broad context of the task and make minor alterations to the context to give the pages a real purpose. For example, the web pages could be produced to inform pupils in Year 6 about the secondary school, and these pages could be published on the school website, provided on CD-ROM, or placed on the feeder schools' intranets as a source of information for prospective pupils. Pupils could then receive some feedback from their intended audience on the usefulness of their pages, although, of course, this would have to be handled sensitively.

An alternative approach might be to create a website for a suitable local organisation – a youth group, a charity, or a leisure or sporting organisation or religious group. If a local organisation is selected, with its agreement, as the context, the project would be enriched in several ways:

- pupils would have a real purpose and audience for their work;
- the needs of the user could be researched and analysed in a more realistic fashion;
- pupils could use actual websites from similar organisations as part of the website evaluation stage of the process.

Any of these alternative approaches would involve pupils in additional research into the needs of the audience and the purpose of the website. Although this would require changes to the proposed lessons and might create additional challenges in managing the unit, it would, without doubt, add to the authenticity of the experience for the pupils and provide greater opportunities for their own initiative and creativity.

Nothing in the unit informs pupils about what happens after a website has been designed and created, including the technicalities and practicalities of publishing the site and keeping it up to date. Perhaps this should be discussed, even though their pages will not be published in this way.

Another consideration for teachers when planning this unit is whether pupils need the experience of web authoring using software other than dedicated web-authoring programs, and, in particular, whether it is appropriate for them to create web pages using HTML. As the unit itself states "The best web authoring packages for use in schools enable pupils to develop their ICT capability without having to master sophisticated techniques" (DfES, 2003). You may therefore feel that the use of HTML as a web-authoring medium is not really necessary, particularly given the availability of user-friendly authoring programs and their widespread use, even among web design professionals. Omitting the use of HTML would still enable the content of the lessons to meet the objectives of the unit.

The importance of design is rightly stressed in the unit. However, because pupils create web pages in two media before using the web-authoring software, they begin to create their home page only in Lesson 4 of the eight-lesson unit, and this may be rather frustrating for them. Some of the activities in the unit, such as the design task in Lesson 3, may require more time than is suggested, so this may also require omissions elsewhere in the unit.

Lesson commentaries

[1a] There may be a better and more active way of approaching this, which may be more likely to support pupils in developing understanding. There is a danger in relying on pupils evaluating website features simply by recalling their use of the Internet, or looking at a website without actually using it. This is actually quite difficult, as the features and aspects we find useful can be taken for granted. If pupils are given an opportunity to look briefly at a well-designed website and one that is badly designed, their discussion of these issues will be better informed. Poor examples of website design can be seen on http://www.worstoftheweb.com/. Ask pupils to evaluate some websites and list good and bad features. This will also get them thinking about good design features early in the unit, and these can be drawn out in the whole class discussion. As they will go on to design a home page for their own school website, it might be useful to evaluate some school websites and recognise the range of different approaches and styles adopted by different schools. A good source of school websites can be found on the Learning Alive website at http://www.learningalive.co.uk/AtSchool/index.asp.

[1b] It is difficult to understand what pupils will learn simply by copying a set of instructions to create the same web page as the one that has been demonstrated. HTML is described in the unit as a "computer language", rather a puzzling term. It is unlikely that pupils will retain the subject knowledge involved in using HTML and understand its structure simply by copying the tags, to complete the task in the time allowed. Many will find it frustrating and alienating. You may feel that pupils need to understand that web-authoring software translates their pages into HTML, and that this is what is read by web browsers. If you want your pupils to understand the function of HTML, then you could show this later in the unit by looking at the HTML view of the pages they have created in Front Page. You may also want pupils to understand the need for accuracy in writing HTML. This is a discipline similar to the one they met when using control commands, with which a parallel could be drawn. As even many web designers no longer create pages using HTML, it seems rather anachronistic to expect pupils in Year 8 to use it, especially at the start of the unit. For the minority who will enjoy writing in HTML, this opportunity could be provided in a computer club.

[2a] Evaluating the children's website "cbeebies" will give pupils a sense of audience, but they may need to

consider one or more further sites which relate to a wider range of audiences. This could include a website from a sports club, a well-known chef, a charity which caters for the elderly, a home improvement retailer, a pop group or teenage magazine or a youth organisation.

Unfortunately, this evaluation is not followed up at this point and it might be preferable to delay this activity until pupils are about to use the understanding they are developing in creating their own school web page. Pupils then go on to replicate the same web page they made in the last lesson, this time using word-processing software.

[2b] Although some understanding may be derived from creating the same web page using an alternative medium, pupils might find it rather repetitive and this exercise could be omitted. You could set an alternative task, or allow them to choose their own context, and still use the activity as an opportunity to make the teaching points suggested, perhaps by creating the same "search engine" page yourself in a word processor so that the pupils can compare this with their own HTML version. The time saved could be used for developing work in the web-authoring program.

[3a] This may be a difficult notion at this stage, as neither the web pages nor the files themselves have yet been created. Understanding file structure can be problematic as the user needs to have created some files before recognising the need to organise them into a structure. You could choose to leave this until later in the design process, when pupils are more likely to understand the need to organise files, rather than tackle it in a more abstract fashion at this stage. They could then make a connection between the organisation of files in the website with what they understand about the organisation of files and folders in general. Some pupils may not have developed their own file system despite extensive use of ICT.

[4a] There are some significant issues relating to timing in this lesson and the time allocations suggested in the lesson notes extend beyond one hour, so you will need to look carefully at the content and decide which section can be reduced:

- The lesson starter is allocated 15 minutes in the lesson details and recorded as 10 minutes in the outline. It is likely to need at least 10 minutes, or longer if approached in a more practical, evaluative fashion than is suggested;
- 25 minutes are allowed for a demonstration of web page creation software, and for pupils to create their own home page at the end of the demonstration. Of this time allocation, only 5 minutes are allowed for pupils to create their own home page, with a few minutes more for them to insert a logo and save their work; again, it is most unlikely that pupils will be able to complete the practical task in the time allocated.

It is likely that you will need to allow more time for the activities in this lesson, both of which are key elements of the web-creation process. If you wish to do this, the work on style sheets could be postponed to Lesson 5, or later.

[4b] Rather than providing page layouts as printed outlines of structures, you could approach this by asking pupils to look at some websites and work out for themselves how screens are typically organised and what the advantages are of different layouts. They are then more likely to come to an informed choice of layout for their own home page. Evaluation of the effectiveness of different formats is an important part of the design process. Provided that access to computers can be ensured for all pupils, this could be set as a homework task earlier in the sequence of lessons.

[4c] The creation of the web page may be easier for pupils if the demonstration is split into several steps which are alternated with pupils' activity. However, there are also management issues here, as the pupils are in groups of four, and you will need to ensure that all of the group have an opportunity for hands-on work and to develop an understanding of the techniques involved.

The use of tables to set out information on a web page is important, and this should be emphasised. Pupils may not have met the use of tables prior to this, or may not know that a table can be used in this way to control layout, with its gridlines greyed out. They also may not be aware of the usefulness of this strategy in a word-processed document, and so it would be useful to draw this to their attention.

[5a] The notions of "white space" and "being too busy" are introduced here for the first time. This understanding is essential if pupils are to grasp the principles of whole page layout. You may need to show examples of layouts and discuss these features to ensure that pupils understand their importance. Ideally, pupils should review websites that provide good and bad examples of use of space, as well as other visual aspects, and evaluate these for themselves before designing their own pages.

[5b] However you decide to organise this part of the lesson you will need to ensure that all pupils have the opportunity to use the web-authoring software. There will be further work with this application in subsequent lessons, and if pupils miss out on these early stages they may be disadvantaged later.

The way in which you manage the organisation, saving and sharing of the web pages will depend on the structure of your school network. This will need to be discussed with colleagues and an overall policy developed before the unit is taught.

[7a] There is no direct reference to the use of sound files in the lesson notes and no support materials are provided. The use of sound files is introduced in Unit 7.3, but only as an extension activity.

Pupils may have identified sound files as one of the features that contribute to a website's effectiveness and planned to include sound in their own pages. Sound files are not generally difficult to create or use, but recording some types, such as "voiceover" commentaries, would be difficult in a busy classroom. You will need to decide whether you have the subject knowledge and resources to support pupils who wish to use sound files in their pages. Pupils could record their own sound files and bring them to the lesson ready to use, download sound files from the Internet, or use sound from recorded sources (bearing in mind copyright restrictions). If some pupils used sound in Unit 7.3, this might be an appropriate task for peer tutoring. It is important that pupils understand the issues of file size and download times when using sound files.

[7b] Providing a printout of the web pages for each pupil at the end of the lesson may be problematic. Ideally, as they are working on several pages each member of the group should take home a different page, and this adds to the difficulty. You may have to make arrangements to provide these printouts after the lesson, or set this as an introductory activity at the start of Lesson 8, when pupils could review the pages together on screen. Alternatively, they could review the pages produced by another group, on screen, and provide feedback to that group.

[8a] Unfortunately this is the only opportunity for pupils to show their work. As this work represents a substantial effort for pupils, you could consider other opportunities for them to show or publish their pages. This is important for pupil confidence and motivation. Would it be possible for the pages to be uploaded onto the school intranet so that pupils can explore them? Could they be published on the intranets of feeder schools, or made available on CD-ROM? The pages could also be used as exemplars when the unit is taught again.

8.3 Information: reliability, validity and bias

KS3 STRATEGY FRAMEWORK OBJECTIVES

Finding things out

Using data and information sources

- Understand how the content and style of an information source affects its suitability for particular purposes, by considering:
  - its mix of fact, opinion and material designed to advertise, publicise or entertain;
  - the viewpoint it offers;
  - the clarity, accessibility and plausibility of the material.
- Devise and apply criteria to evaluate how well various information sources will support a task.
- Justify the use of particular information sources to support an investigation or presentation.

Searching and selecting

Extend and refine search methods to be more efficient.

About this unit

In this unit, pupils learn to evaluate the validity of electronic sources of information in terms of assessing accuracy and reliability and detecting possible bias. They also learn how to search for information using key words, explore more advanced methods and evaluate a range of search engines. Finally they consider fitness for purpose and the importance of ensuring that the information meets the needs of the audience. They are looking for information for Pat, a Year 6 pupil who is researching useful information for a local history project.

Pupils do not require many prior skills for this unit, other than having a basic understanding of accessing an Internet site and the ability to cut and paste text and graphics. As a broader understanding of the role and function of the Internet in society is not a consideration in this unit, there is no specific knowledge requirement. It is interesting to note that similar skills, knowledge and understanding are addressed in Unit 7.2.

The subject knowledge required by the teacher is a basic competence in using the Internet, presentation and word-processing software, as well as in techniques such as cutting and pasting graphics and text. The lesson plans are detailed and, in some cases, very long. The teacher should develop knowledge of these in advance to ensure all of the suggested teaching points are delivered.

Teachers also need to be alert to the number of pupil resources based on a table structure, causing them to look very similar. These will need to be carefully organised. They are used by pupils while investigating search engines and Internet sites, and it may be that the teacher chooses not to include some of them. In addition, sites change regularly, so it is important for teachers to check them before the lesson, and it is recommended that there is an alternative plan in the case of Internet failure.

Pupils normally work in pairs in this unit as the activities require them to make judgements involving extensive dialogue. This is then fed back and shared in whole class discussion.

The unit is intended to take four hour-long lessons, and it is expected that most pupils will be working at Level 5. The suggested activity timings are shown in the table below. Most of the time is spent in teacher-led activity, considerably more time than that spent in independent learning and problem-solving.

	Taught as a whole class	*Pupil work away from the computer*	*Pupil work at the computer*
Lesson 1	40 mins		20 mins
Lesson 2	40 mins	5 mins	15 mins
Lesson 3	35 mins	5 mins	20 mins
Lesson 4	40 mins		20 mins
Overall balance	**2 hrs 35 mins** 65%	**10 mins** 4%	**1 hr 15 mins** 31%

LESSON BY LESSON

Lesson 1: Criteria for evaluating information

In this opening lesson, pupils consider the differences between fact and opinion and go on to consider the need for information to be accurate, reliable and valid.

Starter: Distinguishing between fact and opinion

The lesson starts with a discussion to ensure pupils are aware of the differences between fact and opinion, and then they move on to give reasoned judgements about specific statements. The last slides consider the accuracy and reliability of the statements as well as their context. Fact and opinion are linked to the idea of bias and the need to consider the context.

This activity includes some very useful discussion points which must be included, even if you have an alternative context.

Development: Evaluating validity; and criteria for considering reliability

The teacher explains that information needs to be accurate and reliable to be valid. Pupils are asked to consider the information found on five websites and rank them in order of reliability and accuracy. This is followed by a discussion of their responses using the terms accurate, reliable and valid.

This is a very difficult concept. Are Natwest and the *Guardian* necessarily sites of interest for pupils? See page 92. [**1a**]

The lesson continues with a class discussion about indicators of reliability.

It is important that pupils do not assume that a .gov URL identifier means a site is completely reliable. There is further comment about this on page 92 in Lesson commentaries. [**1b**]

Pupils investigate five more sites and write a brief evaluation of each site's reliability.

Two minutes per site is not long enough to make a meaningful judgement. Could this task be integrated with the previous task, ranking sites in order of reliability and accuracy? See page 92 for comment. [1c] **and** [1d]

Plenary and homework: Evaluating clarity and accessibility; and comparing information features

The teacher uses a Worldnews website and pupils discuss the ease of navigation and clarity of information on the site.

Again, you may feel that pupils could undertake one comprehensive task, comprising all of the skills addressed in the development tasks and this discussion as opposed to a series of activities; each considering a different aspect of evaluation of information.

Pupils have to find two versions of a news story, one electronic and one paper-based, and compare them considering:

- the differences between them;
- the extra facilities available to the electronic publishers;
- whether this affects the reader's judgement of the reliability and accuracy of the story.

This needs supporting discussion, as it is a highly sophisticated task which many pupils will find too difficult to address appropriately. You may need to give pupils a specific example to investigate and provide guidance through a resource to structure their approach.

Lesson 2: Using searches

In this lesson, pupils revisit the notion of Boolean operators and look at different ways of searching for information on the world wide web.

Starter: Using AND/OR/NOT

The first activity aims to convey the concept of Boolean logic using AND/OR/NOT in searches. Pupils are given a shape card which is a black or white square or circle. Pupils stand up if their particular shape meets the criteria specified by the teacher, such as: square AND black. NOT is also introduced.

A clever introduction to Boolean logic – why not follow it up now with a practical web activity to reinforce the concept? See page 93. [2a] **and** [3b]

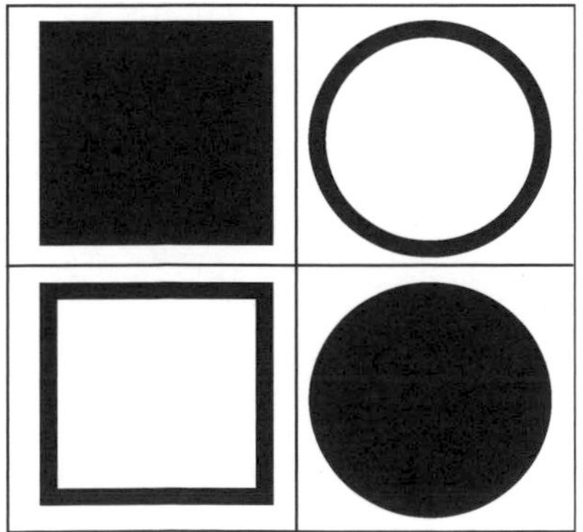

Development: Searching a website and CD-ROM; key word and full text searches; and Internet search engines

The lesson continues with an introduction to built-in search facilities, using the BBC weather site as an example. There is also a demonstration of interrogating a CD-ROM.

The purpose of this would have to be made explicit; most pupils will have used CD-ROMs at primary school and at home. You may want to check that this is absolutely necessary.

Key words associated with websites are now introduced. Pupils read information about whale sharks and identify key words that could be associated with the text. Simplifying the text is a useful suggestion for differentiation.

This is a really valuable activity, but it may be made more relevant by finding a topic the pupils are studying in another subject.

The teacher then uses the "find" facility in Microsoft Word to demonstrate a full text search.

It is important that you check understanding of the term "string". It is not mentioned in the vocabulary cards.

The next part of the lesson provides an introduction to using search engines to find information on the Internet. Each pupil pair evaluates one search engine by looking for information to solve two specified problems. They make notes on the search engine, the key words they used and what they found.

It may be an idea to demonstrate an initial example, as it is quite tricky to work out the appropriate key words for the examples given.

Plenary and homework: Evaluating search engines; and research task

One pair feed back to the class about the website which was the most useful source for the first problem and describe the value of the search engine in the two searches.

You might want to give this more than the suggested 5 minutes as so few pairs will be able to feed back. It may also be useful for pupils to describe any surprises in the behaviour of the search engine.

For homework, pupils complete a paper resource (Pupil Resource 4) listing a series of information requirements. Part of it is reproduced below. They develop possible queries to input to the search engine and ideas for the use of Boolean logic to narrow down the search.

The requirements for the query column need to be carefully explained as this is the first reference to the term and it is not clear whether it is simply key words. It will also be important to make a link to the pupils' experience of Boolean operators at the start of the lesson.

Homework: Searching for information

For each question, write a query that you could type into a search engine. Use AND, OR and NOT where appropriate. Add a few notes about how you could narrow down your search.

Information needed	Query for search engine	How to narrow down the search: brief notes
You need information about the history of your local area between 1800 and 1900.		

Lesson 3: Extending and refining search methods

In this lesson, pupils continue to investigate ways of searching for specific information by refining their interrogation techniques.

Starter: Using the advanced search facility

The teacher demonstrates the need for efficient searching, initially using Google with key words and building up to using AND and NOT in the advanced facility to reduce the number of hits.

> Is a list of 20,000 hits really any more useful than 500,000? You may feel that the skills of skimming and scanning the initial hits for those which may be useful are equally important here. See further discussion on page 93. [3a]

Development: Using precise strings and synonyms to refine a search; and using search engines and Boolean operators

Pupils are introduced to the use of inverted commas around more than one word for an exact phrase search.

> In terms of progression, you may wish to look at this before Boolean logic as it is more likely to be used on a daily basis in major search engines. See further discussion on page 93. [2a] **and** [3b]

This is followed by a pupil activity to divide given words into possible key words, synonyms of those words, and other words that are relevant but unlikely to help in a search.

> Perhaps they should test their keyword choices using a search engine.

Next is a pupil activity using different search engines to find information to answer given questions, followed by a discussion/feedback on findings.

> What happened to the previous lesson's homework task? This is an important discussion, but we should also consider reliability/accuracy and bias here.

Plenary and homework: Describing how to make Internet searches

The teacher summarises what has been learned in the last three lessons. This focuses on a recap of the differences between search engines and formulating queries to find specific information.

> This is very similar to earlier activities; see Alternative approaches, page 91.

The clustering search engine Vivisimo is an example of a different type of search engine which was introduced in Unit 7.2. Perhaps this is an opportunity to remind pupils of it.

Lesson 4: Independent application of new learning; searching and evaluating

This lesson deals with the need for consideration of audience and purpose when searching for information.

Starter: Purpose and audience

Pupils are reminded that when they search for information they must think about their audience and purpose, and they are told that this will inform which search engine they use.

This is the first real mention in the unit of the fundamental issue of audience and purpose. It is unlikely that this will inform which search engine they use, as most people have a preferred search engine and try others only if it does not find what they want. For further discussion, see page 93. [4a]

Pupils are shown the "ajkids" site as an example of a different type of search engine.

It may be better to introduce "ajkids" in Lesson 3 when considering the differences between search engines. Many pupils will be familiar with it already.

Development: Finding information for a report; and selecting Information

Pupils are given a task relating to Pat, a Year 6 pupil who is writing a report on the local history of the town. The period she is researching is "as long as possible" and any maps or illustrations would help enhance her report. Pupils are given an electronic pro forma to collect the information and 20 minutes research time.

An appropriate cross-curricular task may be more useful here. It is likely that the activity will need longer to be completed to a satisfactory standard. See Lesson commentaries, page 93, for further comment. [4b]

This is followed by a discussion of the information found and the search engines used. Pupils are asked whether they have found suitable information and why they chose particular sources in terms of reliability and audience.

Pupil Resource 9 does not refer to reliability and bias, so the need to consider this would have to be made explicit when the task is discussed.

Plenary and homework: Review of learning

The unit ends with a review of what has been learned using Teacher Resource 4.

You may want to note that the information in Teacher Resource 4 provides prompts which may be very useful for discussions earlier in the unit.

Alternative approaches

Although this unit tackles some very important and useful concepts in terms of information handling using the Internet, its approach is fragmented. It also misses the opportunity of linking to a realistic and meaningful context which could be related to some aspect of the school curriculum. Instead, it uses a range of contexts for searching, many of which are not particularly relevant for pupils of this age and the results of which appear to be of limited practical or constructive use for them. In addition, it makes no attempt to consider the nature of the Internet and its impact on contemporary society, a valuable discussion point for any age group. Teachers may wish to look at the parallel unit in the QCA scheme of work. This suggests an alternative approach in which pupils have a specific topic in mind when searching the Internet. Pupils are presented with the challenge of taking a particular stance on an issue and producing an argument to support their viewpoint. This underpins their thinking behind the interrogation strategies used and provides a consistent theme and purpose throughout their investigations. Pupils consider the reliability and status of information, and the identification of bias is an integral element of their remit. It gives them the opportunity to investigate a topic from another subject and use the information they have gathered to create a persuasive presentation. This is an extremely valuable activity which reinforces the notion that information is retrieved from any source, such as the Internet, for a specific purpose. It is this purpose that will influence the search methods used and the information selected for the required outcome. In order to produce a valid argument, pupils have to consider the reliability of their information. Teachers may well wish to combine the more structured methods recommended in this unit with those suggested in the scheme of work.

Lesson commentaries

This initial lesson looks at the reliability and accuracy of sites. This is a notoriously difficult area to grasp with clarity and confidence, so it is optimistic to expect pupils to look at five sites in five minutes and rank them in order of reliability. The following activity requires six sites to be accessed in twelve minutes and a comment made linked to previously discussed indicators of reliability. Follow-up discussion, which could be of value, is omitted. This is a complex issue that you may feel deserves a more generous time allocation. This would give pupils the opportunity to analyse what they see and discuss issues to help develop their understanding. Perhaps one activity giving pupils a longer period to investigate one or two sites, using the same kind of criteria, may be more appropriate. In addition, it is essential that the sites used in activities, as well as those for demonstration purposes, are relevant and their content is of interest to, and accessible by, pupils.

Alternative approaches are considered in the comments that follow. Perhaps it would be worth teachers considering local circumstances and finding sites that are more suited to their purpose. It is interesting to see that the issues of reliability, validity and bias, which are the subject of the unit title, are barely mentioned after the first lesson yet they must continue to be considered. It would be valuable to ask pupils to apply the suggested criteria to assess the possible source and reliability of all sites they visit in subsequent lessons. The issue of clarity and accessibility of sites, also a very useful area to consider, is given brief attention via a demonstration at the end of Lesson 1. It could, however, be incorporated into the subsequent activities in which pupils access and examine a variety of sites.

[1a] The whole issue of the contexts used for developing the skills of effective searching is worth considering. Constructive use of the Internet always has a purpose, yet in order to teach search skills in this unit, pupils are asked to retrieve random pieces of information unrelated to their other studies. In this respect it is similar to Unit 7.2. Again, some consideration of more appropriate topics could yield more productive and richer results.

[1b] You may wish to discuss organisations which present information as reliable when there is a body of evidence, or even conclusive proof, to suggest it isn't. There are a number of conspiracy theories from events in recent history ranging from the harrowing example of the Holocaust denial sites to the groups claiming that Princess Diana was murdered as a result of an official government-sponsored plot. Pupils may well be familiar with the latter example and be motivated to verify the source of information presented on such sites.

[1c] and [1d] The unit engages with a number of important issues including effective assessment of site validity, consideration of the clarity and accessibility of sites, evaluation of search tools and the development of efficient methods for using these tools. Each of these aspects is approached with similar but individual activities. It is advised that teachers check the timings of the Internet-based tasks in this unit as some activities have been allocated minimal time. In some cases, only one or two minutes is allowed for pupils to access, scan, select, read and evaluate information as well as reflect on the methods they used to obtain it. It would seem sensible to consider whether some activities could be combined to make more challenging and meaningful tasks using an issue of real interest, as discussed above.

[2a] **and** [3b] The use of Boolean operators is another important issue here. While the activity using the coloured shapes at the start of Lesson 2 is an excellent introduction to understanding the logical operators, this needs to be followed up by application of this new understanding. Alternatively, it could be decided that this understanding is not actually necessary here for effective searching as narrowing down searches in most engines via the use of inverted commas and the + sign is perfectly adequate.

[3a] The issue of "efficient" searching is a complex one. In Lesson 3, the teacher demonstrates an efficient search using Google, initially with general key words (500,000 hits), limiting the search with specific key words (36,000 hits) and narrowing the search using AND and NOT in the advanced facility (20,000 hits). It is important that narrowing down the search is not proposed as the complete solution to effective retrieval. The right key words are very important, but equally crucial is how the user deals with the results. This includes methods of scanning the initial hits for key words and indicators of useful information. Pupils need to have skimming and scanning techniques so that they can determine the value of the sites as quickly as possible.

[4a] In Lesson 4, pupils are reminded that when searching for information they must think about their audience and purpose as this will inform what search engine they use. However, it is generally accepted that people have a preferred search engine, and while it may not be the best device for every search, the user will be familiar with its characteristics and therefore have more success in using it. Usually it will be the first tool to be employed. Although it is useful for pupils to see a range of search engines, you may question whether they will observe meaningful differences and you may question whether it is worth spending time considering this issue at great length. A quick look at an example specifically for schoolchildren such as "ajkids", a standard engine such as Google, one that employs a categorised directory system such as Yahoo!, and perhaps one which accesses only UK sites should be sufficient. The really valuable aspect is the discussion and feedback to ascertain what pupils have learned about effective searching and problem-solving. This covers the entire process, from identifying key words, adding search conditions, investigating results speedily and efficiently, and accessing the required information in an appropriate form.

[4b] There is no question that pupils' use of the Internet should be structured by the teacher at this stage in order to ensure that all aspects of effective use of the Internet are addressed. However, pupils can learn how to use search engines, consider reliability of sites, and think about their clarity and accessibility in the same activity. This would give them more time to develop meaningful responses to the challenges set. In addition, the final task, in which all of these disparate skills should come together, could be based on an authentic topic in the pupils' curriculum and produce outcomes that would be of value elsewhere.

The major question is whether this unit prepares pupils for independent use of the Internet in their future work. While dealing with some fundamental issues, such as the identification of appropriate key words and the need to question the source of information, it does not deal in any depth with interpreting and restructuring information for a real purpose. It may be useful to consider combining some aspects of this unit with the approach suggested by the Key Stage 3 scheme of work Unit 10. In this, pupils explore the potential of ICT-based information sources while researching a topic relating to a specific brief. The subject chosen should allow different interpretations and viewpoints so that pupils can research the issue and, in doing so, be given ample opportunity to examine reliability and bias. They can then proceed to use the information retrieved for a real outcome such as a publication, a presentation, or a web page for a specific audience. This allows pupils to develop their skills within a meaningful context while using the Internet to find information, before refining and organising it for their purpose. It has the additional advantage that the audience can be used to evaluate the outcomes. The link between the use of the Internet to find information and the resulting selection and interpretation for a purpose is so crucial that it is worth considering extending this unit to accommodate a final outcome with either a peer review or an evaluation by an authentic audience.

8.4 Modelling

KS3 STRATEGY FRAMEWORK OBJECTIVES

Developing ideas and making things happen

Models and modelling

- Develop ICT-based models and test predictions by changing variables and rules.
- Draw and explain conclusions.
- Review and modify ICT models to improve their accuracy and extend their scope.

Finding things out

Organising and investigating

- Explore and interpret collected data in order to draw conclusions.

About this unit

Unit 8.4 is designed to develop pupils' understanding of modelling and presenting numeric data; concepts which have already been introduced in Unit 7.4. In this unit, pupils investigate and develop their own model using spreadsheet software. They reinforce basic spreadsheet skills, knowledge and understanding from prior experience and then go on to learn further spreadsheet skills such as selection of non-adjacent data, producing and editing charts, and copying formulae. They use absolute and relative cell references (also addressed in Units 7.6 and 8.1) and Goal Seek. Some pupils will also tackle functions such as RANDBETWEEN and IF . . . THEN. Teachers will obviously need to be confident in the use of all of these features and have a clear understanding of their function and purpose in a variety of contexts. In addition, teachers should be familiar with the broad range of applications of modelling and simulations to enable rich and diverse discussion of wider issues.

It is advised that pupils work in pairs in this unit. This seems sensible, as would pairings of similar ability. The nature of modelling means that different groups of attainers will probably be attempting tasks at different levels in the unit. Mixed-ability pairings could lead to the more able pupil monopolising the development of the model without involving their partner, so the second pupil fails to learn at their level. Spreadsheet modelling is a good focus for collaborative work, as through investigation pupils can help each other build an understanding of new concepts.

There are a lot of resources in this unit, so advanced planning in terms of cost and management of reprographics is advised. It may be that teachers decide that some paper resources could be combined and some omitted. It is also advisable to check the printing of the electronic resources and pupils' work, including the charts, as some of the originals do not print well due to the display methods used. It is also worth noting that the gridlines are not visible in the Moby model, so identification of individual cells can be quite difficult.

Specialist skills, knowledge and understanding are needed and will require considerable effort by those without a mathematical background. It is important that the teacher has worked through the creation and development of the models in advance, so they are familiar with all stages. The answer sheets are useful but are no substitute for the teacher identifying the likely problems first. If there are areas that teachers find difficult, it is likely some pupils will too.

Clear and accurate instructions and demonstrations are essential when explaining tricky modelling concepts. It may be felt that a broad understanding of the place of spreadsheet modelling in the wider context of models and simulations is more important than the more advanced functions in this unit. Many pupils will not be ready to tackle these functions, and they are not strictly necessary for the fulfilment of the objectives. Although some pupils may be able to master the mechanics of using these tools in this narrow context, it is unlikely that many will develop a comprehensive understanding of them and be able to apply this knowledge independently in other contexts. However, if some pupils are very confident and knowledgeable, the unit should be planned to ensure they are appropriately challenged.

By Year 8, pupils should be increasingly independent in their study and use of ICT. Successful teaching and learning in this year requires a careful balance between teacher-devised structure and pupil independent discovery. Pupils are moving towards the design and realisation of ICT systems, and as such need to be given a certain amount of freedom to design and create their models, followed by the opportunity to review and test what they have done and make changes in the light of further understanding.

It is anticipated that the unit will take five hour-long lessons. The suggested lesson time breaks down as shown in the table below.

	Taught as a whole class	*Pupil work away from the computer*	*Pupil work at the computer*
Lesson 1	35 mins	10 mins	15 mins
Lesson 2	45 mins		15 mins
Lesson 3	20 mins	20 mins	20 mins
Lesson 4	25 mins		35 mins
Lesson 5	35 mins		25 mins
Overall balance	**2 hrs 40 mins** 53%	**30 mins** 10%	**1 hr 50 mins** 36%

Lesson 1: Introducing the unit

This lesson provides the opportunity to revise previous modelling work and then go on to consider additional features, such as Goal Seek, using a school fête model.

Starter: Revising modelling

This lesson starts with a revision of the features of a typical spreadsheet. A presentation is used to reinforce the explicit and less evident components of the screen:

- the concept of cell references;
- the idea that different types of data can be input to a spreadsheet model;
- basic formulae using a range;
- copying of formulae from cell to cell;
- identifying formulae;
- sorting of data.

This represents some important learning. It is discussed further in Alternative approaches on page 102. [1a]

It is suggested that pupils work in pairs on the accompanying starter worksheet, followed by a brief discussion of the issues raised.

Development: The aim of the unit; using and interrogating a model; and using Goal Seek

Pupils are asked to recall any previous modelling work, leading into a revision of the concept of modelling. They are reminded of the benefits of using a spreadsheet model in terms of speed, accuracy and ease of editing, as well as the key area of automatic recalculation when data are changed. The zoo example, used previously in Unit 7.4, provides continuity.

You may want to keep the zoo example on screen and reinforce key concepts by predicting the effect of a change of data on the zoo costs.

The school fête model is displayed and a worksheet used to bring out the important learning points. There is a series of questions the teacher should ask while circulating, and some useful advice on appropriate differentiation by challenging individuals at different levels.

You will need to give the lower attainers a lot of support in completing this. You may find that talking them through the worksheet is more successful. The fifth question, asking the pupils to explain how the formula is calculating the profit or loss, is a key one.

Goal Seek is introduced as a progression from the trial and improvement approach used so far. It is a useful and powerful automated function, but it is essential that the teacher demonstrates an example fully before pupils use it.

Most children would need each step meticulously modelled through an example. These issues are examined further in Alternative approaches on page 102. [1b]

The pupils then work through problems in a Goal Seek worksheet which refers to a school fête model. The differentiation suggestion will almost certainly need to be implemented.

You may want to simplify this and break down the process into smaller steps for pupils to follow. See page 102 for details. [1b]

Pupils are also invited to identify the drawbacks of Goal Seek, for example, that it gives an exact answer. In this case it shows that the number of people needed to enable the organisers of the fête to break even is not a whole number, so some interpretation of figures will be necessary.

Plenary and homework: Reviewing the model

The plenary asks pupils to discuss the validity of a good model, a very difficult concept to grasp given their limited experience.

Pupils are asked to collect information about mobile phone deals and to identify similarities and differences. It is suggested that a frame is created to structure thinking for lower attainers.

Lesson 2: Developing a new model

Pupils develop a new and more complex model: the Moby phone model.

Starter: Identifying variables

The teacher leads an important discussion about different companies, tariffs and offers to bring about identification of a set of variables.

It is useful to have some example leaflets for those who have not brought any information. The suggested presentation slide is not visually attractive, so it may be more appropriate to find an Internet site or an alternative poster with a more appealing display of mobile phones.

Development: Comparing tariffs; structuring, developing, exploring and analysing the model; and input and output values in a model

The idea of finding best value is introduced and the pupils suggest which variables would need be considered. The teacher leads them to the idea of setting up a model to help them find best value. The idea of variables is presented through reference to a familiar example, the school fête. This will help with the identification of possible variables for their mobile phone model.

The teacher shows the Moby model on screen to ensure pupil understanding of the different elements. Pupils are asked to identify certain aspects of the model.

While the Moby mobile phone model represents a realistic and relevant context, you need to be aware that some pupils will have an intricate knowledge of such tariffs and may find it difficult to accept this inevitably simplified model. You have to decide how to deal with this.

Pupils load the basic model and are given an accompanying worksheet. The teacher discusses the initial formula and reinforces understanding. Pupils work through the problems, with the teacher supporting where necessary. The teacher identifies pupils to explain their problem-solving methods in the plenary.

This is essential teaching. The subsequent worksheet has a lot of complex tasks so some pupils will struggle to complete it. You may want to simplify it for this group, unless you can devote a considerable amount of time to support them.

The pupils are told to leave question 11 as this will be homework.

The class has a discussion about the use of Goal Seek and the teacher explains its two-way operation.

The traditional input/output diagram doesn't reflect the complexities of the operation of Goal Seek very well. You may prefer to develop something more appropriate.

Plenary and homework: Evaluating the model

Two pairs describe how they solved the various problems set in the previous task, and the discussion is widened to incorporate suggestions and comment from other pupils. The teacher summarises what has been learned.

Pupils are asked to complete the last question on the worksheet about identifying the most important factors to consider when choosing a phone and are given pointers to help their thinking. It is suggested that some pupils are given a more limited scenario to help structure their thinking.

This is a very useful suggestion for differentiation.

Lesson 3: Using graphs to model with spreadsheets

This lesson revisits the use of charts for presenting data. Pupils then extend their mobile phone model and consider the function of absolute cell referencing.

Starter: Using charts

The teacher starts the lesson with a presentation of charts comparing monthly tariffs based on the mobile phone model. The first is a simple bar chart to show the costs of the various tariffs when using 600 minutes a month. Pupils are asked to consider the advantages of showing data in a graphical format and to compare the table of figures and the chart. They then go on to look at a line graph which shows more information, such as the minutes used against the cost for three different tariffs. It is, of course, then possible to make comparisons between the different providers.

The unit instructs teachers to tell the pupils that this graph is easier for making comparisons, but it would be preferable to prompt pupils to recognise this independently by comparing the line graph with the bar chart.

As in several other units, pupils do not reinforce this learning by creating their own charts here. You may consider changing this. See Lesson commentaries on page 102. [3a]

Development: Cell referencing; extending the model; and reviewing the model

The lesson then uses the school fête model to explore the concept of absolute and relative cell references. The teacher runs through the steps to create a formula to calculate the amount of money taken for 400 visitors.

Be careful: you will need to change the sheet options in page setup if you use paper copies of the resource for your preparation or with pupils in the absence of a suitable display method. The unit instructions refer to row and column headings which do not print (see above). Cell referencing is discussed in Lesson commentaries on page 102. [3b]

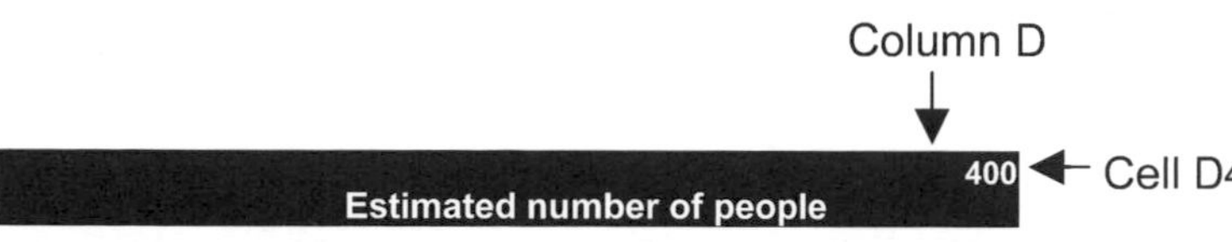

INCOME		No. bought per person	
Entrance	£2.00	1	
Tea/coffee	£0.50	1	
Cakes	£0.30	1	
Hot dogs/burgers	£1.00	1	
Rides	£0.75	4	
Games	£0.40	3	
Raffle	£0.50	2	
Plants	£1.50	2	
Tombola	£0.50	2	

Cells D4 – D12

When the formula is copied down to calculate the money taken for the various attractions at the fête, the results will be incorrect, as it will calculate according to the invalid relative values of descending cells (D4–D12) as opposed to the valid absolute value representing the number at the fête (D4).

Ask pupils to direct you in carrying out each instruction, including the copying of the formula. Most of them will not realise the need for an absolute cell reference. It is an interesting exercise for the pupils to work out what went wrong.

The lesson reverts to the Moby phone model, in which pupils are shown a new and extended model with additional columns referring to different totals of call minutes.

You may want to display the spreadsheet grid as it is quite difficult to identify cells in the middle of the sheet.

Pupils are asked to describe the formulae needed to work out the cost of the first mobile phone tariff, Talk 15, for the first total number of call minutes: 100. As advised, it is essential to go through the first formula, describing actions in "natural" speech before referring to spreadsheet terminology. This is an opportunity to embed understanding of the use of an absolute cell reference. Mobile phone worksheet 2 is distributed and pupils begin to work through it.

Perhaps rename mobile phone worksheet 2, "Extending the Moby Mobile Phone Model", so that it is clear to which stage in the development of the model it refers. You may wish to let some pupils move on independently and talk through the first two questions with the rest of the class.

Questions 3 to 5 give instructions for creating a line graph and then prompt pupils to consider some of the drawbacks of this way of displaying information. A suggestion of how to use the chart follows.

It may support understanding to work through this with certain pupils. The Lesson commentaries refers to this chart activity on page 103. [3c]

Plenary and homework: Evaluating the use of charts and graphs

The plenary looks at the advantages and disadvantages of using ICT to produce graphical representations.

Lesson 4: Investigating models

Most of this lesson is devoted to the introduction of the RANDBETWEEN function to generate random data for testing the pupils' models.

Starter: Tossing a coin

The lesson starts with pupils being asked to think about the probability of throwing heads or tails when tossing a coin ten times. Pupils are shown a model to help them prove their hypothesis. This uses the RANDBETWEEN function in Excel which generates random numbers which can be used to test their Moby phone model.

Development: Testing a model with a random number generator; and exploring an online model

Pupils are asked to consider changing the model to account for the random nature of phone usage from month to month. The teacher then guides them through the creation of the RANDBETWEEN function and asks which tariff is best value if the pupils use between 300 and 400 minutes per month. After experimenting and finding this a difficult question to answer confidently, the pupils are encouraged to create a bar chart which responds to changes in their data and shows the best value tariff over a number of test cycles.

This activity, while providing a challenge for some pupils, is not an essential tool for use by the whole class. Other pupils could produce their own data to test their models, or these could be teacher-generated. See Lesson commentaries, on page 103. [4a]

Pupils go on to explore a commercial online model which is designed to help people choose their mobile phone. The teacher asks pupils to think about the variables used in the online model and how they differ from those they have used in their own model. They also consider the accuracy of the user profile.

This is a useful exercise, but check the site just before the lesson to ensure it has not changed. It is still a suitable site at the time of writing.

Plenary and homework: Reviewing the mobile phone model

The lesson ends with a whole class discussion about the differences between the online models and an evaluation of the pupils' models. Pupils are asked to summarise their understanding of the term "simulation" and think about other models or simulations they have used.

There is an extension activity at the end of this lesson, this is discussed briefly in Lesson commentaries on page 103. [**4b**]

Lesson 5: Simulations and models

This final lesson gives pupils the opportunity to investigate the broad spectrum of simulations and models beyond the spreadsheet.

Starter: Defining simulations and models

Pupils give examples from the homework task of models and simulations with which they are familiar. These are recorded, and a definition for the word "simulation" is agreed.

Development: Explaining the objectives; setting and demonstrating the task; and investigating simulations and models

Pupils are told they will use a range of models and simulations and make predictions about what will happen if they change variables. Examples of the models are:

- planning a train journey;
- checking holiday costs;

according to set criteria.

Three simulations are suggested. One of them, a game, is demonstrated and some variables and their functions are indicated in the process. It is suggested that a link is made to the model of the school fête.

> Make sure these resources are still on the Internet and that you are familiar with the sites and activities.

Pupils are given a series of web links leading to simulations or models for use online. Each pair makes a choice from two groups, A and B. The help sheet for Group A asks them to identify the real-life situation that is being simulated and to investigate some of the variables being used. The help sheet for Group B gives two scenarios relating to holiday travel for pupils to explore. It is suggested that some pupils are directed to appropriate sites, according to their reading ability.

> It is probably best to avoid those that require previous registration or email addresses, such as trainline.com.

Plenary and homework: Reviewing the unit; and key vocabulary

Pupils are asked to suggest as many different types of simulations and models as they can. This is followed by a general review of all activities and objectives for this unit, along with a check of key vocabulary. They are asked to write a brief account of the unit and a prompt sheet is suggested for some.

> This could be covered in Lesson 4 at the end of the related teaching. Pupils may enjoy spending a lunchtime looking on the Internet for further simulations linked to other subjects.

Alternative approaches

Finding appropriate contexts for spreadsheet modelling is a challenge, and development of models, even at this level, is quite a complex and time-consuming task. The contexts used in this unit are appropriate for the age range and perhaps any additional preparation could be put into developing the broader view of modelling and simulations. It may be useful to consider starting the unit with this broad overview, before focusing on the fairly restricted example of conventional spreadsheet models. It is important that the online simulations are not seen as light entertainment after the serious work has ended. Presented as it is, with attention to other types of modelling tacked on the end, pupils may see spreadsheet modelling as authentic modelling and fail to gain an understanding of the other aspects of modelling and simulations.

The processes and concepts underlying modelling will be grasped by some pupils with no difficulty. However, this unit is challenging and complex in places and it is essential for you to identify from the outset those individuals who will struggle. You will need to plan carefully how to provide the necessary support from the start, or lower attainers will gain very little from this unit.

Lesson commentaries

[1a] Lesson 1 begins with pupils working on a revision sheet, which may be an appropriate way to settle the class, but you may decide you want to involve the whole class in the task immediately. If the spreadsheet is displayed on an electronic whiteboard, this offers a useful opportunity for pupil involvement in dragging the correct label to its location or identification of particular cells holding different types of data.

The introductory exercises have some useful revision points which will challenge misconceptions. Some of the questions asked in the school fête worksheet could be partly replaced by class discussion. They could form the basis for some pertinent discussion about the capabilities of a spreadsheet and what may be the most effective tool for other named tasks. Pupils often type in the cell reference rather than clicking on the cell. Sometimes they are not aware of the fact that numeric data only are valid for a calculation, and that the introduction of an alphabetic character such as a unit (for example, cms) will render a formula worthless. Pupils also need to adopt the habit of identifying the contents of cells by checking the name box at the top of the screen, and the method of representing a range of cells should also be reiterated here. When sorting data, it is important to remind pupils exactly what sorting in alphabetical order and numerical order actually mean. Often this is best explained by providing a tangible manual sorting exercise. It is also essential that the teacher discusses the idea of hypotheses and explores pupils' understanding of the term "variable" as well as the notions of "profit and loss" and "breaking even". It is easy to assume pupils understand these ideas, but in reality they are difficult to grasp. Yet this understanding is vital for much of the spreadsheet modelling they will do in the future.

[1b] Although Goal Seek is a useful automated function for pupils to see, it is important that it is not introduced until they have fully understood the process that is taking place in their trial and improvement approach. A parallel can be seen in the need for pupils to understand the addition formula before they are shown the autosum button. The suggested discussion about which data to enter into the options in the Goal Seek dialogue box for accurate results is vital. It would also be useful to provide a space on the Goal Seek worksheet for pupils to explain how it operates in subsequent questions. It may well be necessary to go through this process again with some pupils while others move ahead. Again, it is vital that pupils check their answers to see if they are viable, as sometimes in the heat of competition they become careless and fail to notice nonsensical outcomes.

[3a] At the beginning of Lesson 3, a presentation is used to compare two charts and a sheet of figures showing information about mobile phone tariffs. While this is a useful exercise in itself and demonstrates the key point that graphical representation is often far easier to decipher than figures, the lesson then returns to the mobile phone model without any reinforcement or practical follow-up. It would seem sensible to omit this activity and continue with the model based on figures and return to the issue of graphical representation later when the whole concept can be explored in a meaningful way. This will aid understanding and allow independent use of charts in the future. This is the fourth time over Years 7 and 8 that charts have been approached, but learning has not been consolidated for pupils. There is further consideration of charts relating to [3e] **and** [3f] below.

[3b] Some comment is needed about absolute and relative cell references, which are considered in a useful way in this module. It is important to remember that absolute and relative cell references can only

be understood when shown in an appropriate context; it is impossible to explain them successfully in the abstract, so do not be tempted to try. It is also essential for pupils to learn the syntax of the absolute cell reference. This is the same as learning the rules of any language and, although it may be daunting to some teachers and pupils, after a few applications of the concept it becomes easy to use.

[3c] We return to consider charts later during the use of mobile phone worksheet 2. Although creating a line graph is a useful exercise at this stage, it is worrying that the pupils are given step by step instructions to create it. The instructions are quite difficult to follow, and many, while achieving the expected outcome, will be unclear about how the final graph relates to the initial spreadsheet. For example, rows rather than columns are selected as holding the source data, and the "Y" axis is rescaled. While some pupils will find it easy to relate these actions to the data, they may need to be supported in recognising this. A significant number of pupils will require these points to be exemplified and related to the context in order to see exactly what they have done to create the chart and why they have done it. Only then will some pupils be able to understand the process and apply this new learning independently to other contexts.

There is plenty of evidence of a failure to teach an understanding of electronically produced charts in displays all over the country. They often show over-complex chart types and inappropriate or incorrect data being graphed. This results in confusing and ineffective outcomes which are difficult to interpret or which communicate nothing of value. It would be advisable to discuss the issue with Maths staff and perhaps develop some sort of agreement that addresses this vital area of learning. This unit does not teach pupils about electronically generated charts; it merely gives mechanistic instructions for the creation of one particular chart type. It would be far more effective if pupils have already covered this area prior to this unit and are able to suggest a chart type and create it without the step by step instructions. They could then go on to make a useful analysis of the information it displays. This work could then be seen as a useful reinforcement and application of their prior learning.

The plenary looks at the advantages and disadvantages of using ICT to produce graphical representations. Again, pupils have created one chart type about one specific type of information, so although it may be a useful discussion, this is not enough to ensure real understanding. Teachers need to consider where these advantages and disadvantages are discussed in a wider context.

[4a] Lesson 4 uses the RANDBETWEEN function in Excel to generate random numbers to test the mobile phone model working with a wide range of data. Some less experienced ICT teachers may understand the concept of random numbers being used to test the model, but equally, may not feel confident in teaching this particular activity. The National Curriculum in ICT and the ICT framework objectives do not require the use of this sort of function, and while it is not difficult to use in this context, it is unlikely that many pupils will have a full understanding of its wider use. It could be left until pupils are studying at GCSE. At that stage, thorough testing could involve the use of randomly generated numbers, but in Year 8, self-generated test data would be perfectly acceptable. As the unit says, people are usually quite consistent in their mobile phone usage, so the RANDBETWEEN function could be considered a diversion. Perhaps it could be used with the most able pupils as an extension or computer club activity.

[4b] The substantial extension activity provided at the end of Lesson 4 may be an appropriate way to stretch the higher attainers, although it is not made clear where this additional teaching could take place. It would be appropriate for only a limited number of pupils and many teachers, particularly those with non-mathematical backgrounds, may find the complexities of the model quite daunting. The nature of the tasks undertaken by the pupils during the lesson are such that many will require considerable support and guidance, so it is unlikely the teacher will be able to deliver this additional work. It is also doubtful whether many pupils could explore it unaided. The new model incorporates some quite complex formulae, and it is not clear whether pupils are to recreate the model or use it to explore various issues to extend their understanding. This is an interesting exercise, but not by any means necessary to meet framework objectives. It is also slightly puzzling as extension work, as this much higher level is not suggested in other units.

8.5 An ICT system: integrating applications to find solutions

KS3 STRATEGY FRAMEWORK OBJECTIVES

Finding things out

Organising and investigating

- Understand:
  - how data collection and storage are automated in commerce and some public services;
  - the impact of electronic databases on commercial practice and society;
  - potential misuse of personal data.

Developing ideas and making things happen

Analysing and automating processes

- Automate simple processes by:
  - creating templates;
  - creating simple software routines.
- Consider the benefits and drawbacks of using ICT to automate processes.
- Represent simple design specifications as diagrams.

Models and modelling

- Develop ICT-based models and test predictions by changing variables and rules.
- Draw and explain conclusions.
- Review and modify ICT models to improve their accuracy and extend their scope.

Control and monitoring

- Develop and test a system to monitor and control events by:
  - using sensors effectively;
  - developing, testing and refining efficient sequences of instructions and procedures;
  - assessing the effects of sampling and transmission rates on the accuracy of data from sensors;
  - understanding how control and monitoring has affected commercial and industrial processes.

Exchanging and sharing information

Fitness for purpose

- Recognise how different media and presentation techniques convey similar content in ways that have different impacts.
- Understand that an effective presentation or publication will address audience expectations and needs.
- Devise criteria to evaluate the effectiveness of own and others' publications and presentations, and use the criteria to make refinements.

Refining and presenting information

- Plan and design presentations and publications, showing how account has been taken of:
  - audience expectations and needs;
  - the ICT and media facilities available.
- Use a range of ICT tools efficiently to combine, refine and present information by:
  - structuring a publication or presentation.

About this unit

This unit involves a feasibility study for a local charity fund-raising project to grow bedding plants from seedlings to maturity for sale to the public. The school would be responsible for the financial aspects of the project, controlling the conditions for growing the seedlings, and the advertising.

During the first three lessons, the pupils develop a financial model to manage and predict their costs. During Lessons 4 to 6, they explore the possibilities of a control system for the school greenhouse to cover the hours when they cannot check the seedlings. In Lessons 7 and 8, they design a marketing strategy to attract customers to buy their plants.

This unit represents the culmination of the learning in the first years of Key Stage 3 and is a considerable challenge. Pupils have a little more autonomy than in previous units, and they have the opportunity to work on a realistic integrated system which is of relevance to them.

The unit demands a broad spectrum of skills, knowledge and understanding, both in ICT terms and generic knowledge from other disciplines. This ranges from knowledge of the life cycle of plants, an understanding of financial modelling, appreciation of the thinking involved in developing control systems, and the creative flair required to produce quality publicity documentation. There are few secondary teachers who can offer such a range of knowledge and skills at the required level, so it is likely that teachers will have to spend considerable time developing their command of all themes. It is also necessary, as in previous units, that the teacher is very familiar with the practical elements and has worked through the entire unit in advance, noting any areas where problems might occur or timescales need to change.

Although it is suggested that most pupils will be working at Level 5, it may be that some pupils would be able to reach higher levels than anticipated if given appropriate support and time. The work relates to many earlier units, and care will have to be taken to support any pupils who have not studied or have struggled with the previous units in the ICT strategy. Various differentiation strategies are suggested, although these may not meet the needs of many pupils at the lower end of the achievement scale. For those pupils the unit may need remodelling.

As in other units, there are many resources to be reproduced and organised, and again it may be felt that some are surplus to requirements. Pupil management of their resources is also of great importance, although hopefully the previous units will have prepared them for the task. Although a shared storage area is recommended during other units, it is essential here because pupils' ideas and outcomes are frequently displayed to the class and used for feedback and discussion. In addition, there needs to be a system for housekeeping in terms of deleting those files no longer required, to avoid exceeding the capacity of the shared area.

Pupils work in pairs organised by the teacher throughout this unit. Although there is no recommendation, similar-ability pairs would seem most sensible. Mixed-ability pairings over this period of time, and for such a variety of activities, would inevitably mean that some pupils would be held back whereas others would not participate fully. In Lesson 1, there is a recommendation that the teacher works with the lower attainers, so similar-ability pairings are obviously assumed. Occasionally pairs work together for an evaluation exercise when it is useful to seek an objective opinion. As before, it is recommended that pupils are reminded of the criteria used by "critical friends".

It is recommended that the ICT teachers liaise with other departments to check where they have embarked on similar activities. Pupils may have used sensors in Science and control technology in Science or Design and Technology, and will have used spreadsheets for modelling in Mathematics. Some aspects of data privacy may have been addressed in PSHE or Citizenship, and the generic knowledge relating to design and marketing will also have been considered in Design and Technology.

The unit suggests a duration of nine lessons of 60 minutes each. However, on two occasions an extra lesson could be inserted into the schedule; there is a comment about this in the Alternative approaches section. The following table shows the suggested breakdown of lesson time on the basis of teacher-led whole class teaching, paired or small group-based work away from the computer, and practical, computer-based activity. It can be seen that nearly half the lesson time is spent in teacher-led, whole class activities, approximately a third on group work away from the computer, and just under a quarter on practical, computer-based work. The taught element and teacher support is absolutely crucial in this unit, and the focus on the systems life cycle for organising and managing the project is a valuable element. However, the amount of computer-based work representing autonomous problem-solving is minimal. Pupils may be given more decision-making power than in previous units, but they spend only a quarter of their time at the computer developing their models, control systems and publicity materials. There is a comment on this in the Alternative approaches section.

	Taught as a whole class	*Pupil work away from the computer*	*Pupil work at the computer*
Lesson 1	45 mins	15 mins	
Lesson 2	30 mins	15 mins	15 mins
Lesson 3	30 mins		30 mins
Lesson 4	40 mins	20 mins	
Lesson 5	30 mins	15 mins	15 mins
Lesson 6	15 mins	25 mins	20 mins
Lesson 7	30 mins	15 mins	15 mins
Lesson 8	15 mins	25 mins	20 mins
Lesson 9	20 mins	25 mins	15 mins
Overall balance	**4 hrs 15 mins** 47%	**2 hrs 35 mins** 29%	**2 hrs 10 mins** 24%

LESSON BY LESSON

Lesson 1: Revising systems and introducing the project

This opening lesson revisits the concept of a system. In addition, pupils are introduced to the project, and they begin to develop their financial model.

Starter: Looking at systems and sequencing events

This lesson is mainly used to consider what a system is. Pupils are shown a PowerPoint presentation in which they identify the input, process, and output cycle of a series of control systems. They then go on to look at some simple methods of organising processes using a systems flowchart and a Gantt chart.

> They are, in fact, only considering control systems, which represent a very narrow definition of a system. They do not go on to use a Gantt chart later in the unit, so they do not have the opportunity to reinforce their understanding of it. This is discussed in Lesson commentaries on page 117. [1a]

Main activities: Introducing the project

The systems life cycle is demonstrated to the pupils, and they are reminded of their previous experience in developing a public information system in Unit 8.1. They are then introduced to the unit brief, that is, an activity in which they model a possible system involving the growing of plants to raise money for charity.

> This does not relate exactly to the content of Unit 8.1 so this reminder needs to be carefully planned.

Pupils then consider the information they need in order to develop the three parts of the model and decide which ICT applications might help them. The lower attainers will require some guidance to focus on the relevant issues.

Plenary and homework: Reviewing the learning; and identifying the elements of a financial model

In pairs, pupils discuss their understanding of a system, share their thoughts with another pair and report back any variations in their definitions. The homework involves pupils in identifying the costs they will need to consider in their financial model. They are given a pro forma to help them.

> The resource is ill-defined and most pupils will need a more structured resource.

Lesson 2: Modelling the finances

The main activities in this lesson are a revision of pupils' understanding of financial modelling, followed by the development of an automated spreadsheet to represent their seedlings project.

Starter: Thinking about the finances of the project

The lesson begins with pairs of pupils pooling their homework ideas on a new pro forma.

Development: Selecting data; and constructing a model

The teacher shows a PowerPoint presentation to guide a whole class discussion about the information required for a financial model for the seedlings project. Pupils are shown an example of the customer file relating to the previous time this project was run. They identify the relevant items of information, and the teacher leads a discussion of how to develop a financial model for this project in which different incomings and outgoings are considered, as well as the profits for the charity.

> There are a number of assumptions relating to the plants and the trays in which they are grown that need to be stated at the start of this phase of the unit. This is a key consideration in Lesson 3.

The pupils are then grouped in pairs, which will be maintained for the whole project, and they begin to develop a simple model.

> An example of a possible outcome is provided for you, but you may feel this task could be omitted and prefer to wait to start developing the model using the authentic Amstead website data. This is discussed further in Lesson commentaries on page 117. [2a]

Pupils print two copies of their initial spreadsheet model.

> You will need to organise the printing carefully, as they will have been working on this for only 15 to 20 minutes and some may not have finished. You need to choose a few pairs to describe their plans to the rest of the class, so make sure you decide who they will be in advance and print their spreadsheets first.

Plenary and homework: Reflecting on progress; reviewing the model; and suggesting improvements

Selected pairs explain their thinking to the class and the teacher relates it to the systems life cycle. This theme continues with the distribution of a systems life cycle record sheet on which pupils complete a description as to how they have addressed each stage of the cycle during the development of their models. For homework, the pupils are asked to annotate their printouts to justify their decisions and think of some questions their model will aim to answer.

> As with the earlier exercise, you may want to omit this and concentrate on the model based on the Amstead data. You would need to give considerable additional support to the lower attainers, as many pupils will not have a clear idea of the process of growing and selling plants. This is discussed further in Lesson commentaries on page 117. [2a]

Lesson 3: Developing the financial model

In this lesson, pupils develop their model using information from a garden centre website, create necessary formulae and test a prediction.

Starter: Identifying the required data

Pupils begin by exploring the Amstead Garden Centre website to identify information that will help in developing their model.

It is important that you carry out this task of retrieving the data from this site in advance and check how long it takes. You may well decide to increase the time available for completion of this task. See further discussion on page 118. [3a]

Main activities: Developing the financial model

The class reviews the homework and some pupils talk about questions to which their models will provide answers. Pupils then develop their models in their pairs in order to meet the following requirements:

- the cost of producing a tray of plants;
- how much they should charge for a tray of plants with a forecast profit of 20 per cent;
- how much profit they expect to make if people buy the same amount as last time;
- the smallest number of trays of plants they must sell in order not to lose money.

Some further questions are asked of those who complete the four requirements.

There are some questions about this data set meeting the requirements of the task, without certain assumptions being specified in advance. See Lesson commentaries, page 118, for further comment. [3a]

Plenary and homework: Reporting the feasibility of the system; and annotating the financial model

A whole class discussion looks at the financial feasibility of the project, and the teacher draws out issues about different sales scenarios and possible comments to be made to the head teacher in the final report. The pupils also consider how their work on the financial model relates to the stages in the systems life cycle and what it contributes to the project as a whole.

The homework asks pupils to show the development of their work by annotation of various printouts and planning sheets.

The requirement to show the project development in terms of the systems life cycle is useful, but is likely to take more than the allocated time. It will require additional support, as pupils like to show their "best work" and sometimes do not recognise the importance of the process as opposed to the end result.

There is a note at the end of the lesson which indicates an extra lesson could be added at this point to allow pupils to demonstrate work at a higher level.

See Lesson commentaries, page 118, for further comment on this suggestion. [3b]

Lesson 4: Using control systems to automate a process

In this lesson, pupils will begin to develop their control systems to enable the plants to be grown successfully.

Starter: Control in real life

Initially, pupils are asked to comment on a series of images as to whether the processes depicted should be controlled by a person or a computer.

The word "should" is misleading, and you may decide to replace it with "could" and let pupils respond with "either" as long as they can justify this decision. Some of the pictures are not very clear, so you may want to replace them or add extra hints.

The pupils then move on to place various cards on a grid to show whether specifically named systems should be controlled by a computer or person and give reasons.

It isn't clear why both activities are included, although the second can be seen as more complex. You may wish to ignore the first and go straight into the second, more substantial task.

After pupil feedback, the discussion focuses on the two lists summing up the type of circumstances when computer control or human control is first choice. The project is reiterated; that the pupils need to develop a system whereby they can control the conditions in the greenhouse remotely when they are not in school.

Main activities: Conditions in the greenhouse; and using software to regulate the temperature in the greenhouse

Pupils are asked to think about what plants need to grow and to identify the conditions in the greenhouse which may need to be varied over time. After feedback and recording of ideas, the teacher explains the difference between analogue and digital sensors. Pupils are invited to record on a template (Pupil Resource 9) the different variables that could be monitored and measured and the type of sensor which would be required to fulfil the function.

This will be a real challenge for both teacher and pupils as it may be optimistic to expect pupils to have such a broad knowledge of plant growth. See Lesson commentaries, page 119, for further comment. [4a]

The teacher then uses the software to show the development of the flowcharts relating to an electric heater and a cooling fan used during Unit 7.6 the previous year. Pupils consider how they could be adapted to meet the conditions in the current project.

Plenary and homework: Controlling the greenhouse; and starting to draft the report

Pupils draft a short statement explaining why the greenhouse should be controlled by a computer.

Surely pupils would find this easier if they had already completed the work to develop a control system for the greenhouse? Applying these ideas is essential to embed understanding.

The objectives of the lesson are reiterated, as are the reasons why computers are better at some control tasks and humans at others. An initial draft of the element concerned with control in the head teacher's report is set as the homework task. A resource listing the points to include is available.

You may think the resource is valuable but wasteful of paper! Either copy and paste it so you have three copies on an A4 sheet or write the requirements on the board for pupils to copy! You may also feel they have not yet engaged sufficiently with the problem to begin this report unsupported.

Lesson 5: Programming and testing the solution

In this lesson, pupils consider the efficiency of their control system. It is suggested that a webcam is set up to take a time lapse sequence of the pupils entering the classroom. This will be used later in the lesson when considering the possibility of time lapse monitoring of the seedlings.

Starter: Controlling the greenhouse

Pupils are reminded of the conditions in the greenhouse that need to be monitored. They are given a set of parameters relating to temperature, light and water levels.

There is nothing to explain why these particular parameters have been chosen. The temperature range, for example, does not relate very closely to the temperatures required for the plants being considered in this unit.

Then pupils are shown a list of possible scenarios against which they consider the stated control criteria and decide on an action.

There are a lot of scenarios here to which pupils have to react very quickly. It will show the range of ability in the class, as some will find the challenges relatively simple and others will need additional time to work through the problems to develop a real understanding. It will be important to target lower attainers to check understanding.

Main activities: Developing the control system; and frequency of sensing

Pupils work through the control planning sheets (Pupil Resources 13 and 14) to develop precise descriptions of actions and identify appropriate flowchart symbols.

The initial instructions are entered to show what is expected. You may wish to enter more prompts for the lower attainers.

When the first planning sheet is complete, pupils use the software to build and test their flowchart for temperature control. They then move on to develop the flowchart for the light control, working through the same "design, implement, test" process as defined by the systems life cycle. At an appropriate time, specified pupils will demonstrate their flowcharts and explain their decisions as part of a whole class discussion led by the teacher.

There is a mismatch between the temperature range to be used and that which is required by these plants as shown in the Amstead website. Some pupils may notice this fact, so you need an answer ready! There is further discussion of the information needed and what is provided in the Alternative approaches on page 118. [3a]

The teacher then introduces the idea of checking the values in the control system at longer intervals by altering the sampling rate. The time lapse video sequences are shown to exemplify this and a discussion follows to consider the varying sampling rates required by different systems.

Plenary and homework: Improving the efficiency of the system; and developing the solution

For the last 10 minutes, pupils are asked to consider an appropriate time lapse when monitoring conditions in the greenhouse, and contribute their ideas to a class discussion.

There is no suggestion about what the optimal interval might be! You may need to ask a keen gardener who has used such a control system.

Pupils are asked to add the necessary instructions to reduce the sampling rate on their control planning sheet (Pupil Resource 14). This shows the position and content of the symbols used to produce the desired effect on their flowchart printout and annotate accordingly.

Lesson 6: Extending the control system

The final lesson in this phase considers the extension and refinement of the system, and pupils consider the feasibility of the project in a report.

Starter: Key words wordsearch

Pupils settle into the lesson with a key words wordsearch relating to control systems, followed by a discussion of words identified and their meanings.

Main activities: Refining and programming the final control system

The focus of the next activity is to discuss the advantages of less frequent sampling and to move on to the idea of making the system more efficient. This is shown by defining an upper and lower temperature limit, so that a heater is switched on only when needed. The pupils are given a status table (Pupil Resource 16) on which they record the status of the heater according to different input values. The accuracy of their predictions is demonstrated through the use of the software, by entering various input values and observing the response.

There is only a brief mention of a fan being used to reduce the temperature once the upper temperature threshold is reached. If this is not part of the final system, it isn't clear why it was discussed in Lessons 4 and 5.

Pupils then go on to edit their own flowcharts to include a time delay and improve efficiency by entering two values to provide an upper and lower temperature threshold within which the heater will be switched off. It is suggested that lower attainers may need copies of the demonstration flowchart.

You may need to think of a variety of differentiation strategies to develop understanding of this exercise.

It is suggested that higher attainers are asked to add a counter to their water level sensing flow-chart or asked for their suggestions on refining and improving their systems. All flowcharts are to be printed and saved in the shared area.

Supporting resources would need to be developed for most pupils (and teachers) to enable them to add a counter. For further comment, see page 119. [6a]

Plenary and homework: Reporting on the feasibility of the system; and completing the greenhouse system section of the systems life cycle report

Pupils consider their control system in terms of the stages of its construction, possible improvements, whether the system is feasible, and what information would be required by the head teacher.

They collect together their documentation and annotate any recent additions to show the ongoing development of the system. The lesson ends with a reminder of their progress through the systems life cycle in this element of the unit. This theme continues for homework, where pupils complete the appropriate column on their system life cycle report sheet (Pupil Resource 17) to record their progress during the development of the control system.

Notice that this activity was a homework when relating to the modelling element and it is now completed in the lesson, and vice versa with the updating of documentation task. This is a wise approach, as if an activity is constantly consigned to homework, pupils may devalue it.

Lesson 7: Marketing the product

This lesson is the first in which pupils consider the marketing needs of their project as well as the associated data privacy issues.

Starter: Marketing methods

The initial activity involves pupils thinking of possible marketing methods for the sale of their seedlings. This is then compared with a list that is provided in Teacher Resource 12. The teacher explains that a mixture of methods would usually be employed, and pupils move on to complete an Advertising Media Analysis (Pupil Resource 18) in which they think about complementary products and marketing methods. Their findings are discussed, and the importance of effective marketing in a campaign such as this is emphasised by the teacher.

Main activities: Targeting advertisements; developing the customer database; and privacy issues

The value of targeting advertising is discussed, and pupils are reminded of the list of previous customers (Pupil Resource 5). Ways of attracting these customers are discussed and the topic is widened to look at the abundance of "junk mail" and the ways in which it can be generated. A mailmerge system is demonstrated, either using a PowerPoint presentation (Teacher Resource 12) or by using the word-processing software and the data file of names and addresses, to produce personalised letters.

A demonstration using the actual software is far more appropriate than showing a dynamic system via a series of static slides. It is important that pupils are aware of possible pitfalls and where precision is crucial. It is also best for pupils to apply what they have seen soon afterwards. They will not remember the detail and advice about avoiding pitfalls if the demonstration is isolated from the application. See page 119 for further discussion. [7a]

Pupils move on to consider data privacy, and the Data Protection Act is briefly discussed.

It is important here to talk about the principles in pupil-friendly language or this could become very tedious! The legal status of the data file may not be completely clear, so you will need to discuss an agreed approach to this with colleagues beforehand. There is also scope for a discussion on the ethical and environmental issues, which are equally noteworthy.

Pupils create a data file for their use which can be used to record and track orders, record when they are completed and calculate the cost. They need to design and create a data structure, a data entry form and a report to generate an invoice for customers. They are given up to 18 minutes to carry this out.

This is an extraordinary expectation. See page 119 for further comment. [**7b**]

It is suggested that lower attainers use a prepared database.

This seems to be a case of all or nothing. In order to ensure lower attainers do experience these valuable data-handling and collection skills, perhaps you could offer a partially developed structure for these pupils to complete.

Plenary and homework: What information is held about us; and documenting the system

The last 10 minutes are devoted to a discussion of possible organisations that hold information about individuals and what they might use it for.

This could have been addressed when the Data Protection Act was discussed. The plenary could be used to consider the database structures and data-collection forms they have produced.

For homework, pupils annotate a data entry form to show what data types they have included and why. They also identify cases in which the subject's permission would need to be sought.

It is the data (field contents) for which permission is required, rather than the data type. The resource "Documenting the database system" (Pupil Resource 19) is useful here, although it is important to explain why both the field and the field type have been chosen.

In addition pupils are asked to write a paragraph to explain the advantages of their computerised system over a manual system recorded on paper. It is mentioned that teachers wishing to give the data-handling aspects of the unit more of a focus could insert an additional lesson here.

Lesson 8: Developing a marketing package

In this lesson, pupils begin to create a corporate image to help them market their plants to the appropriate audience.

Starter: Key characteristics of a corporate image

Pupils are reminded of the issues addressed in Unit 7.3 in which they designed and created a logo to convey a company image.

> The logo was not designed for a company, it was a logo for a subject at school. If you want to avoid the business environment suggested by "corporate image", you could refer to it as the "house style" or the "branding flow".

Pupils identify the main items of information they need to impart to potential customers about their plants and think about possible ways of doing this.

Main activities: Creating the corporate image; and designing the publicity materials

Pupils start by creating some draft designs for a "piece of material to illustrate corporate image", and then move on to think about an advertisement. While designing their corporate image material, pupils are asked to annotate their work to show where it meets the four aspects set out in slide 2 of Teacher Resource 13, which are:

- to raise money for charity;
- the quality of the plants;
- grown by pupils of St Egberts;
- value for money.

They are also asked to address any technical issues connected with, for example, images, and their choice of software for the realisation of the publicity materials. Each pair of pupils then reviews the work of another pair and they share feedback. Slide 4 of Teacher Resource 13 shows the guidelines for sensible and sensitive review.

> Due to the time limits, it has to be assumed that the pupils will create only draft designs and will not carry the process through to fully implement the materials. This is discussed on page 120. **[8a]**

Once the "corporate identity" materials are complete, pupils move on to design their advertisement, which can be in the form of a poster, a leaflet, a multimedia presentation, a website, a short video or a radio advertisement.

> Many schools will not have the facilities to offer the full range of alternatives. You may have multimedia software, but of course this has not been explicitly addressed in the strategy, so although pupils may have ideas for implementation, it is unlikely they could produce a product of a satisfactory standard in the time available.

Pupils are to use the storyboard technique to develop their ideas, and the 'storyboard resource' (Pupil Resource 20) is available for use. For those developing a website, a site map used for the virtual school visit in 8.2 (Pupil Resource 21) is available. Pupils have to negotiate their chosen approach with the teacher so they can be guided to an appropriate publication. Some ideas for dealing with pupils during this activity are suggested.

In order to manage this successfully, you may find you can only offer a limited choice of task, although it would be important to retain the opportunity to provide a more demanding activity for higher attainers. This is discussed on page 120. **[8b]**

Plenary and homework: Audience and fitness for purpose; and reviewing the publicity materials

Specifically chosen pairs display their work, and its fitness for audience and purpose is discussed. For homework, pupils are asked to annotate their advertisements to show ways in which they could be developed next lesson.

Lesson 9: Producing the project report and analysis of the result

This is the final lesson in the unit, in which pupils complete their marketing material. They create their report about the feasibility of the study for the head teacher and the charity representative, evaluate their work and consider their own future progression in terms of ICT capability.

It is important that pupils come to this lesson with all of their documentation showing the development of the three elements of this unit.

Starter: Key words

The lesson starts with a simple but useful task. Pupils select cards displaying a key term and place them on the relevant system life cycle diagram referring to an element of the unit; financial model, control system or marketing. Their responses are discussed.

Main activities: Completing the marketing materials; and preparing the final report

Pupils spend 15 minutes completing their marketing materials in the light of suggestions made in their homework. Some pupils may only complete one task.

Pupils get frustrated when they are given insufficient time to complete their work. Intense creative work using the computer is time-consuming, and account should be taken of this in planning the unit schedule. There is further discussion on page 120. **[9a]**

Pupils are gathered together to discuss the purpose and content of the final report for the head teacher. The report is produced as a display or a portfolio, showing progression through the steps of the systems life cycle in each of the three elements of the unit. Pupils use their annotated documentation, completed resource support sheets and printouts of their computer-based work to think about possible improvements to their system. They finish with a discussion about the feasibility of the project. A writing frame is available if needed (Pupil Resource 24) for the feasibility report.

This is an innovative idea which will motivate pupils, although they will need to have completed all of the preceding tasks which combine to constitute this final outcome. With appropriate discussion and time for realisation, completion of this would take at least a lesson.

Plenary and homework: Reviewing the project; and setting personal targets

Pupils work in groups of four to evaluate their work. They think about where the investigations could be extended and reflect on the groupings in which they worked. The class come together for a final review of the work of the past weeks. Pupils carry out a self-evaluation for homework. They consider their performance and work with others, as well as their own ideas about the success of the three elements and how they employed ICT in the project.

Alternative approaches

This is an interesting unit in that it suggests that it will give pupils more autonomy in a number of areas. However, it could be argued that this is not the case. The integrated aspect is a strength and enables pupils to both revisit and further their learning in an extensive range of skills, knowledge and understanding. This is a complex unit, and in order for pupils to achieve the learning objectives they will need time to develop their thinking, both individually and collaboratively. The suggested time schedule will not allow many pupils to gain maximum benefit from the tasks in this unit. If extra lessons are included, this work would be a very useful preparation both for Year 9 and later for those who decide to continue their ICT studies at GCSE level. The scenario may be seen to be of interest, although many pupils will require a lot of discussion about the background detail and the issues that need consideration, as few will have any real knowledge of the bedding plant scenario. It is essential that they gain a holistic view of the project in order to participate fully in the various opportunities it offers.

Although there are wide-ranging and useful resources for pupils and teachers in this unit, one notable omission is examples of possible systems which would give a much needed guide to expectations. Other than an example of the initial simple model, there is little to suggest what outcomes teachers may expect in terms of the modelling and control systems and possible marketing materials. This is demanding teaching for less practised ICT teachers, who may not have previous experience or familiarity with Key Stage 4 ICT to help them gauge levels of expectation.

Appropriate differentiation is an enormous challenge in this unit, and some pupils will find it difficult to access some of the concepts addressed. The resources have not been designed with the needs of these pupils in mind, and you may find that you need to develop an alternative unit for the lower attainers with supporting resources. At the same time, some high attainers may want to develop their work further. This can be accommodated by allowing a lot more independence for these pupils to follow their own ideas, or by providing specific computer clubs to allow them to progress further.

The parallel unit in the QCA scheme of work is based on the same idea of an integrated project in which pupils set up, organise and run a fund-raising event. Although it acknowledges that this may not be possible in reality, it does suggest that full implementation is seen as a strength. This is not recognised in the same way in strategy Unit 8.5, and it may be that teachers wish to use a context that could be realised in reality.

Lesson commentaries

[1a] A look at systems is useful as a starting point, but it needs to address a broader definition than simply control systems. The consideration of flowcharts and Gantt charts could be relevant, but pupils do not apply these tools in organising their work schedule (there is no further mention of either in this context). You may feel you want to apply their use, change the context to something more relevant or omit this altogether and leave it until they are used for project planning in the Year 9 case studies.

[2a] It is suggested that pupils start developing an initial model based on test data provided by you. However, it would be completely acceptable to wait until they have the full picture of the data on the

Amstead website before they start creating their models, which provide the focus of this modelling stage. There is a mention of ensuring the pupils understand the mathematics, but this can be developed when creating the model using the "real" data. The subsequent homework is useful but again, could be applied to their actual model. As the lesson notes suggest a limited time for discussion, you may want to omit these initial tasks and set the scene in more detail, providing additional support for the development of the main objective for this phase of the unit, the model based on the Amsted data. The lesson notes also appear to over-estimate the levels of knowledge pupils will have about growing seedlings, so this may also influence your decision.

[3a] It is very difficult to get a complete picture of the data pupils need and where it can be found, as the website is not organised for easy data retrieval. To find information about Zinnia, you can choose the S–Z choice on the "Browse a section of the catalogue" option, which takes you sequentially through the records of each plant starting with the letters S through to Z. This takes some considerable time. Alternatively, you can display the whole catalogue. However, once you have scrolled to Zinnia, the column headings are no longer on screen (so make a note of them first). In order to see the price, which is the furthest column on the right, the first column on the left, showing the name of the plant, is no longer on screen. As Zinnia is the last record, this isn't too much of a problem, but with the other plant records located centrally in the data, you need to read across the fields very carefully. Whatever approach is taken, it certainly takes far longer than 5 minutes to access the appropriate data.

Name	Type	Seed count per gram	Where to sow	Sowing temp	When	Time to germinate	Transplant	Flowers	Variety	Description	Price code
Geranium	Half hardy perennial	220	Under glass	21°C	Jan–Feb	1–3 weeks	2–3 weeks	July–October	Paintbox Mixed	Near F-1 qualities, weather resistance, long lasting extra	J
Lobelia	Half hardy annual	30000	Under glass	21°C	Jan–March	2–3 weeks	3–4 weeks	May–October	Cambridge Blue	Pale Blue	G
Pansy	Hardy biennial	120	Under glass	10–15°C	Feb–May	3–4 weeks	4 weeks	June–September	Viola	Clear, bright colours	F
Phlox	Half hardy annual	500	Under glass	16°C	March–April	2–3 weeks	2–3 weeks	June–September	21st Century Magenta Mixed	White, Red, Magenta & Rose shaded flowers	Q
Zinnia	Half hardy annual	100	Under glass	20°C	Feb–April	2–3 weeks	4 weeks	June–September	Profusion	Flowers profusely over many weeks. Enjoys sunny positions	T

The table above shows the records of some of the plants to be grown using the "Browse the whole catalogue onscreen" option. (This is a condensed version which shows more than can be viewed onscreen.) As you can see, there is a significant variation in the required temperature, which is not acknowledged when pupils are developing their control system. The month of sowing is also difficult to determine, as some plants, such as the Geranium, need to be planted in January or February, whereas the Phlox should be sown in March or April. These kinds of anomalies need prior consideration, and decisions or assumptions made which are subsequently explained to the pupils.

There are also a number of variables that do not receive any consideration, but of which pupils may become aware. We assume that they will grow the same plants that appear on Pupil Resource 5, which is the list of previous orders. This is not made explicit. The idea of trays is introduced, but there is no obvious discussion of their cost or their size in terms of the number of plants they can hold. You can see from the table that the Amstead website shows the price of plants per gram and the number of seeds per gram. It is not made clear how many plants will make up a tray, how much wastage there is due to seeds failing to germinate, the cost and amount of compost required and who will be paying for the electricity used. These difficulties will need to be resolved before the unit is taught.

[3b] The suggestion of an extra lesson is certainly useful; primarily for the many pupils who will find this project extremely demanding. It may also help you to ensure that the models are fully implemented by every pair of pupils. It is unlikely they will all be completed in the allocated time, even if the exercise developing an initial model in Lesson 2 is omitted as suggested. The lesson could also be used as an opportunity to provide a further challenge for the more able, although you may find that this is a more appropriate task for a computer club specifically targeted at higher attainers.

[4a] The teacher's notes have high expectations of both teachers' and pupils' knowledge of growing bedding plants from seed! You would need considerable whole class discussion around the context, and it would be very useful to check exactly when, where and how this topic has been addressed elsewhere in the curriculum. It is also unlikely that the majority of pupils will gain any real understanding of the characteristics of analogue and digital sensors simply from a short explanation, as this has not been addressed explicitly in previous units. This is complex subject matter and deserves due consideration. It will need careful explanation, and pupils will require support to apply what they have learned.

[6a] On screen flowchart software is obviously a cheap and easily managed option, but nothing can replace the powerful nature of collaboration and intense engagement that pupils experience when controlling real models. Although the use of software with on screen representation teaches the necessary skills and knowledge, the development of genuine understanding is more likely to take place using models, where possible. This means that the troubleshooting process is more immediate and the process of refining and improving the systems becomes more intuitive.

[7a] As already suggested, a demonstration of the actual mailmerge process is more useful than a PowerPoint presentation, but even this is not satisfactory if pupils do not follow up with practical application of the process. It is this that enables understanding when an explanation of the theory cannot. You may feel there is little point in showing this process in isolation. It would be better placed in the following lesson, when pupils are developing marketing materials and could be given the chance to try it themselves afterwards. Some sort of support material will be needed as they are unlikely to implement the whole process successfully from memory. It is worth noting that the equivalent QCA unit in the Key Stage 3 scheme of work suggests that pupils both design and implement simple mailmerge letters.

[7b] The bulk of previous data-handling work was carried out in Unit 7.5. Unless there has been considerable cross-curricular reinforcement, pupils will need to be reminded of the subject knowledge relating to database structures. Topics such as efficient design in terms of data entry forms, as well as a brief reminder of the software techniques, will be needed in addition to the prompt cards suggested. The context needs reinforcement through discussion, and pupils will also need some time for design considerations before implementation. What data should they use? What is the point of this if they use the data from the previous implementation of this scheme, which is already stored electronically? Are they going to be able to attract new customers? You may like to have some "dummy" data available in the form of completed address forms for pupils to work with.

If you wish this unit to be a truly integrated project, incorporating all areas of ICT, it would be useful to include extra time for data handling so that this activity can be fully designed and implemented. Data handling using database software teaches many useful cognitive skills, such as hypothesising, sorting, categorisation and analysis, and does need to be addressed appropriately during Years 7 and 8. It may be that you would prefer to use database software for Unit 7.5, which requires complex searches using Boolean logic, for which, in general, database software is more efficient and actually easier to use. That unit also introduces much of the necessary subject knowledge relating to database structure. In a real implementation of this unit, however, there would be some calculations linked to the customer details, so a spreadsheet may be the most suitable tool to use here. However, if there was a need to interrogate the data, database software would be the best tool to use. It may be that teachers wish to revisit this aspect of the equivalent unit, 8.12, in the QCA scheme of work, where it suggests that pupils design a structure for a simple database, create a data file, update the information and interrogate it to produce reports.

[8a] Perhaps different groups of pupils could produce publicity materials in an assortment of formats. The issue of attracting new customers does not appear to be given particular significance, and although pupils examine how marketing literature can be targeted, they do not relate it predominantly to this project. You may wish to give pupils some creative freedom to think about ways in which they could sell the product and develop complementary marketing methods. After an initial reinforcement of guidelines for good design from Unit 7.3, and a reminder of the aspects that need consideration (slide 2 of Teacher Resource 13), you could support the pupils in designing and creating publicity materials for a purpose. This could be followed by a full review, possibly carried out with the help of potential customers. Templates, with partially developed ideas, could be used to support lower attainers.

[8b] It is interesting that the unit mentions the use of hardware and software that has not been addressed thus far in the strategy. It may well be that you choose to incorporate the use of some of these other tools in some units or to replace units which you feel are of less value.

[9a] The timings suggested here are inadequate for pupils to produce work of really high quality. It appears that data handling using data files and the more creative uses of ICT are given less emphasis in the strategy than the modelling and control aspects, as many of the related tasks are left unfinished. It is inevitable, particularly when realising the more creative work, that pupils will need to spend time out of lessons to produce really top-quality outputs, but it is necessary for the teacher to be there for a significant amount of time, providing structure and support and constantly questioning and guiding pupils through the process, at whatever level they are working.

It would certainly seem sensible to add further lessons to this unit to ensure that all areas are addressed appropriately. Although pupils do work more independently than in previous units, of the suggested nine hours duration, only a quarter is actually spent working unaided at the computer. This is a significant concern, as the unit is very teacher-dominated, and you may feel that it does not give pupils sufficient scope to make decisions and develop their work independently. Some extra time could be used to develop the data-handling element in more detail, include a sample mailmerge system and ensure the marketing materials are further elaborated and focused. In addition, more time could be allowed for the final presentation of the project, which could be an informative and impressive classroom display. It is worth noting that the QCA scheme of work suggests 12 hours for a project which does not include the development of a control system. This is due to the expectation that pupils would fully implement both the data-handling and publicity aspects of the project and also carry out a useful evaluation of the ways in which the use of ICT has enhanced the planning and organisation of the event. You may feel it is worth spending some time considering the use of a combination of aspects of both units.

Year 9 case studies

9.1 ICT systems In this case study pupils explore ICT systems within the context of designing a new water ride in a theme park. They assess the requirements of a new ride, then plan and develop a safety control system. They create a presentation for the park manager, outlining the features of the ride and the safety components it includes.

9.2a Development of a data-handling system In this case study pupils develop a data-handling system in which the data are generated from a questionnaire distributed to a class in another location. Pupils develop the system and document it using the standard stages of the system life cycle.

9.2b Development of an online data-collection system In this case study pupils set up an online data collection system to be completed by partner schools either in a different UK location or abroad. They learn data-handling skills, develop and investigate hypotheses using the data set they have generated from their online form. They write up their findings in a final report and make a presentation to a chosen audience in an agreed format.

9.3 Front-of-house theatre booking system In this case study pupils design a front-of-house ticketing system for a school production. They undertake three main tasks:

- modelling a seating plan which enables individual seats to be booked and a total kept of money taken;
- modelling the financial plan so that decisions can be made about ticket price;
- advertising the production to Year 6 pupils and their parents.

They use a design specification as the basis for their work, manage and record progress using Gantt charts and project documentation. In the final stages of the unit they present their project to the user and complete their project documentation.

9.1 ICT systems

KS3 STRATEGY FRAMEWORK OBJECTIVES

Developing ideas and making things happen

Analysing and automating processes

- Automate ICT processes.
- Represent a system in a diagram, identifying all its parts, including inputs, outputs and the processes used.

Control and monitoring

- Use ICT to build and test an efficient system to monitor and control events, including:
  - testing all elements of the system using appropriate test data;
  - evaluating the system's performance;
  - annotating work to highlight processes and justify decisions.
- Review and modify own or others' monitoring and control systems to improve efficiency (e.g. use more efficient procedures, reduce the number of instructions or procedures, add an element of feedback).

Exchanging and sharing information

Fitness for purpose

- Produce high-quality ICT-based presentations by:
  - creating clear presentations, sensitive to audience needs;
  - justifying the choice of form, style and content.
- Use knowledge of publications and media forms to devise criteria to assess the quality and impact of multimedia communications and presentations, and apply the criteria to develop and refine own work.

About this unit

In this case study of ten lessons, pupils explore ICT systems within the context of designing a new water ride in a theme park. The ride must be water-based, involve some kind of boat or raft and be planned so that one or more boats can move through the water channel safely and under control. The context of the work is similar to that of Unit 13, Control Systems in the QCA scheme of work for Year 9, and there are aspects of that unit that could be usefully incorporated into this work.

Having assessed the requirements of the new ride, pupils plan and develop a safety control system, which could include a feedback loop. Pupils are expected to produce:

- a schematic design of the ride;
- a complete control system for the ride, containing one or more boats;
- a presentation to the park manager outlining the features of the ride and how safety features have been included.

Having planned the ride, pupils develop their system using control software such as Flowol. They use ICT-based applications such as Gantt charts, project diaries and presentation software in the planning, recording and presentation of their project. There is no requirement for them to build models, and though the use of a variety of input and output devices to test their procedures is suggested, this is optional. Once the project is complete, pupils present their system to the park manager, outlining the features of the ride and its safety components. They evaluate each other's presentations using previously agreed criteria.

The central task of the unit, the design of the water ride for the theme park, is similar to that included in the QCA scheme of work. This unit also requires the use of ICT in the planning, documentation and presentation of the project, an expectation of skill and understanding which is similar to that required for GCSE project work.

The unit builds on work in control undertaken in Units 7.6 and 8.5. It develops work on systems flowcharts and Gantt charts, although it should be recognised that the control systems developed in the previous units represented quite a narrow definition of a system and that Gantt charts are referred to only in Lesson 1 of Unit 8.5.

Prior to starting the unit, pupils will need a knowledge of flowchart conventions, which are introduced in Unit 7.6 and to be able to plan, design, test and evaluate a control system, based on problem identification and needs analysis. To complete the unit successfully they will need to have an understanding of systems life cycles and be able to undertake ongoing planning, evaluation and documentation of the project, while monitoring and managing progress. They will need to be able to use generic ICT tools as part of this process, and at the end of the project, be able to present their solution for a specific audience, the park manager.

In addition to the above, teachers will need to be able to monitor the ongoing project work and support pupils in managing their projects.

Although pupils are brought together in pairs or groups for discussion during the lessons, the impression is given in the unit that each pupil will produce his or her own system, accompanying documentation and presentation. However, this is not stated explicitly, and it is a matter for professional judgement by teachers.

The unit of work is intended to comprise ten hour-long lessons. The balance of whole class teaching and individual or paired work at and away from the computer is as follows:

	Taught as a whole class	*Pupil work away from the computer*	*Pupil work at the computer*
Lesson 1	35 mins	25 mins	
Lesson 2	10 mins	50 mins*	
Lesson 3	10 mins	50 mins	
Lesson 4	15 mins	45 mins*	
Lessons 5 and 6	20 mins		100 mins
Lessons 7 and 8	20 mins		100 mins
Lesson 9	20 mins	20 mins	20 mins
Lesson 10	60 mins		
Overall balance	**3 hrs 10 mins** 32%	**3 hrs 10 mins** 32%	**3 hrs 40 mins** 36%

* Some brief use may be made of ICT in these sessions, for activities such as maintaining records or amending Gantt charts.

LESSON BY LESSON

Lesson 1: Introducing and planning the project

This lesson revises prior work in control, sets the context for the project, and pupils begin to plan their project.

Starter: Computers in control

This is a paper-based activity intended to revise pupils' understanding of control systems and the vocabulary associated with control.

Development: Thinking about the project

The project is presented to the class.

It is suggested that pupils could access a website showing theme park rides to help them understand the control systems involved. This is discussed on page 130. [**1a**]

The system life cycle is revisited and pupils are reminded about Gantt charts, which they met briefly at the beginning of Unit 8.5.

It might be useful to have some specific examples to illustrate the system life cycle. One based on the tasks undertaken in Unit 8.5 would be appropriate. You could show a Gantt illustrating the timing of tasks in Unit 8.5. Unit 9.3 begins with a practical exercise developing a Gantt chart based on buying a new car. That task might be useful here.

Pupils begin planning their own project using a Gantt chart (Pupil Resource 2). The tasks and suggested blocks of time are outlined on the chart and pupils merely have to sequence the tasks and time allocations.

The suggested Gantt chart is simple and sequential, with no time overlaps on tasks. It might be useful to discuss with pupils that in reality projects are often much more "messy". Examples could be drawn from television house or garden "makeover" programs or their own experience of parents' DIY projects, where some tasks have to be completed in a particular order but others may overlap.

Plenary and homework: Initial ideas

One or two pupils feed back their ideas, and issues arising from them are discussed. They print out their uncompleted Gantt charts and complete them for homework.

If they are completing their Gantt charts electronically, as suggested by the use of an online resource, it seems a backward step to print them and then complete them in pen. It might be better to save them as a draft and revisit them in a future lesson. An alternative homework could focus on analysing the elements of a control system required in a water ride or some other theme park ride.

Lesson 2: Analysing the elements

The planning is continued, pupils analyse the features of a ride and begin to represent these schematically.

Starter: Gantt charts

Pupils discuss their homework in pairs, justifying their decisions. One or two pupils present their partner's Gantt chart to the class.

If this has not been completed as homework, it could be completed now. Alternatively, pupils could present their analysis of the control features of other theme park rides.

Development: Features of theme park rides

The main part of the lesson focuses on the processes involved in theme park rides and the safety precautions associated with the features pupils identify. It is suggested that they are shown videos of theme park rides or visit the websites listed to help support their analysis. Pupils make a list of the elements and associated safety features of a water ride. These ideas are shared and pupils develop their own ideas, on paper or on the computer as a schematic diagram.

A log flume schematic, Teacher Resource 3, is intended as an example here. You could also show the simpler hand-drawn schematic drawing included in the QCA unit of work. This is discussed on page 131. [2a]

This activity is intended as an individual activity.

It might be helpful to allow pupils to work in pairs or small groups at this stage to encourage them to share and develop ideas collaboratively.

Plenary and homework: Controlling the ride

One of the pupils' diagrams, or a further developed schematic diagram (Teacher Resource 4), is used to discuss where computers could be used to control the ride.

This lesson has covered a lot of thinking, and the completed schematic diagram (Teacher Resource 4) is complex. More time may be needed if pupils are to understand it properly.

Pupils complete and annotate their diagrams for homework.

If they have been sharing ideas, it may be necessary to photocopy their work so that all can take a copy home, or allow time for them to make their own copy of the shared work so far.

Lesson 3: Devising the theme park rides

Work continues on system inputs and outputs, and pupils evaluate their schematic diagrams together.

Starter: Input or output?

This is a lively activity intended to revise pupils' understanding of inputs and outputs.

Development: Controlling the ride

The main part of the lesson introduces some very important new aspects of the system. These include the placement and function of sensors, switches, timers and gates, as well as particular features of this type of ride such as the camera, fountain and water bucket. This development is illustrated in a series of increasingly developed schematic diagrams (Teacher Resources 3, 4 and 5). Pupils work in pairs to adapt and annotate their own diagrams to include these features.

There is a great deal to do in the time allowed, and it is important for pupils to go through this process for themselves. This is discussed in more detail on page 131. [3a]

Plenary and homework: Evaluating the designs

In the plenary, pupils choose suitable criteria for evaluating their schematic designs. Working in their pairs, they use these to evaluate each other's designs.

As they have been involved in helping to develop each other's designs through discussion, it might be better for them to work with another pair for this evaluation task.

For homework, they annotate their diagrams in the light of this feedback and complete their project diary.

This is the first mention of the project diary. It is discussed in greater detail on page 132. [3b]

Lesson 4: Design and programming the control system

In this lesson, pupils continue to design their ride and begin to program the control system.

Starter: Using flowcharts

Pupils are reminded of flowchart conventions.

These conventions were introduced only briefly in Unit 7.6, more than a year earlier. If pupils have not had the opportunity to consolidate and apply this knowledge in other curriculum areas, you may need to allow longer to revise this understanding.

Development: Designing the ride

Pupils move on to using control software to design their ride. A paper-based support (Pupil Resource 7) encourages them to think about the outputs and motors included in their systems. In this part of the lesson they are asked to use subroutines to develop different sections of the system. The lesson notes suggest that the teacher demonstrates the creation of these subroutines.

It will be important to remind pupils of the use of subroutines at this point, as they have met them only briefly in the last lesson of Unit 7.6. This learning will need to be revised and consolidated. It will also be essential to demonstrate the programming of subroutines to support pupils as they begin this for themselves. This is a substantial task and may not be completed in the time allowance suggested.

Plenary and homework: Evaluation criteria; and updating the documentation

In the plenary session it is suggested that pupils agree criteria for evaluation of the completed subroutines and use these to evaluate each other's work.

> It is not necessary to overcomplicate this discussion of criteria. Pupils should be encouraged to ask themselves some simple questions such as: "does it work and is there a shorter, neater or more efficient way of programming it?"

For homework, they update their schematic diagrams, using a fresh printout to show development in the light of this evaluation. Project diaries are also updated and pupils refer to their Gantt charts to monitor progress.

Lessons 5 and 6: Testing and developing the control procedures

Pupils now have a substantial period of time to test and develop their control procedures.

Starter: Progress check

Pupils report on their progress since last week, referring to the system life cycle to identify the nature of the task or activity.

> Only 10 minutes are allowed for each pupil in the class to give three examples. It might be a better use of time to ask pupils to work in pairs or small groups, giving their three examples to their partner or other members of the group. The teacher can then select a few pupils to give feedback to the whole class.

Development: Implementing and testing the refinements

The pupils are reminded that they should continue to develop each section of the ride independently and bring them together into a complete system later. A number of support resources (Teacher Resources 13–19) are available to exemplify sections of the ride. The lesson plan suggests that pupils have access to predefined mimics, mimic creators, on-screen controls or external devices to support this development work.

> The provision of such resources is vital if pupils are to be able to test and refine their procedures. The provision of external devices, while not essential, would be of value. Some higher-attaining pupils may include the use of feedback in their systems.

Plenary and homework: Variations on the theme; and updating the documentation

The work of one or two pupils who have taken an interesting approach to the project is shared with the class. For homework, the schematic diagram and project diaries are updated.

It is important that a fresh printout of the schematic diagram is used to show the progressive changes.

It is acknowledged in the lesson notes that additional time may be needed to complete these activities.

Lessons 7 and 8: Completing the system

In these lessons pupils test their procedures to ensure that they are efficient, and then combine their procedures to create a complete system.

Starter: Room for improvement

Some pupils demonstrate one of their procedures and others give feedback on one factor that makes the procedure work well and one suggestion for improvement.

> This is a very public forum for providing feedback and will need to be handled with sensitivity.

Ideas for improving procedures are shared on a flip chart.

Development: Pulling it together

Based on the strategies explored in the starter, pupils continue to work on their own procedures in order to make them more efficient.

Once they are happy with each of their procedures, pupils combine them to create a complete system. They are asked to test them at each stage, using the criteria agreed in the starter session. Further resources (Teacher Resources 20–22) are available to support pupils who are able to extend and refine their work.

> Use of some of these resources may be problematic. This is discussed in Lesson commentaries on page 132. [7/8a]

The lesson notes suggest that additional lessons may be needed to enable pupils to finish this work.

> Professional judgement will be needed to determine how much additional time should be allowed and when pupils should be asked to consider the work complete.

Plenary and homework: Efficiency; and documentation

In the plenary, pupils are asked to consider how subroutines have made the system more efficient, and for homework the project documentation is updated.

Lesson 9: Developing the presentation

The focus of the unit now changes and pupils begin to work on the presentation of their system.

Starter: Criteria for a good presentation

Pupils reflect on and then discuss the criteria for a good presentation.

> The lesson notes make reference to the audience for the presentation. This is discussed in greater detail on page 135 in Lesson commentaries. [9a]

Development: Content of the presentation

In the main part of the lesson, pupils first make lists of what they think should be included in the presentation and then develop criteria for judging what is essential information. The teacher reminds them of the material already produced which could be included.

Pupils consider the content of the presentation and evaluation criteria in small groups. They will be required to present their solutions individually in Lesson 10, so after this initial discussion they should work on their own presentation for the rest of the session.

Plenary and homework: Evaluation of the presentation

In the plenary the teacher reviews the information that should be included in their presentations. The lesson notes suggest that the peer evaluation form (Pupil Resource 8) is developed to include pupils' own criteria. For homework, pupils annotate their presentations in response to evaluation.

This could pose organisational difficulties. See page 135 for a discussion of these. **[9b]**

Lesson 10: Presentations

In this lesson pupils present their new ride to the park manager.

Starter: Ideas for evaluation criteria

Pupils are asked to develop evaluation criteria for the presentations, based on those discussed in previous lessons. They are also asked to work in groups to think of questions that the park manager might ask.

Development: Presentation to the park manager

Pupils make their presentation to the park manager. They are reminded that all aspects of the ride should be presented, including the schematic diagram, safety features, developments and reviews along with a clear justification of the choices they made. It is suggested that each is followed by questions and that open questions should be encouraged. Each presentation is evaluated by pupils, using the agreed criteria.

This task needs clarification, and it is discussed on page 135. **[10a]**

Plenary and homework: Selection of presentation; and feedback

Pupils select the most effective presentation and justify their decision, and presenters have the opportunity to respond. The teacher draws out key features. Pupils are encouraged to review their own presentations in the light of others' feedback. For homework, pupils annotate their work and hand in all documentation.

Alternative approaches

This is an interesting context for pupils to work in, and a good one for exploring control systems. It extends the use of control beyond the contexts used in Units 7.6 and 8.5. The use of peer evaluation is a strong feature of the unit. Pupils establish criteria for making judgements at each stage of the process. This unit centres on control systems and this is its main focus, although pupils are also given opportunities to use ICT to plan and document the project they are working on.

It is important that pupils are encouraged to reflect on the design, creation and testing of their system. They are asked to use Gantt charts and a project diary to plan and record this process, and the use of these, particularly the setting of targets for future tasks, may need to be discussed with pupils explicitly early in the project. Reference should be made to these throughout the project, with specific reference each lesson, as appropriate.

If the case study plan is followed closely, pupils spend the first four lessons planning their control system. While the importance of planning should be recognised, you will need to think carefully about whether the use of control software should be delayed until Lesson 5. This means that pupils are asked to plan the ride in its entirety without having the opportunity to try out any of its sections using the control software. It is worth noting that they have used the software only in Unit 7.6. The programming task which forms the central focus of the unit is challenging, and some pupils will need a lot of support if they are to tackle it successfully. Such pupils will need to be realistic about the features they include in their ride design.

Care is needed with the use of the teacher resources. Specific comments on some resources are detailed below, but it is worth looking at all of the resources and deciding which to use before beginning the unit. For example, there are nine control programs written using Flowol. Three of them (Teacher Resources 10, 12 and 14) are relatively simple programs to control a part of the ride, such as the camera. A further three control the same parts of the ride, but are more developed and extended programs (Teacher Resources 16, 18 and 19). The remaining Teacher Resources (20, 22 and 23) are complex solutions controlling the entire ride, some using subroutines.

You will need to decide which resources you are going to provide as examples. You could consider not using the extended sections of the ride, and continue with the simpler sequences of commands, at least for some pupils.

Lesson commentaries

[1a] There are three websites suggested for pupils to look at before planning their ride.

http://www.somecoasters.com
http://coaterclub.org
http://crystalbeachpark.net

The first two contain pictures of various theme park rides. The third includes video clips, but is not suitable for use as the ride shown in the video is not, in fact, a water ride and the voiceover includes some unsuitable language.

[2a] The resource suggested for use here is Teacher Resource 3:

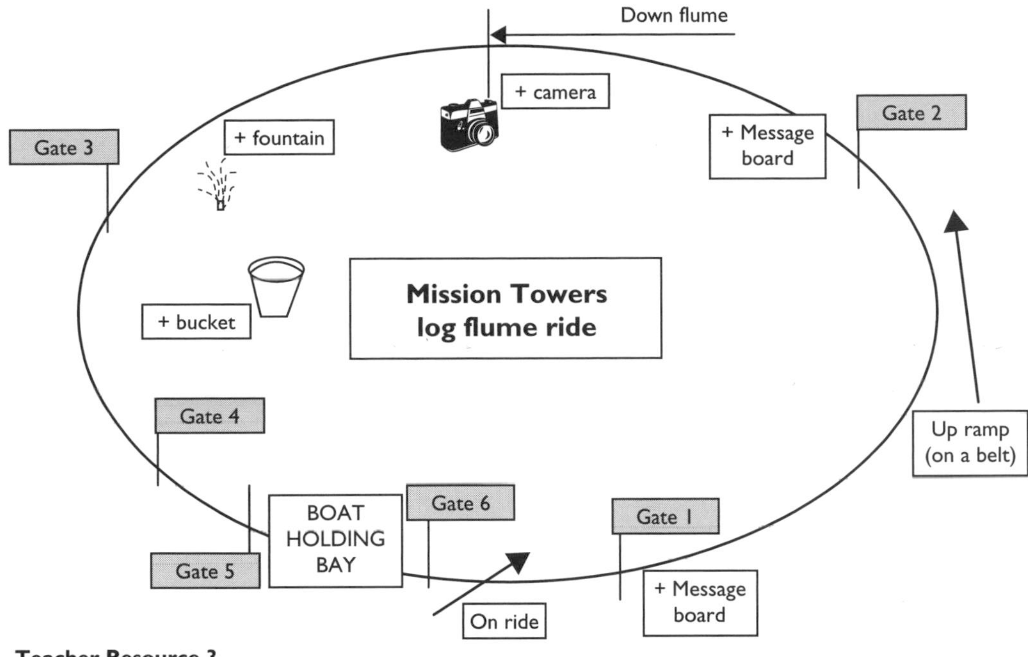

Teacher Resource 3

It looks complex and may be off-putting for pupils if they have not had a good opportunity to tackle the thinking and problem-solving involved for themselves. It might be helpful to start with the simpler diagram from the QCA (shown below) and ask pupils to develop something similar for themselves first before moving to the more conventional schematic representation. There is an opportunity to revisit the schematic diagram in Lesson 3, and it might be better to introduce it at that later stage.

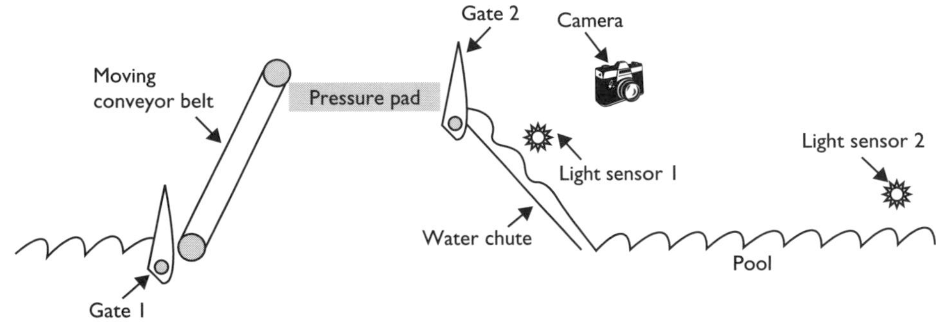

[3a] This is a substantial development task, and pupils are working in pairs, although each is producing his or her own version. Only 40 minutes are allowed for the discussion of key terms with the whole class, for the teacher to pose a number of questions to support pupils' thinking about their own diagrams, and for them to develop both of their diagrams to include sensors and switches. There are examples for pupils to see, including Teacher Resource 5, shown below. This is even more complex and you may need to suggest that pupils tackle a simpler ride, leaving out unnecessary features, such as the fountain and bucket, and limiting the number of gates.

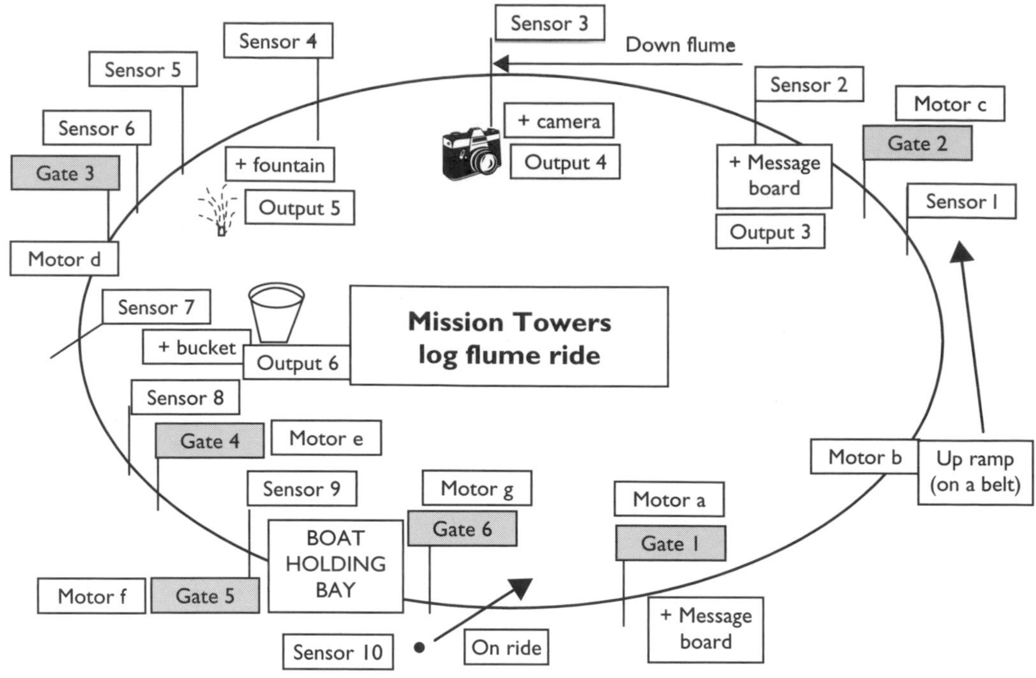

Teacher Resource 5

Pupils will need to work through their own examples before considering the example given. It will be important for them to have been through this process if they are to be able to work through the example shown and use this as a stimulus to improve their own diagram.

You may also decide to use control software to allow pupils to test their system as they develop it, rather than expecting a system planned to a relatively finished state without the opportunity to test it. As yet, they have had little opportunity to use computers as part of the design process or to explore the practical effects of their ideas. They may not have used control software since completing Unit 7.6 at the end of Year 7 and may have to refresh their knowledge of its application before they can think their way into the task.

[**3b**] It is clear from the format of the project diary that it is intended to have a front cover printed with the pupil's name and project title, with the pages of the diary completed on paper. You could allow pupils to complete this as an online document if resources allow. Printing of the title page will need to be organised in advance, perhaps completed in Lesson 2 and made available in Lesson 3. The diary makes reference to tasks completed, targets for future tasks and completion dates. This will need to be discussed and carefully set up in the lesson, which will put additional pressure on time allocations. Perhaps it could be postponed until Lesson 4.

[**7/8a**] Some of these resources, such as Teacher Resource 20 (overall solution), are daunting, as the screenshot opposite shows.

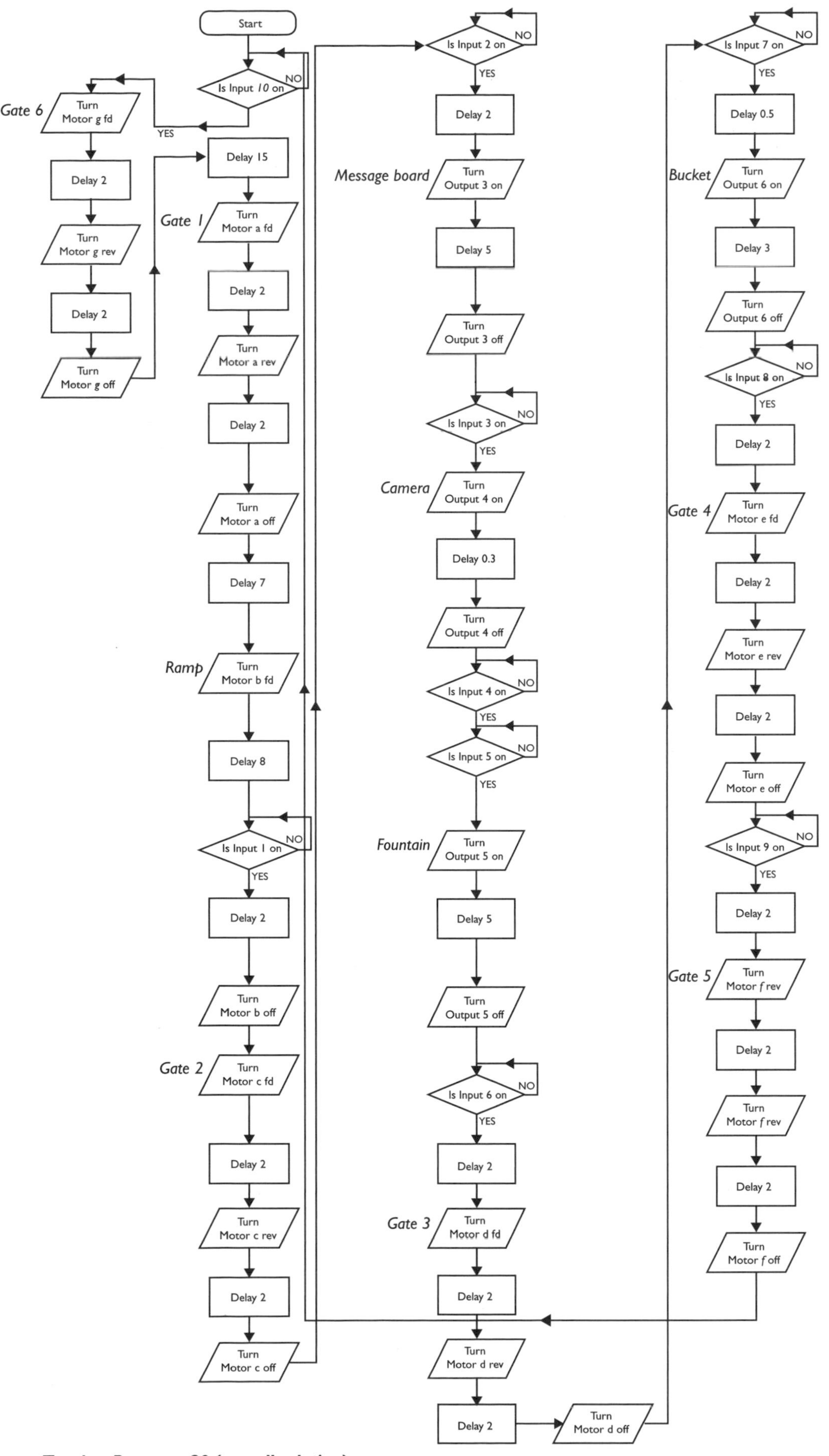

Teacher Resource 20 (overall solution)

It is questionable whether this resource would be supportive to pupils. Perhaps you could use the separate subroutines, routines such as those in Teacher Resource 22, or continue to use the earlier simpler resources such as the camera section shown below. This could be used to help pupils tackle any problems they have with their own subroutines.

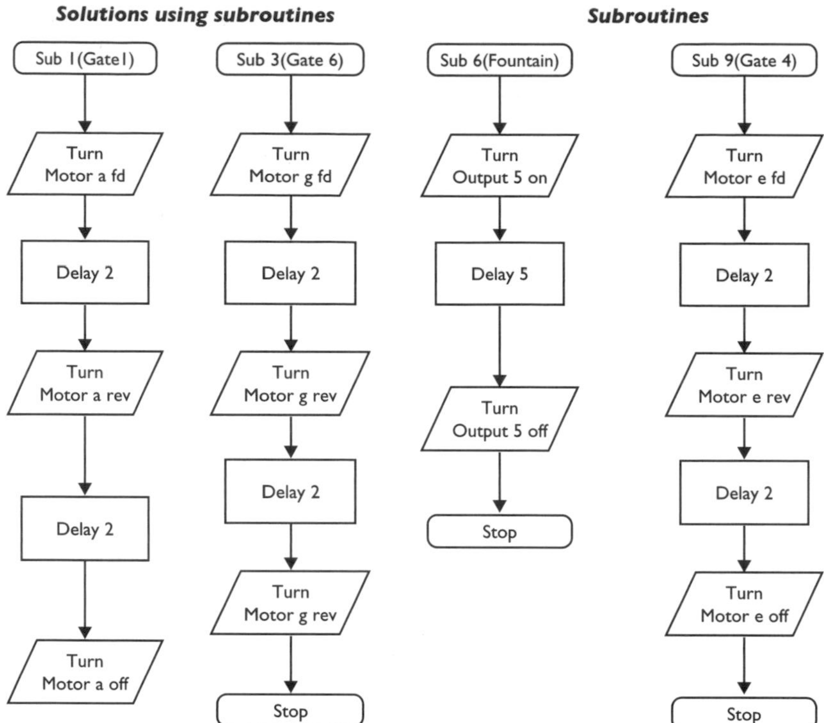

Teacher Resource 22

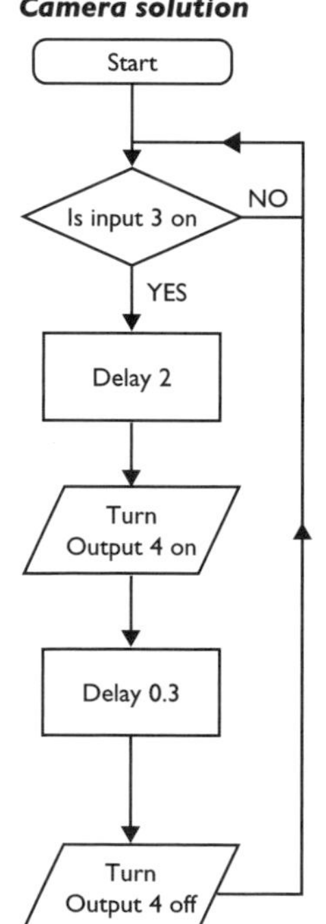

Teacher Resource 10

[9a] The audience for the presentation is the park manager. The lesson notes suggest that you remind the pupils that the audience for the presentation could change, but it is difficult to think of an alternative audience. When planning the presentation, it might be better to ask pupils to think about the different perspectives that the presentation should cover to persuade the park manager to adopt the new ride. This could include the views of young people who enjoy theme park rides, safety officers or parents concerned about safety, or the public relations team who are preparing publicity material for the new ride.

[9b] For homework, pupils are asked to update their project diaries and annotate their presentations. Annotating presentations could pose organisational difficulties because it means that each pupil will need a printout of their presentation. Perhaps these could be provided for collection later.

[10a] There are a number of issues that may need clarification and professional decisions. Firstly, it is unlikely that up to 30 pupils can present their work fully, given the suggested content, in 40 minutes. If pupils are to maintain interest and provide feedback, you should limit the number of presentations. A maximum of five is probably sensible. Also, it is important that the evaluation criteria are clarified. Pupils will have to take on the role of park manager in evaluating the presentations, and this will need to be discussed carefully with them in advance. Are they judging the ride and its associated control system or the quality of the presentation? Pupils who do not have an opportunity to present their ideas for this project should be given an opportunity to present work from other units later in the year.

9.2a Development of a data-handling system

KS3 STRATEGY FRAMEWORK OBJECTIVES

Finding things out

Using data and information sources

- Select information sources and data systematically for an identified purpose by:
  - judging the reliability of the information sources;
  - identifying possible bias due to sampling methods;
  - collecting valid, accurate data efficiently;
  - recognising potential misuse of collected data.

Searching and selecting

- As part of a study, analyse high-volume quantitative and qualitative data systematically by:
  - exploring the data to form and test hypotheses;
  - identifying correlations between variables;
  - drawing valid conclusions and making predictions;
  - reviewing the process of analysis and the plausibility of the predictions or conclusions.

Organising and investigating

- Construct, test and document the development of a database system which shows:
  - a design specification;
  - appropriate means of data input and validation;
  - systematic testing of processes and reports;
  - evaluation of the system's performance and suggested modifications.

Exchanging and sharing information

Fitness for purpose

- Produce high-quality ICT-based presentations by:
  - creating clear presentations, sensitive to audience needs;
  - justifying the choice of form, style and content.
- Use knowledge of publications and media forms to devise criteria to assess the quality and impact of multimedia communications and presentations, and apply the criteria to develop and refine own work.

Refining and presenting information

- Use a wide range of ICT independently and efficiently to combine, refine, interpret and present information by:
  - structuring, refining and synthesising information from a range of sources;
  - selecting and using software effectively, justifying the choices made.

Communicating

- Understand the advantages, dangers and moral issues in using ICT to manipulate and present information to large unknown audiences (e.g. issues of ownership, quality control, exclusion, impact on particular communities).

About this unit

This case study aims to bring about the exchange of questionnaires and thus of information between two groups of pupils, ideally in different locations or countries. It addresses the strand of ICT capability relating to data handling and advocates the use of database software tools.

Pupils are set the challenge of designing a questionnaire to collect data and then carry out an enquiry and present their findings. They initially discuss the form and structure of questions and the effect this has on the data they capture. They then use this knowledge to design a questionnaire related to the context in which they are working. This questionnaire is then exchanged with another set of pupils, preferably in a different location. A data structure is developed based on the questionnaire using database software, and the data generated by their questionnaire are input for interrogation and analysis. Pupils then develop a set of hypotheses which they test using the data set they have created. They then draw conclusions from their findings. Each stage in the process is documented using the accepted stages of the system life cycle as a framework.

No context is specified for the unit, so pupils and teachers can choose a setting and purpose that is of interest to them. The exchange of questionnaires between two classes will produce sufficient data to create 20 to 30 records. This could be increased if more than two classes were involved in the exchange.

The case study assumes previous knowledge of database software, although the opportunity is given to increase skill and knowledge levels during the course of the unit of work. It should be noted that although data structures have been considered, the use of database software has not been advised or addressed in the previous units of the ICT Key Stage 3 strategy.

It is evident that teachers of this unit require a sound knowledge of the theoretical issues connected with database structures and of their creation within an appropriate database software application. In addition, teachers need to be familiar both with the development of system documentation and strategies for supporting pupils in their understanding of this challenging process.

Pupils work individually, in groups and in pairs at different times during this project. It is expected that a record is kept of individual contributions to group outcomes to inform assessment. Ideas for assessment opportunities and differentiation are indicated throughout, although the summative assessment is largely based on evidence of understanding of the process as demonstrated in the documentation.

The unit documentation does not specify an expected range of attainment levels. However, from the tasks within the unit, it would appear that pupils could attain a level in the range of Levels 5 to 7.

The unit is expected to take about ten hours. The balance of time in lessons is as follows.

	Taught as a whole class	*Pupil work away from the computer*	*Pupil work at the computer*
Lesson 1	50 mins	10 mins	
Lesson 2	30 mins	20 mins	10 mins
Lesson 3	45 mins		15 mins
Lesson 4	40 mins	20 mins	
Lesson 5	25 mins	15 mins	20 mins
Lesson 6	20 mins		40 mins**
Lesson 7	15 mins		45 mins**
Lesson 8	15 mins	15 mins	30 mins**
Lesson 9	20 mins		40 mins
Lesson 10	15 mins	45 mins	
Overall balance	**4 hrs 35 mins** 46%	**2 hrs 5 mins** 21%	**3 hrs 20 mins** 33%

** This is time for individual work on computers. If the pupil, computer ratio is 2:1 this time using the computers will be halved.

There is a large proportion of teacher-directed, whole class teaching in this unit. In the first five lessons, pupils spend long periods of time being taught as a class, and although there is plenty of opportunity for interaction, some pupils may find this is not their preferred learning style. Although pupils are working autonomously during lessons six to nine, largely using computers as and when they need to, some will require extensive support and carefully planned guidance.

LESSON BY LESSON

Lesson 1: Introducing and planning the project

This lesson sets the scene for the project. Pupils revisit the idea of testing hypotheses through interrogating data in a database. They also plan their work for the project using a Gantt chart.

Starter: Online questionnaires

Pupils are shown the online questionnaire from *CensusAtSchool* and attention is drawn to the ease of data entry and validation.

Some sort of recap of the function and usage of data validation would be necessary here.

Pupils are asked to consider the advantages and disadvantages of entering data online as opposed to manual collection of data followed by data entry at a later time.

Development: Review of effective search techniques

Some test data from the *CensusAtSchool* project are provided in the form of an Excel file or a comma separated variable (.csv) file. The teacher demonstrates the process of interrogating the database to find the answers to a range of questions.

It is necessary, prior to the lesson, to ensure the file is imported successfully into your chosen database package. You would need to check that you are very familiar with the search facility in the software and have thoroughly investigated the searches in advance.

This serves as an introduction to the idea of using the database to test hypotheses followed by analysis of the results to reach conclusions. It is suggested that questions are given to pupils according to their ability.

As data handling using databases has not been the focus of prior units during Key Stage 3, the distribution of the questions will need to be considered carefully. There is further comment about the time allowance and scheduling of this activity in Lesson commentaries on page 147. [1a]

The context for the project is now introduced.

Ten minutes is suggested for this task. An in-depth discussion initially of the underlying purpose of the project followed by an exploration of issues and related ideas is required in order to motivate the pupils and provide a secure foundation for future work. This is likely to take more than ten minutes.

The stages of the project are considered and these are discussed to ensure understanding of the process. The use of a Gantt chart is introduced. Using the electronic Gantt chart incorporating some automated features, pupils are asked to organise their work by allocating appropriate blocks of time to each stage. This will form a project plan.

This useful tool was introduced in both Units 8.5 and 9.1. It will need to be revisited every lesson. It may be useful to relate the stages to the context of the unit. See the Lesson commentaries section on page 147. [1b]

Plenary and homework: Whole class Gantt chart and questionnaire

A whole class Gantt chart is created through discussion with the teacher taking responses from pupils.

Pupils are asked to complete the online *CensusAtSchool* questionnaire and to draft some possible hypotheses for a class questionnaire.

It is suggested that the homework could be an assessment opportunity in that it could require written evidence of understanding of the term hypothesis. This is explored in Lesson commentaries on page 147. [1c]

Lesson 2: Developing a questionnaire

This second lesson starts by looking at which particular questions in the data set would provide the evidence for specific hypotheses. Pupils then move on to look at how careful design of the structure of questions can make them more effective by gaining an accurate response and generating unbiased data.

Starter: How we survey to test hypotheses

Pupils examine a series of hypotheses based on the *CensusAtSchool* data. Using a questionnaire relating to the data, they decide which questions will provide the proof for their proposition. An extension activity is suggested in which some pupils have to develop their own question to obtain the additional data required to answer a particular hypothesis.

This is a useful activity, but perhaps it would be better placed during Lesson 1, before the pupils develop their own hypotheses for homework. It is essential to emphasise the link between the data required for the hypothesis and the data collected by the question.

Development: Developing a questionnaire

Pupils share the hypotheses they developed for homework. The class discusses the questions that would be needed to collect the appropriate data required to prove or disprove each premise. The need to avoid confusion or bias is explained.

Pupils then discuss their suggestions and questions in groups and develop a shortlist of five appropriate questions. Groups then swap questions and test each other's for effectiveness within the context.

Plenary and homework: Effective questions

The class discusses examples of effective and less successful questions and investigate the reasons for this. They go on to identify different types of questions, including multiple choice, yes/no, numeric and so on, and discuss how the data collected by these questions could be analysed and which questions lend themselves to easier analysis. It is suggested that use could be made of some resources from Unit 7.5 at this point, as well as slides from Teacher Resource 6, which looks at analysing data and representing results using charts.

It may be unwise to start discussing graphical representation here as there are many issues connected with different types of questions that need to be addressed. See the Lesson commentaries section page 148 for further comment. [2a]

For homework, pupils are asked to refine their questions to ensure they are unambiguous and free from bias. It is indicated that this individual work can be used to assess understanding of issues surrounding bias.

Lesson 3: Refining and collating the questionnaire

In this lesson pupils' questions are refined and merged to produce a suitable questionnaire, which is then sent to their partners in this project.

Starter: Questionnaire development techniques

The teacher shows pupils questionnaires in different stages of development and asks for ideas to improve them. This will chart the development from open-ended questions through to questions with multiple choice or key word answer choices where appropriate.

Development: Forming hypotheses and refining questions; and producing the final questionnaire

The questions produced by pupils in the previous lesson are displayed, with those on similar topics grouped together.

> It will be necessary to plan sufficient time to merge these files containing the questions and sort them into appropriate topics.

Pupils are asked to consider the possible responses to the questions and what hypotheses they could test. They then consider any further hypotheses that they may want to test and refine their questions using their homework ideas.

> These questions were designed as a result of making hypotheses in the first place, so this activity may well be rather repetitive. See further comment in Lesson commentaries, page 148. [3a]

The questions are then rationalised so that any repeated ideas are merged and a final questionnaire is produced. Pupils are then asked to format the questionnaire and consider ease of use and suitable graphics.

> The development of the actual questionnaire based on the ideas discussed in the starter of the lesson will probably take more than the time suggested. It would also be important to ensure that the pupils do not change the questions in any way or the data collected will not be consistent, a requirement for a shared file.

Plenary and homework: Sending the questionnaire

Questionnaires are sent to partner schools via email or an alternative method. Pupils are told that they will start writing up their documentation in the following lesson.

Pupils are asked to draft an outline of the problem.

> Where has the documentation been explained or referred to? If all pupils are going to do this successfully, a lot of explicit reference to the documentation will need to be made here or in previous lessons. As this is considered, rightly, to be an assessment opportunity, it is important that the requirements of the documentation are made clear to pupils.

Lesson 4: Developing the project documentation

In this lesson, pupils revisit the different stages of the system life cycle. They begin to document their work, starting with the "identification and analysis of their problem".

Starter: Processes and cycles

In groups, pupils are given a specific task, such as making a cup of tea. Each pupil is given a card showing a sub-task involved in making a cup of tea, such as "Put tea into teapot". They are asked to arrange themselves in the order in which the sub-tasks are implemented in carrying out the main task. Their final order is fed back to the class and discussed. This is then linked to the order in which their work could be organised to ensure the task is completed successfully.

Development: Developing the project documentation

The teacher runs through the separate processes that make up the system life cycle using Teacher Resource 9. It is explained that pupils are developing a system to solve a problem and the importance of documenting the development of their system is made explicit.

> This is useful preparation for both further study at Key Stage 4 and sixth form. However, each stage needs to be related to your context to make the exercise meaningful for pupils. See further comment in the Lesson commentaries section on page 148. [4a]

The "identify" and "analyse" stages of the problem are considered and pupils are asked to write up these stages individually. A template is provided (Pupil Resource 9). It is suggested that the template could be revised to provide more support for lower attainers.

> This is a useful suggestion for differentiation, and some illustrations are shown in the three versions of Pupil Resource 9. Some pupils may need a writing frame showing the different points they should address, with some suggestions they could use to get started. It would also be important to clarify the "problem", as this may be a slightly novel usage of the word.

Plenary and homework: Documentation so far

Pupils are reminded that the documentation forms an important part of the assessment for the unit. The teacher explains the importance of considering the process as well as the outcome of the project in the final assessment to evaluate an individual pupil's understanding.

For homework, pupils are asked to evaluate the effectiveness of the questionnaire from their partners in another class or school. They are asked to complete the questionnaire for homework.

Lesson 5: Planning the database structure

This lesson focuses on the development of an efficient database structure. Pupils are also introduced to the design stage of their systems development documentation.

Starter: Coding data

The start of the lesson considers the need to code data to allow for ease of processing. The *CensusAtSchool* data are used to illustrate this point. Pupil Resource 1, a sheet showing the system for coding this data, is used alongside Resources 10 and 11, which provide some sample data and some questions relating to the coding scheme.

This is such an important issue that it may need more than 10 minutes to explore thoroughly. The amount and type of coding used depends on the data types and the way it is to be presented. Coded data are excellent for graphical displays but not so useful for tabular displays. You may feel that only limited coding for particular fields needs be introduced in this unit. It will also depend on the features available in the package you use. **[5a]**

Development: Planning the database structure; and testing it

A comparison is made between the use of a database program and a spreadsheet program for this kind of project.

It is interesting that a spreadsheet was used in preference to a database in Units 7.5 and 8.5. The work in 7.5, in particular, did not include any calculations, so it would lend itself to the use of a database. You may choose to use a database in that unit so that pupils have prior experience to bring to this unit of work.

The process of setting up a file structure is demonstrated, including the possible uses of validation.

This may be the first time that pupils have come across the concept of validation of data. This will require further discussion and the provision of some examples to support understanding.

Pupils complete a planning sheet (Pupil Resource 12) on which they record their field names, lengths, and types, as well as any validation they intend to use. They then set up their structures using the database software.

If you do not have one computer per pupil, either develop an alternative task for those not using the computers and swap them over halfway through the time allowance or ask the pupils to input their structures in pairs.

Pupils then compare their structures in groups and one is proposed for saving in the shared area.

Pupils test the structures in terms of entering data and check the validation rules. The structures are refined accordingly, printed and annotated.

It is not clear whether pupils test their own chosen structure or the structure generated by another group. You will need to make a decision about this. The annotated outcomes can be developed into an assessment opportunity as suggested, although some supporting guidance may be required. It would also be useful to observe pupil discussions during the refinement process if they are not working individually.

Plenary and homework: Class database structure

It will be necessary before the next lesson to assess the five or six database structures from the groups and create a final structure for use by all pupils.

Producing a common structure for use by all pupils is sound practice at this stage. The construction of the contents will still be familiar to pupils.

The design stage of the system life cycle is introduced in relation to the project documentation. The key questions in the design stage are considered and pupils are asked to write a first draft for homework.

A meaningful discussion about the expectations of the design phase of the documentation will take more than the few minutes allowed here.

Lesson 6: Entering data into the database and planning an enquiry

Pupils enter data from the partner school questionnaires and begin to plan their enquiries.

You will need to make sure that you have received and checked the data from your partner class/school before this lesson.

Starter: What do we mean by personal data?

Pupils are asked to judge whether various data items could be classed as personal data. This develops into a discussion of different aspects of personal data and the importance of keeping it private. The point is made that some types of data, such as medical records, do not in themselves identify an individual, but, when stored along with someone's name, become sensitive data that should not be disclosed.

Development: Entering data into a database; and planning an enquiry

Pupils enter their data into the pre-prepared structure.

There is a note reminding you to organise the lesson around the data entry. If you are using a package that doesn't allow multi-user access, a carousel of activities will be necessary.

Pupils begin to develop their enquiry individually, based on the hypotheses discussed in Lessons 2 and 3. If they complete this, they can progress to their implement and test stages. They are reminded that the testing takes place at intervals during the process.

You may find that many pupils need further guidance on these stages of documentation both here and for homework. It may be useful for them to see an example of a documented system or an alternative enquiry strategy. It will also be important that you are totally clear about your own expectations.

Plenary and homework: Continuing the enquiry plan

Pupils report back on their progress in planning their enquiry. For homework, they are asked to annotate a hard copy of their enquiry plan and continue the design, implement and test stages of their documentation.

Lesson 7: Carrying out the enquiry, developing and framing queries

In this lesson pupils carry out their planned enquiries and write the implementation and test stages of their documentation.

Starter: Effective queries

Pupils are shown how to interrogate a database to find evidence to prove or disprove their hypotheses.

> This will take longer than 10 minutes. If pupils have not used database software previously, ongoing support and guidance will be needed.

Main activity: Carrying out the planned enquiry

Pupils work on their own enquiry. They test their stated hypotheses following the interrogation strategy set out in their design. They also work on their implementation and test sections of their documentation.

> This will require a significant amount of teacher support.

Plenary and homework: Key findings

Pupils report back on their findings. They are to continue to develop their documentation for homework.

Lesson 8: Comparing findings, refining the enquiry and planning a presentation

Starter: Progress so far

Pupils are asked to contribute to a class discussion to share findings so far.

Main activity: Refining the enquiry

The evaluation stage of the project is introduced and pupils continue to implement and test their systems and write up their findings.

> Pupils will be accustomed to the idea of evaluation and review of their work if they have followed the strategy during Years 7 and 8.

Plenary and homework: Key findings

In groups, pupils identify the key findings from their enquiry to present to the class.

For homework, pupils are asked to plan a presentation slide to present their findings. They are to remember audience, form, style and content.

Lesson 9: Preparing a presentation

In this lesson, pupils agree evaluation criteria for the presentation of their findings and work to develop their presentation slides.

Starter: Criteria for evaluation

Pupils are reminded of the need to have an agreed list of evaluation criteria for the presentations.

Development: Preparing the presentation

Each pupil prepares a slide to present their findings as agreed with the rest of the group. A consistent format for the presentation within groups must be agreed.

Plenary and homework: Preparing for evaluation

Next lesson's presentations and subsequent evaluations are discussed. For homework, pupils are asked to prepare notes for the presentation of their personal slide.

Lesson 10: Presenting findings

In this lesson, pupils present their findings to the rest of the class.

Starter: Evaluation criteria

The criteria for evaluation are reinforced and a checklist is distributed.

This could become tedious. Many of the findings will be similar as pupils worked together to identify hypotheses. You may wish to limit presentations to certain pupils and allow the other pupils to present findings on a different project at another time. See Lesson commentaries, page 148, for further comment. [10a]

Development: Presenting findings

Each group presents their findings on an individual basis. The pupils evaluate the presentations of the other groups.

Plenary and homework: Evaluation

Pupils are asked to evaluate their own progress throughout the whole project. For homework, they are asked to complete their project documentation.

Alternative approaches

This case study contains some extremely useful skills, knowledge and understanding which are essential for the development of authentic, broad-ranging ICT capability. The unit addresses the tricky but interesting issue of questionnaire design and the nature of the data it generates. It also revisits the concept of file structure and uses a sound approach in allowing pupils to design their own configurations but, by an evaluation and review process, choose the most appropriate final structure for use by the whole class. It is only by doing this that a sufficient number of records can be created and interrogated in order to produce useful results.

The unit provides useful resources and advice to help teachers support pupils through the initial process of designing questions and developing appropriate hypotheses. However, in later lessons they are left relatively unsupported in designing and implementing their test and interrogation strategies in order to generate data to prove their hypotheses. They are also expected to be relatively independent in tackling the complex process of analysing their findings and drawing conclusions from the data, as well as writing up their documentation. This requires high-level skills, and many pupils will find it beyond their capability unless carefully guided. It is likely that any teacher embarking on this unit with pupils will need to provide a range of supporting materials to guide lower attainers through the latter steps in the process.

The case study assumes a basic familiarity with database programs, yet this is not explicitly addressed earlier in the strategy. Most pupils will have experienced data handling only in primary school or when using Excel at Key Stage 3, unless their teachers have autonomously developed extra lessons in Unit 7.5 or 8.5. In addition, it is the first time that pupils have to keep a record of their systems according to the stages of the system life cycle. Although it is stated that this should be brief, it does have a major influence on the final level assigned for the project, so some exemplar materials would be beneficial both to teachers and pupils to indicate expectations.

The choice of context is left to individual schools, but the examples in the unit documentation all relate to a class survey. It is to be hoped that schools do develop their own contexts for this project, as this will radically affect pupil motivation and learning. The class survey is a very familiar context that most pupils will have encountered, albeit in a less sophisticated way, at primary school. It is the context of the sample file provided with the Information Workshop package used widely at Key Stage 2. If pupils are to develop their own useful hypotheses and gain a sound understanding of the value of data handling, it may be more constructive for them to tackle a fresh, less limited issue, about which they have important and genuine questions to ask. This matches the expectation that contexts and audiences will become less familiar as pupils progress through the key stage.

Pupils could survey other pupils' responses to a common issue in the news or a local issue that affects other nearby schools. Alternatively, it may be valuable to link with another curriculum area such as languages or geography. This may enable the data to be represented in another language and possibly link with a school in another country or with a different culture. This would also fit well with the Citizenship curriculum. Unit 10 of the Key Stage 3 Citizenship scheme of work is concerned with a debate about a global issue, and Unit 17 is about school linking. Either of these could add an extra dimension and be of additional interest for the pupils, allowing them to develop an enquiry consisting of real questions and theories which they are motivated to investigate.

It is also important to remember that the first three lessons dealing with the development of hypotheses and questionnaires must be translated so that they refer to the actual context used for the unit rather than the *CensusAtSchool* or "class survey" data. Any reference to the system life cycle and stages of documentation must also be delivered through this context, which will have been discussed at length and therefore represents a real problem to the pupils. If the problem is not real, the exercise becomes meaningless for pupils, who will not remain motivated or focused for the full ten-week duration of the unit.

Lessons in which pupils work autonomously will need to be carefully planned, with a regular evaluation of progress informing the plan for the following lesson. Teacher direction of pupils to the appropriate operating level for their ability will be crucial here. Concepts will need reinforcement, either on a whole class level or with groups of individuals. Pupils will constantly need reminders of the tasks for the lesson and the approach they should use. Even at GCSE level, pupils need a framework for their project development; it will not happen unless the teacher organises and communicates a schedule and keeps a careful watch on individual progress.

Lesson commentaries

[**1a**] Although a recap of search techniques is essential at some point in this unit, it could be considered that the first activity in the first lesson is not the most appropriate time. Interrogation is shown as the 8th and 9th stages of the development of the data-handling system in a list of 12 shown in the lesson plan for Lesson 1, so a very brief reminder at this stage would suffice.

[**1b**] If it is considered that the Gantt chart is a useful scheduling tool for project management, then it should be used for that function. It is set up in the first lesson but it is never mentioned again. It is important that teachers remember to refer to it on a regular basis and discuss whether the project is keeping to the planned time and if not, why that is so. Its completion with comments should also be part of the final requirements for documentation so that pupils perceive its value.

[**1c**] You have modelled the idea of setting and proving hypotheses using a data file earlier this lesson.

You then went on to "set the scene" for the whole unit and in doing so, you have established the purpose and problem the pupils are going to investigate. Now you need to make it clear that the hypotheses they develop for homework should relate to the scenario underpinning this unit. It may well be that pupils will need some support here. An additional resource showing the type of data they are likely to collect and a few examples to show the sort of premise they may develop would be useful here. If you wish to use this as an assessment opportunity you could ask pupils to provide a rationale for their choice of each hypothesis, why they think it is valid, what data they will require to provide evidence for it and their estimation of the likely result.

[2a] There are a whole range of issues relating to the nature of the design of questions and analysis of data that will take much longer than the time suggested in the documentation for the second lesson. The discussion about varying approaches to the analysis of different types of data is absolutely essential, but further examples would be required to assist understanding. Pupils also need additional input relating to different types of questions and the answers they elicit. Some further discussion, relating to open-ended answers as opposed to limited choices may be useful. This is particularly important where value judgements are required, leading to the need for limited answers to ensure consistent data are collected. This is demanding subject matter, requiring sufficient time for consideration if real understanding is to be achieved.

[3a] The process of analysing question types, responses and making hypotheses in Lessons 2 and 3 needs to be rationalised so that it can be approached in a logical order. You will need to be clear in your own mind whether the suggested schedule is the most logical sequence. In addition, all of these issues must be taught and applied within a realistic context.

[4a] (*also of relevance for Lessons 6, 7 and 8*) This is useful preparation for further study, but you will need to return to each stage in later lessons. Additional guidance relating to your own context will be required by some pupils, and examples to show the level of expectations would be useful. This unit is very skimpy on detail and advice on the actual teaching relating to the various stages of documentation. Any teacher who has not taught GCSE may have difficulty and will need to look carefully at the course work expectations of any of the major examination boards at that level. They provide illustrations of outcomes for training examiners and teachers, so these may be useful. It is important, however, to remember that less extensive documentation is expected here. Some pupils will require further supporting materials to guide them through the processes of implementing the system and developing the documentation. It is also important to schedule progress carefully, as it requires vigilance and discipline from both teacher and pupils to keep within the suggested timetable. Teachers need to make expectations clear to pupils so they can demonstrate their understanding in their documentation through the use of annotation and explanation. It may be useful to ask pupils to try and write their documentation as a guide for a teacher who was not party to the development of the project, so they could follow what happened and the thinking behind the process.

[5a] Packages such as Flexi DATA, Information Workshop, Junior Viewpoint and Pinpoint all have a chart generation facility. However, if you are using Microsoft Access, you will need to check that the additional graph-generating package has been installed. Pinpoint would be a suitable choice for this project as it includes a questionnaire-development feature for data input. It also offers a suitable progression in moving towards the use of an industry standard package such as Access.

[10a] You may wish to revise the schedule for the last few lessons, in which pupils are developing their presentations of their findings. It is likely that some pupils will not have managed to complete this demanding system development and accompanying documentation in the time allowed. In addition, the time schedule for the presentations is very tight and may be impossible to adhere to. You may wish to limit presentations to certain pupils and allow the other pupils to present findings on a different topic at another time. This may give useful additional time for completion of the system and documentation for those who need it.

9.2b Development of an online data-collection system

KS3 STRATEGY FRAMEWORK OBJECTIVES

Finding things out

Using data and information sources

- Select information sources and data systematically for an identified purpose by:
  - judging the reliability of the information sources;
  - identifying possible bias due to sampling methods;
  - collecting valid, accurate data efficiently;
  - recognising potential misuse of collected data.

Searching and selecting

- As part of a study, analyse high-volume quantitative and qualitative data systematically by:
  - exploring the data to form and test hypotheses;
  - identifying correlations between variables;
  - drawing valid conclusions and making predictions;
  - reviewing the process of analysis and the plausibility of the predictions or conclusions.

Organising and investigating

- Construct, test and document the development of a database system which shows:
  - a design specification;
  - appropriate means of data input and validation.
  - systematic testing of processes and reports;
  - evaluation of the system's performance and suggested modifications.

About this unit

In this case study, pupils plan a long-term project to gather a large amount of data through an online questionnaire. The pupils should be linked with another class, ideally in a different location or country.

The unit addresses development of ICT capability through data handling and advocates the use of database software tools.

Pupils are set the challenge of designing an online questionnaire to collect data and then carry out an enquiry and present their findings. They initially discuss the form and structure of questions and the effect this has on the data they capture. They then use this knowledge to design a questionnaire related to the context in which they are working. This questionnaire is then exchanged with another set of pupils, preferably in a different location. The data generated by their questionnaire is imported to a database software package for testing a hypothesis and analysis of the results. Pupils then draw conclusions from their findings. The project is documented using an ongoing diary and the schedule is managed using a Gantt Chart.

The context of the unit is related to investigating the lifestyles of pupils in another region or country. Alternatively, pupils and teachers could choose a setting and purpose that has a particular interest for them. The online questionnaire should generate sufficient data to create a substantial data set for interrogation to prove a hypothesis. If one of the partners is unable to input and exchange data electronically, some input may have to be carried out manually, although this should be limited if possible.

The case study assumes some previous knowledge of database structure, as this area is not explicitly addressed. The opportunity to revisit skills and knowledge relating to data interrogation and reporting is built into the unit and it does suggest that extra lessons could be added if other skills and knowledge are required. It should be noted that although data structures have been considered, the use of database software has not been advised or addressed in the previous units of the ICT Key Stage 3 strategy.

It is evident that teachers of this unit require a sound knowledge of the theoretical issues connected with database structures and of their creation within an appropriate database software application. In addition, teachers need to be familiar both with the creation of an online data-collection questionnaire and tools for managing the development of the project.

Pupils work predominantly in pairs during this project. Ideas for assessment opportunities and differentiation are not indicated throughout, as in Unit 9.2a, and there is little indication of possible ways of organising the summative assessment.

The unit documentation suggests that pupils will be working at National Curriculum attainment Levels 5 to 6.

The unit is expected to take about ten hours. The balance of time in lessons is as follows.

	Taught as a whole class	*Pupil work away from the computer*	*Pupil work at the computer*
Lesson 1	50 mins	10 mins	
Lesson 2	45 mins		15 mins
Lesson 3	35 mins	10 mins	15 mins
Lesson 4	35 mins		25 mins
Lesson 5	35 mins		25 mins
Lesson 6	40 mins		20 mins*
Lesson 7	40 mins		20 mins
Lesson 8	35 mins	5 mins	20 mins
Lesson 9	30 mins		30 mins
Lesson 10	25 mins		35 mins
Overall balance	**6 hrs 10 mins** 62%	**25 mins** 4%	**3 hrs 25 mins** 34%

* Some of the timings for this lesson are missing in the author's copy of the documentation.

There is a significant proportion of teacher-directed, whole class teaching in this unit. There is also a substantial proportion of practical, computer-based work, although it is only in the last few lessons that pupils are working autonomously rather than working on specific tasks following teacher directions. During the times in Lessons 9 and 10 when they are developing their reports independently, some will require extensive support and carefully planned guidance.

LESSON BY LESSON

Lesson 1: Introducing and planning the project

This lesson sets the scene for the project. Pupils think about who holds data about them. They revisit the idea of testing hypotheses through interrogating data in a database. They also plan their work for the project using a Gantt chart.

Starter: Who holds information about you and your family?

Pupils work in pairs to record the names of people and organisations that hold data about them. They combine with other pupils to develop group suggestions which are fed back to the class.

A useful exercise, but it requires linking to the context and further discussion to explore potential misuse and so meet the related objective for this lesson.

Development: How are data collected?

Pupils are shown a range of appropriate questionnaires, and some examples of data-collection methods are displayed.

The *CensusAtSchool* project which has generated a large collection of data is shown, either live from the web or via a series of presentation slides (Teacher Resource 1). The point is made that these data were collected by a questionnaire.

A hypothesis relating to mobile phone ownership is considered and tested using the data on the site. The results of the investigation are discussed.

The teacher then outlines the project. Pupils will collect a large amount of data about the daily lives of people in the UK or abroad. They will then investigate this data by developing and testing hypotheses and draw conclusions based on the evidence they find. Project development is discussed with reference to previous experience in Units 8.5 and 9.1, and pupils are asked to think of the stages that will be undertaken.

At the end of the project they will present their findings to a specified audience and an appropriate presentation format should be decided here.

This is an exciting challenge. It will be important to find an appropriate final presentation audience.

Plenary and homework: Project management tools; and Gantt chart

The idea of project management tools is discussed and the use of a Gantt chart is introduced. An example chart based on building a settee is discussed (Teacher Resource 2). The pupils then see a skeleton example relating to their project, and for homework they are asked to organise their work by allocating appropriate blocks of time to each stage. This will form a project plan.

The pupils have met Gantt charts on a number of occasions. It is essential that this useful tool is actually used in the planning of their project. It may be useful to rewrite the steps of the project in the context of the unit so that pupils link the stages with what they are actually doing.

Lesson 2: Planning the project

This second lesson starts by looking at the Gantt charts pupils have developed. They then examine the stages of the system life cycle and they are introduced to the use of a project diary to record their progress through the stages.

The development of the system in this unit does not appear to adhere strictly to the system life cycle. If this is to provide a framework for the development it will need to be mentioned on a regular basis and the final report will need to be carefully structured.

Starter: Homework solutions

Pupils compare their completed Gantt charts to one provided in Teacher Resource 3. This is discussed in terms of similarities and differences.

Development: Gantt charts; and the system life cycle

Pupils are shown a possible solution and the function of the Gantt chart reinforced.

The solution Gantt chart in Teacher Resource 3(b) shows Lessons 5, 6 and 7 as being lessons in which pupils learn "Data Structure skills". This is not quite correct as during these lessons pupils are learning general data-handling skills rather than skills relating to data structures.

A revision of the stages of the system life cycle follows and this is linked to the steps in the Gantt chart. Pupils carry out a drag and drop exercise to organise the stages in the correct order.

Plenary and homework: Project diary

The use of a project dairy to record progress is introduced. Pupils are given a diary structure and asked to embed the class Gantt chart in it. They complete the diary to date, for homework. It is indicated that some pupils may require further support for this task.

Lesson 3: Deciding what information to collect

Pupils consider the information they need to collect to answer their hypotheses about differing lifestyles. They go on to design appropriate questions.

Starter: Differences

Pupils are asked to consider the differences in the lifestyles of people in other schools, regions or countries. These differences are discussed and simple, related hypotheses are generated.

Development: Focus for questions; and designing questions

Suitable topics for questions are gathered and categorised under sensible subheadings such as housing, taste in music, amenities and school.

This is a valuable exercise. Considerable discussion of topics and their value would be beneficial for pupil understanding and motivation in this project.

The issue of question design is addressed. The stages of developing a questionnaire are shown and discussed. Pupils work in pairs to consider possible questions relating to one of the subheadings discussed earlier. They record these and then evaluate the questions of another pair. This is followed by a class discussion about designing questions which relate to their hypotheses.

This relationship between questions for the questionnaire and how they will provide evidence to answer hypotheses is a crucial consideration. It is essential that pupils understand this link.

The questions are refined in the light of discussion and saved.

Plenary and homework: Professional questionnaires

The class looks at the questionnaire designed for the *CensusAtSchool* project and discusses the effectiveness of the questions. For homework, pupils are asked to identify two types of questions they could use when framing their questions in the next lesson.

It is important to clarify the stages of development of both questions and hypotheses during this lesson. It is not entirely clear how this homework builds on the work of the main activity in the lesson in which questions were designed to extract specific information. See Lesson commentaries section, page 159, for more discussion. [3a]

Lesson 4: Designing an online form to collect information

During this lesson the pupils learn how to create an online form and identify "dirty" data from a data set.

Starter: Sample form

Pupils are shown a sample online data capture form showing a variety of question types using electronic tools such as drop-down menus, radio buttons and check boxes. This is linked to their consideration of different types of question formats in the *CensusAtSchool* questionnaire.

Development: Creating an online form

The teacher demonstrates the creation of an online form using the elements investigated in the starter. Data validation checks are considered here.

Non-specialist teachers may need more indication of the type of validation checks that may be used here. Pupils may also need to revisit this topic if they are to include them in their online data capture forms.

Pupils then create their own form based on the questions they developed on a specific topic in the last lesson.

Teacher Resource 11 showing this process would need to be reproduced for pupils. See Lesson commentaries, page 159, for further discussion of this issue. [4a]

The pupils save their questionnaire into a shared area so the teacher can collate a final version using the most effective questions developed for each heading.

Plenary and homework: Raw data

A set of data is displayed in a .csv format. The format is explained and pupils are invited to identify problems with the data. Pupils are given a homework resource (Pupil Resource 7) showing the same data set and asked to annotate it to show where improvements can be made.

As Teacher Resource 12 "Data from completed online form" and Pupil Resource 7 "Copy of dirty data", have different headings, it may not be clear that they are in fact the same.

Lesson 5: Using an online form to collect data

In between Lessons 4 and 5, the teacher creates a final online form consisting of the most effective questions from each category developed by the pupils. During this lesson, pupils input their own data using the class data capture form. They then check and make the necessary changes to a file with some missing data entries before importing it to a database package.

Starter: Final form

The teacher displays the final form that has been created.

It will be important to keep as many ideas as possible that have been developed by the pupils so that they continue to identify with the data.

Main activities: Completing the form; and importing a .csv file

The teacher demonstrates how to complete and submit a final version of the form. Pupils are invited to input and submit their own data using the form and are reminded that it will be stored as a single line in a .csv file.

The teacher then demonstrates how to import a .csv file into a database package.

An authentic demonstration would be more effective than showing the presentation slides provided. Any teacher delivering this unit will need to be familiar with the process of importing a .csv file.

Pupils now "clean up" the data in the .csv file (Pupil Resource 8) and import it into the database.

This (Pupil Resource 8) is not the same "dirty data" set as that provided for the homework task (Pupil Resource 7). As the homework has not been followed up at this stage you may wish to link the two activities more explicitly. You may also wish to change this data so that it displays a similar set of problems to the data provided for homework.

Plenary and homework: Review point

Pupils check their progress using the Gantt chart.

It would be important to discuss at this point where and why difficulties have been encountered, keeping to the schedule.

The class discusses how partner schools can respond to the form, as some may not be able to receive it online. This may necessitate some manual input of data.

Pupils are asked to update their project diaries for homework.

Lesson 6: Data-handling skills

During this lesson pupils develop the skills of interrogation of data.

Starter: Searching and sorting

As they enter the room, each pupil is given a card showing a record of pupil data. It is a subset of the data in the .csv file they used in the previous lesson. Database terminology is reinforced and pupils are invited to identify the field types. The pupils then sort themselves into height order according to the data shown on their card. This process is compared to the speed with which a computer can sort data.

Simple searches are demonstrated by asking pupils to stand up if the data on their card matches a certain condition; for example "taller than 165 cms". This is followed by investigating complex queries in a similar manner.

An excellent starter. However, it may well be that you would want pupils to be addressing these interrogation concepts much earlier in the key stage. This starter could be used to help much younger pupils understand the idea of simple and complex queries. It is a similar exercise to another valuable starter modelling Boolean logic in Lesson 2, Unit 8.3.

Development: Demonstration and practice; and sorting data

Using a data set of pupil data (29 records), the teacher demonstrates the sort facility and asks pupils to search manually for answers to quick-fire questions. Pupils are then shown how to input a simple query and the matching records are displayed and checked.

This activity is carried out using Access in the sample lesson plans, but it is indicated that any appropriate database such as Pinpoint, Flexi DATA, Information Workshop or Junior Viewpoint could be used.

Pupils practice simple and more complex queries.

It is important that a comparison is made between the speed with which the matching records are found manually and electronically. **[6a]**

Plenary and homework: Hypotheses

Pupils discuss how they would investigate hypotheses using the interrogation skills they have been developing during the lesson. The lesson plan asks the teacher to end with the hypothesis "Tall pupils have large feet" and explain that this will be checked in the next lesson and displayed in chart format.

This is a similar hypothesis to one of the suggestions for investigating the "My Class" survey file that comes with the Information Workshop package. Many pupils may have tested a similar hypothesis many years before so you may wish to focus on a different area.

Pupils are asked to update their project diaries for homework.

It will be important to check these updates are taking place. See Lesson commentaries, page 158, for further comment.

Lesson 7: Data-handling skills

In this lesson pupils chart their data using Excel and learn to use the COUNTif function.

Starter: Graph activity

Pupils are shown some data relating to the size of named animals and their gestation periods. A hypothesis "Larger animals have longer gestation times" is presented to pupils. A scattergraph showing the result is displayed. Pupil understanding of the chart is checked.

Development: Demonstration and practice; scatter graphs from the database; and using COUNTif

The teacher demonstrates how to use MS Excel to chart data in MS Access.

> The use of Excel to create charts from Access data was originally addressed in Unit 8.1 so this could be a brief reminder. Further comment on this point can be found in Lesson commentaries, page 159. [7a]

Pupils test the hypothesis put to them at the end of the previous lesson. Do taller people have larger feet?

The following hypothesis is put to pupils: "Most pupils walk to school".

The use of the function COUNTif is demonstrated to pupils. This will count the number of pupils using each method of getting to school. A chart of the results is drawn and clearly shows that the hypothesis is not proved and that the most popular way of getting to school is by bus.

> It may be useful to discuss possible reasons with the pupils so they become familiar with discussing and analysing results.

Pupils are then encouraged to test some further hypotheses such as "most pupils have mobile phones" using the COUNTif function.

> Although a useful tool in this context, some pupils may need additional support to understand the use of COUNTif in order to apply it independently.

Plenary and homework: Review points

Progress against the Gantt chart is checked and findings recorded. Pupils are asked to update their project diaries for homework.

Lesson 8: Importing data

Data collected via the online data source will be required for this lesson. Pupils import the data and clean it up. They then evaluate the data and discuss possible surprises. Next, they investigate the data and decide if stated hypotheses can be supported by it.

Starter: Dirty data

Pupils are given a printout of 12 to 15 records and invited to check it and annotate any changes they would make before importing it.

Development: Cleaning up and importing the data; and evaluating the data

The data collected using the online form is imported to Excel from the shared area and cleaned up prior to export to a database package.

> Data can be edited in table view in most database packages, so this step may not be necessary.

The data are discussed and evaluated. This includes a discussion about effectiveness of question design and whether the data matches expectations.

Plenary and homework: Forming hypotheses

Pupils are given the "Yes, no, yes if" cards from Pupil Resource 11. Each card displays one of these three responses. A hypothesis is suggested and pupils respond with a card to show if they think it can be supported by the data they have collected. A variety of suggestions should be made, eliciting all three answers at different times.

> You will need to devise some appropriate hypotheses from your data as this is an important skill for pupils to grasp.

Pupils are asked to study the data collected, decide on a focus for their investigation and create some related hypotheses

> You may need to support some pupils by making some possible suggestions during the lesson.

Lesson 9: Analysing data and reporting on hypotheses

Pupils discuss their hypotheses with others, test them and produce charts and conclusions of their findings. They are reminded of the format for the class presentation of the project.

Starter: Hypothesis check

Pupils share the hypotheses they have developed for homework and check that their data set can provide the evidence required to support it. It is suggested that some pupils may require further support such as some prepared ideas.

Development: Agreeing how to report back; and analysing the data

Pupils are reminded that in the previous two lessons they were producing a report of their findings.

> You may feel that this is not the case. The last two lessons have focused on learning to use the COUNTif function and evaluating the data that has been collected. This appears to be a typographical error in the lesson documentation.

The end of project presentation is discussed. The format and audience for this was decided in Lesson 1.

> It may be that you decide to change this in the light of experience. Only 5 to 10 minutes is devoted to these issues so it may require additional discussion. See Lesson commentaries on page 159 for further comment. **[9a], [10a] and [10b]**

The report of the project is discussed. Pupils will summarise their hypothesis and the evidence they have found to help them draw conclusions. Teachers are advised to provide a template to provide a consistent style for the presentation.

Pupils move on to test their hypotheses and produce graphs to support their analyses. It may be necessary to show pupils how to capture a screen shot to show their findings. While supporting pupils, the teacher chooses an example of good practice to share with the rest of the class during the plenary.

Plenary and homework: Modelling a "good" contribution

Examples of good work are shared with the whole class. The teacher discusses what represents good work. Pupils are asked to update their project diaries and include some comments about improving their work in the light of what they have seen in the plenary.

Lesson 10: Reporting back

Starter: Evaluation criteria

The class agrees a list of criteria to use when evaluating their report.

Main activity: Analysis; and reporting back

Pupils continue to analyse the data and summarise their findings.

Pupils will need support and further guidance about how to proceed here. See Lesson commentaries page 159 for further comment. **[9a], [10a] and [10b]**

Plenary and homework: Peer evaluation

Pupils look at each other's reports and evaluate them according to the agreed criteria. For homework, pupils are asked to respond to the feedback and note how they could improve their part of the presentation. In addition, they are to update their project diaries and submit their completed projects.

It appears that the presentation has to be organised for delivery on an alternative occasion. For further comment, see Lesson commentaries page 159, **[9a], [10a] and [10b]**

Alternative approaches

This is an interesting unit of work which differs significantly from previous units in the strategy. It addresses a challenging opportunity for interaction and exchange of ideas made possible only by the existence of information and communications technologies. The idea of obtaining a large amount of data online for investigation and analysis is a exciting prospect and is likely to motivate pupils of this age. The suggested context is suitable, although it would be important that the information collected offers a genuine insight into other people's lives and that the partners have some real differences in lifestyle. Alternative contexts which are of particular interest to a specific school could be considered, or an issue connected with the Citizenship curriculum may be seen as a possibility for genuine interaction and exchange of differing views.

The unit appears to put more emphasis on practical-based work than some previous units, and most of the ICT skills and knowledge addressed are relevant and appropriate in the context. The unit is less concerned with documentation than the "partner" Unit 9.2a, although this could be seen as an extra challenge to teachers as there is only the briefest guidance about the substance of the report which will constitute most of the summative assessment. Unlike Unit 9.2a, the documentation is not strictly related to the system life cycle, so further support cannot be gained from looking at the guidance which is incorporated in GCSE specification documentation. Teachers will need to be completely clear in their own minds of the structure and content of the report, which is essentially the outcome of this unit.

In terms of data handling, the unit addresses the design of questions with reference to the nature of the data they will elicit and revisits the interrogation of data and presentation in terms of charts. There is little mention of the major area of data structures and other means of reporting. This would possibly be a useful additional lesson in the middle of the unit when data-handling skills are addressed. As data handling with databases has not been the focus of any previous units in this strategy, it may be useful to ensure that the related skills, knowledge and understanding are addressed here. This is an essential component in the development of comprehensive ICT capability and in relation to preparation for more independent study in Key Stage 4.

Lesson commentaries

[3a] In the main activity of the lesson questions were designed to extract specific information according to the headings developed earlier by pupils. It is inevitable that pupils will have raised the notion of different question types and formats such as multiple choice, yes/no, numeric and so on. It is impossible to separate the framing of questions from the prediction of responses, particularly as this issue has been addressed earlier in the strategy in Unit 7.5. Many pupils will be aware of open and closed questions, the difficulties in analysing value judgements and the variety of responses to a question with the same meaning. They would be ready to use different formats during the main activity in this lesson, so the teacher may choose to address these issues and introduce the useful *CensusAtSchool* questionnaire at that time, rather than waiting until the end of the lesson. It is also necessary for the teacher to be clear when addressing questions in the form of questionnaire items as opposed to questions in the form of hypotheses. This is not always totally explicit in the notes and may cause confusion.

[4a] The instructions in Teacher Resource 11 relating to setting up an online questionnaire would need to be reproduced for pupils. It is unlikely that a demonstration will be sufficient for them to carry out the process unaided. If the question development activity in the previous lesson was carried out in same ability groups, some pupils may need further support in finalising their question design during this lesson. If the activity was carried out in mixed-ability groups, it will be important to question relevant pupils to ensure understanding of the group contribution. There is no time allocated for the design of the online form. It may be useful to add 15 or 20 minutes for this before pupils tackle the implementation of the form, as it will save time.

[6a] The project diary is a very useful tool for recording the progress of the system, and this process constitutes an appropriate homework. However, regular checks of these diaries will need to be made. The completion of these diaries will not be a straightforward process for many pupils, and some will just not do it regularly enough! The update needs to take place when events are fresh, so a few minutes at the end of each lesson discussing events and issues for the diaries would be essential.

[7a] The use of Excel to create charts from Access data was originally addressed in Unit 8.1, so this could be a brief reminder. If you are using one of the alternative database packages such as Pinpoint, Flexi DATA, Information Workshop or Junior Viewpoint, this use of an external graphing facility would not be necessary as they have their own chart-generation tools. It would be important to check that the package can provide scattergraphs.

[9a], [10a] and [10b] It may be that you decide to change the presentation in the light of experience. Only 5 to 10 minutes was devoted to these issues in the first lesson, so it may well require additional discussion by the end of the unit. There does not appear to be any time allocated for the presentation within the ten weeks of the project, and it is indicated that it does not take place at this time. This is beneficial, as it means that the presentation is an authentic activity. However, it does mean that an alternative occasion will have to be organised and time allowed for revision and rehearsal at a later date.

In addition, the teacher will need to be clear of the connection between the presentation and the reports that are being developed during the last two lessons. The final lesson notes are not comprehensive, and there is limited information about what constitutes the "completed" project. It may be assumed that the final reports are required for the summative assessment, but this is not explicitly stated. They appear to serve a dual function in terms of the assessment and the presentation but this may be more difficult to implement in practice than it appears. Further work will be required to transform the report into an appropriate presentation as the formats will inevitably be different. Some pupils may also need more support and guidance on how to proceed in the final two lessons than is given in the documentation. You may feel that as well as clarification of the final outcomes, additional support and possibly time for the analysis, production and presentation of the hypothesis test results will also be necessary.

9.3 Front-of-house theatre booking system

KS3 STRATEGY FRAMEWORK OBJECTIVES

Finding things out

Using data and information sources

- Select information sources and data systematically for an identified purpose by:
  - Judging the reliability of the information sources;
  - Collecting valid, accurate data efficiently;
  - Recognising potential misuse of collected data.

Developing ideas and making things happen

Analysing and automating processes

- Automate ICT processes.
- Represent a system in a diagram, identifying all its parts, including inputs, outputs and the processes used.

Models and modelling

- Design and create ICT-based models, testing and refining rules or procedures.
- Test hypotheses and predictions using models, comparing their behaviour with information from other sources.

Exchanging and sharing information

Fitness for purpose

- Produce high quality ICT-based presentations by:
  - Creating clear presentations, sensitive to audience needs;
  - Justifying the choice of form, style and content.
- Use knowledge of publications and media forms to devise criteria to assess the quality and impact of multimedia communications and presentations, and apply the criteria to develop and refine own work.

Refining and presenting information

- Use a wide range of ICT independently and efficiently to combine, refine, interpret and present information by:
  - Structuring, refining and synthesising information from a range of sources;
  - Selecting and using software effectively, justifying the choices made.

Communicating

- Apply knowledge of the technical issues involved to communicate information efficiently (e.g. use mail lists to speed up communication).

About this unit

This is a unit of 14 lessons in which pupils design a front-of-house ticketing system for a school production. They undertake three main tasks:

- modelling a seating plan which enables individual seats to be booked and a total kept of money taken;
- modelling the financial plan so that decisions can be made about ticket price;
- advertising the production to Year 6 pupils and their parents.

They use a design specification as the basis for their work, manage and record progress using Gantt charts and project documentation. In the final stages of the unit they present their project to the user and complete their project documentation.

The project management and documentation develops work covered in Units 9.1 and 9.2. The use of a spreadsheet as a modelling tool builds on the techniques and understanding learned in Unit 8.4.

Prior to starting the unit, pupils will need an understanding of the tools and processes of project management, a high level of skill and understanding in the use of spreadsheets and the ability to design publications for a specific audience. To complete the project successfully, they will need to be able to use a design specification as the basis for their work and devise criteria for judging success. To complete the activities and design models similar to those included as exemplars in the resource pupils, will need a high level of skill and understanding of spreadsheets including the use of RANDBETWEEN and COUNTif. They will need to be able to write a report in an appropriate style, and higher-attaining pupils will produce a solution in which systems are linked dynamically.

Teachers will need to spend time working through the exemplar solutions and gaining a good understanding of them if they are to be able to support pupils in devising similar solutions.

Group organisation is not referred to explicitly in the unit. In Lesson 5 the notes refer to the work of the pupils in pairs. However, there is no reference to collaborative paired work prior to this lesson, and the use of homework for important planning and developmental work suggests that these are individual rather than paired projects.

This unit differs from the others in the strategy in the suggested balance of time allocations to different types of activities. More than half the time is spent at the computer, designing and implementing the solution, as well as planning and documenting the project. This reflects the expectation of pupils' developing independence. Relatively little time is spent on individual or paired tasks away from the computer. The suggested time allocations are shown opposite.

	Taught as a whole class	*Pupil work away from the computer*	*Pupil work at the computer*
Lesson 1	45 mins		15 mins
Lesson 2	22 mins	35 mins*	3 mins
Lesson 3	35 mins		25 mins
Lesson 4	20 mins		40 mins
Lesson 5	20 mins		40 mins
Lesson 6	20 mins	5 mins	35 mins
Lesson 7	20 mins	5 mins	35 mins
Lesson 8	20 mins		40 mins
Lesson 9	10 mins	15 mins	35 mins
Lesson 10	20 mins		40 mins
Lesson 11	25 mins		35 mins
Lesson 12	10 mins	10 mins	40 mins
Lesson 13	10 mins	30 mins	20 mins**
Lesson 14	10 mins	10 mins	40 mins**
Overall balance	**4 hrs 47 mins** 34%	**1 hr 50 mins** 13%	**7 hrs 23 mins** 53%

* This activity could be computer based.
** These are activities which use generic ICT tools: delivering a presentation and updating documentation.

LESSON BY LESSON

Lesson 1: Planning the project

Pupils revise work on Gantt charts, the project is introduced and they begin to determine outcomes and success criteria.

Starter: Gantt charts

Gantt charts are reviewed, using a practical scenario, selling your old car and buying a new one.

If you have taught the units in sequence, this is the fourth time pupils have used Gantt charts. This practical activity, or a similar one might also have been used in Unit 9.1. If this is the case only a brief reminder may be needed here.

Development: Statement of the problem

Having revised pupils' knowledge of the systems life cycle, the project is outlined: developing an ICT system for the school pantomime, which is to be presented to Year 6 pupils and their parents. A paper based resource provides basic information for pupils. The system will need to enable the keeping of records of tickets sold, money taken, income and expenditure. Publicity material will also be required. In discussion the teacher draws out the three main aspects of the system:

The reference to information on income and expenditure available on the intranet or in the library needs clarification. This is discussed in Lesson commentaries on page 173. [1a]

- a financial plan that will aid decision making on ticket pricing based on information on income and expenditure available on the intranet or in the library;
- a simulation of the hall and the seating plan for booking seats, including the possibility of numbering seats so that people can book seats at the front of the hall;
- an information system for advertising the event to two different audiences, pupils and their parents.

It is suggested that higher-attaining pupils could use a database and mail-merge to send personalised letters of invitation to parents.

This is a realistic expectation for higher-attaining pupils, but no support materials for the techniques involved are included, so these would have to be provided, or time made available later in the unit for teaching them.

Pupils begin their planning for these tasks in pairs, each creating a Gantt chart using Pupil Resource 3. Some timescales are suggested, such as how long it will take to print tickets. Teacher Resource 3 gives a completed example, based on the lesson outlines in the unit.

Plenary and homework: Success criteria; and beginning project documentation

The plenary discussion establishes outcomes and success criteria for the project. The examples suggested are:

- a seating plan which allows individual seats to be booked and financial records kept;
- a financial plan to model costs and inform decisions on ticket prices;
- suitable advertising materials, and (for higher-attaining pupils) a database and letter templates for personalised letters to parents.

For homework pupils produce a statement of the problem and success criteria for these tasks.

This is a demanding task, for which students need support even at GCSE and A level. These Year 9 pupils will also need considerable support here.

Lesson 2: Input, process, output

Starter: Keeping people on the dance floor

The starter sets out a scenario in which the manager of a night club wants to ensure an equal number of men and women in the club in order to reduce the potential for trouble. Pupils are given a spreadsheet model to investigate for three minutes and are asked to explain the COUNTIF and IF functions.

The pupils are simply given this as a finished spreadsheet, and they may need support to make the connection between this and the work they are doing. This is discussed in more detail on page 173. [2a]

Development: Information needs

The focus returns to the system life cycle and pupils have to analyse the activities in the system in terms of the input–process –output model. One example is: given:

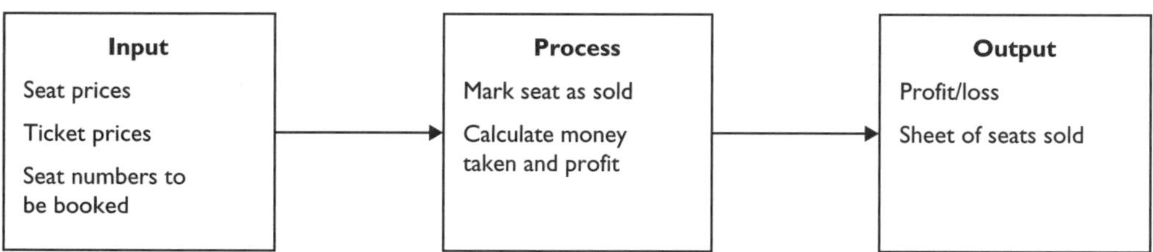

Pupils create charts for each of the products they have identified.

Again this is a demanding task and will need careful explanation and discussion.

Plenary and homework: Success criteria; and designing a financial and seating plan

The whole class discusses what information will be needed and where it can be obtained. It is suggested that pupils gather information from members of staff or that this is gathered for them and placed on the school intranet or in the library.

Professional judgement will be needed about the management of this process, and the extent to which pupils can, in fact, collect the information required.

Success criteria are discussed and for homework pupils are asked to design a financial and seating plan.

This is a demanding task for homework which will need to be set up carefully. It requires access to Excel, and is crucial to the development of the project. It is discussed in more detail in Lesson commentaries on page 173. [2b]/[3a]/[5a]

Lesson 3: Implementing the financial or seating plan

Starter: Progress and next steps

Pupils discuss progress to date with reference to their Gantt charts.

> It is good to see the Gantt charts being used in this way. It is important that pupils realise that they are flexible tools, open to change and refinement.

The Project documentation templates (Pupil Resource 5a–c) are introduced.

> The templates provide useful prompts for structuring the project documentation. This process is important and will need careful explanation and setting up, which may take longer than the time suggested. It will need to be revisited in future lessons.

Development: Finance and seating

Having shared their plans for the financial and seating information, begun as homework, pupils carry on with their implementation.

> If this has not been begun as homework, as suggested in the Alternative approaches, then the comments on page 173 should be considered at this point. [**2b**]/[**3a**]/[**5a**]

Plenary and homework: Ticket prices; and evaluation

The plenary provides an opportunity to discuss any problems and pupils are encouraged to consider flexible and adaptable approaches such as using the symbols "a" and "c" to represent adult and concessionary ticket prices. For homework they review their work, consider how it could be improved and write up their project documentation.

Lesson 4: Random numbers, refining the financial or seating plan

Starter: Random number activity

The dance floor activity is revisited at the start of Lesson 4. The Dance floor random number model (Teacher Resource 10) is displayed.

> Like earlier models, this is supposed to generate random numbers when the function key, F9, is pressed. This function appears not to be properly set up.

Development: Refining plans for the pantomime

In the main part of the lesson, pupils continue to refine and develop their models. Now in the testing and evaluation stage of the system life cycle, they are encouraged to consider ways of automating the trialling of different combinations of ticket types.

> As in Unit 8.4 when RANDBETWEEN was used to generate random numbers to test a model, this complicates the process unnecessarily. Possible approaches are discussed on page 175. [**4a**]

The lesson notes suggest that higher-attaining pupils could investigate having three different ticket prices (described as pensioner, adult, child).

> This seems to be making the model less realistic, as generally the same concession applies to anyone entitled to a reduced ticket price.

Plenary and homework: Review plans

The plenary session reviews work to date and links this to pupils' Gantt charts. For homework, they reflect on and document the implementation, testing and evaluating part of process.

Lesson 5: Testing and refining the financial or seating plan

Starter: How are we doing?

In the starter pupils discuss progress to date and make any necessary changes to their Gantt charts.

Development: Models

Work continues on pupils' own solutions. Teacher Resources 6 to 9 are available to prompt refinements to their models.

The comments about these resources on page 173 also apply here. [2b]/[3a]/[5a]

Pupils work in pairs, and then join with another pair to test their models and refine their work based on this feedback.

Plenary and homework: Reviewing the models

The work of some pupils is shared to highlight features and review work done. For homework, they document their work and collect examples of different types of tickets in preparation for the next stage of the project.

These are to be used in the next lesson to analyse the information on business cards and tickets and consider effective design. If you think your pupils may not be able to bring in a range of different tickets you will need to be prepared with examples for the class to work with.

Lesson 6: Further refinement and user documentation for the financial or seating plan

Starter: Suitable information

The starter looks at the information contained on business cards and tickets Pupils undertake an analysis of both formats, using Pupil Resource 7. The distinction is drawn between what *could* and what *must* be on a ticket.

Development: Implementation

In the main part of the lesson pupils are given time to finish their seating / financial plan and their project documentation. If the work is complete they are asked to begin producing user documentation.

Plenary and homework: Information needs and ticket design

The homework, designing two tickets, is set up in the plenary session. Pupils are reminded that their system and user documentation should be ready by Lesson 8 for pupils in Year 10, who will be the users of the system.

The medium for the design is not stated. You will need to decide whether this should be completed using ICT and whether the use of design wizards or templates such as those available in MS Publisher are acceptable.

Lesson 7: Common forms and conventions (logos), creating tickets

In Lesson 7 the focus of the work changes to the design of tickets and publicity for the production.

Starter: Common forms and conventions (logos)

The teacher runs a projected display of some logos as a continuous loop. Using Pupil resource 8, Common forms and conventions – logos, pupils evaluate a series of logos in projected and monochrome printed formats. Some key points for effective logos are drawn out in discussion.

This is very similar to an activity completed in Unit 7.3. It is discussed in Lesson commentaries on page 175. **[7a]**

Development: Creating a logo

The main part of the lesson is given over to reviewing their ticket designs, based on peer evaluation, identifying the appropriate places for logos and implementing their ticket designs. They are asked to make reference to the implement, test and evaluate parts of the system life cycle.

Pupils have only 35 minutes to review previous designs, create a logo and implement their ticket designs, presumably using an ICT application. These are demanding tasks, particularly the creation of a logo, and the time allocation is insufficient.

Plenary and homework: Review and project update

For homework, pupils update their documentation

Lesson 8: Refining the financial or seating plan in the light of user feedback, implementation of ticket design

The focus now returns to the financial / seating model.

Starter: Review of plans

Pupils review their plans in the light of the users' feedback.

The starter refers to the review of the models following this feedback. There are significant organisational issues which are not addressed explicitly. Pupils have been told that their models should be ready for Year 10 pupils to use. This is discussed on page 175. **[8a]**

Development: Extending the plan

Pupils now have some further time to refine their plan in the light of feedback.

They continue to work on their tickets and documentation.

Plenary and homework: Progress review; and design of publicity materials

Pupils' progress is discussed in relation to their Gantt charts.

If some pupils need to rework their models substantially following feedback from users you will have to decide which activities they should omit from those that remain, or whether this reworking is practicable.

For homework they are asked to design publicity such as posters or a website, explaining what software will be used and why it is appropriate for the task.

This is potentially a considerable task and an unrealistic expectation for one homework. They are expected to have completed their posters or websites ready for use in the next lesson!

Lesson 9: Publicity for the production, mail merge and personalised letters

Starter: Considering appropriate styles for audiences

Pupils work in pairs, identifying the main features of two magazine covers, one for iMac computer magazine, and the other for Barbie.

This is an interesting exercise, but important issues arise, which are discussed in Lesson commentaries on page 175. [9a]

Development: Refining and reviewing

Pupils are asked to annotate changes to their posters or websites in the light of the starter exercise. They then continue to refine their tickets and documentation.

This is a totally unrealistic expectation in the time allowed.

Plenary and homework: Publicity

The plenary focuses on a discussion of how pupils can ensure that the publicity materials reach their audience.

It is suggested that this also includes discussion of mail merge and personalised letters. Again, this raises important issues and is likely to need far longer for proper consideration of the issues involved.

For homework pupils document decisions taken about publicity material. Higher attaining pupils tackle a mail merge exercise, planning their data structure and letter template.

The task for higher attaining pupils is a huge undertaking. It will be vital to plan and prepare some introduction and resources for the task, as well as materials or teaching to support them.

Lesson 10: Implementing publicity

Starter: Gantt charts

Pupils return to their Gantt charts, reviewing and updating them.

Development: Work on publicity

Work continues on the publicity materials.

There is a presentation for higher attaining pupils on the use of mail-merge.

> Teacher resource 13, a PowerPoint presentation on mail-merge is intended to support this. This is discussed on page 176 in Lesson commentaries. [10a]

Plenary and homework: Presenting documentation

The pupils are going to present their solutions and project documentation to the Year 10 users. The plenary focuses on the presentation of supporting documentation and in discussion the class agrees a list of features, described as "do's" and "don'ts" for presenting documentation.

> This is difficult. There is no indication of what these features are, and in reality they will vary according to the purpose of the presentation and the needs of the audience. Pupils will need to focus on the needs of the users of this specific system.

For homework, they plan their presentations.

> Pupils return to presentations in the next lesson when they evaluate multimedia presentations. We can only presume that it is the content of the presentation that they are working on here.

Lesson 11: Preparing a presentation for the user – features of a presentation

In this lesson the focus changes again. Now pupils consider the uses and features of a multimedia presentation.

Starter: Refining and presenting information

The teacher outlines the different ways in which presentations can be used.

> This is important information, as often alternative uses of presentations (such as a moving display or "kiosk" presentation) are overlooked.

Pupils then look at some PowerPoint presentation accessed via the Internet and evaluate them.

> There are some problems with the resources suggested. These are discussed on page 176. [11a]

The lesson notes contain a useful summary of the important features of multimedia presentations.

> Only 15 minutes is allowed for the teacher's input as well as the pupils' research. There are some very important issues to be considered here, and their discussion may take longer.

Development: Preparing the presentation

The pupils continue to prepare their presentation.

Plenary and homework: Successful presentation and review

The criteria for a successful presentation are discussed.

It will be useful to refer back to the attributes of effective presentations identified in the lesson starter.

Lesson 12: Preparing a presentation for the user

Now the focus is on the skills of the presenter, rather than the design of the PowerPoint presentation.

Starter: What makes a good presenter?

The starter is a brief discussion of what makes a good presenter.

This is a huge area of learning, and it is unlikely that a brief discussion will impact on pupils' ability to apply the points made. You could consider a more co-ordinated and dynamic approach to this, perhaps in co-operation with colleagues from other subjects such as English or Drama.

Development: Presentations

Pupils continue to prepare their presentations. The lesson notes suggest that they also prepare an evaluation sheet for the users of their system.

No guidance is given for this activity. You will have to decide whether it is the presentation or the system which is being evaluated, or both. See page 176. [**12a**]

Plenary and homework: Gantt chart review; and writing the script

Pupils review their Gantt charts and write the script for their presentations.

Asking pupils to write scripts for their presentations raises issues which are discussed on page 176. [**12b**]

Lesson 13: Presenting the solution to the user

The systems are tested by users.

Starter: Success criteria

There is a final opportunity to review the success criteria produced in Lesson 11 before the users test the system.

Development: Presentation to the user

The lesson notes state that each pair or group makes their presentation. This is the first suggestion of pupils producing a solution as a group. It is likely that paired work is the only possibility here.

Plenary and homework: Report

Pupils report to the class identifying one success and one improvement they need to make.

It is unrealistic to expect that these reports can be given in the 10 minutes allowed. There are likely to be a minimum of 12 and a maximum of 30 reports to be delivered, each addressing two aspects of the work. More time should be made available.

For homework, pupils add feedback to their project documentation.

Lesson 14: Completing and compiling project documentation

Starter: Success criteria

Pupils review their success criteria, making reference back to Lessons 1 and 2.

Development: Completing documentation

The main part of the lesson gives an opportunity for pupils to complete documentation.

Plenary and homework: Reflect on the process of completing a project

Pupils are asked to reflect on the process of completing a project.

Ten minutes are allowed for discussion and feedback on the whole unit of work The lesson notes end with an enigmatic "looking forward to Year 10". If pupils are to make the most of their learning in this project, a fuller discussion will be needed.

For homework, pupils complete their documentation of the project.

Alternative approaches

This is an interesting unit of work which provides opportunities for pupils to explore various ICT applications and develop models in a school-based context. The time available for pupils to develop their own work means that they have the opportunity to work independently, developing their own systems. While this is to be welcomed, there is little reference in the lesson notes as to how pupils will be supported to develop their own solutions. On some occasions, crucial planning and development work which is central to the success of the project, such as the design of a financial and seating plan, is set as homework. It is likely that many pupils would need support with this, so it should be completed in class. On another occasion, pupils are asked to design a poster or website as homework. While a poster may be a reasonable expectation in this respect, a website is not.

While the problem set in the unit may be appropriate, the expectation that most pupils will be able to produce models of the level of sophistication of the exemplars is unrealistic. Higher-attaining pupils should be able to complete the mail-merge activity, but bear in mind that they will need to be provided with a database and teaching materials in order to be able to do this.

Lesson commentaries

[1a] The aim is that the production makes a small profit. Pupils are told that there is information available about expenditure and income, but none is provided. Income presumably comes from ticket sales, and this will be modelled using the spreadsheet, but there is no information at all about expenditure. A number of items could incur expenditure including:

- production costs for scripts, music scores, materials, costume hire, set and prop construction and so on;
- licensing costs for copyrighted materials;
- staffing costs, such as overtime payments for caretaking, time spent by office staff on printing;
- premises costs, such as heating, lighting and cleaning.

It will be necessary to provide information on at least some of these costs, if the goal of modelling income and expenditure so as to arrive at a small profit is to be realised.

In reality, of course, there are additional costs and income involved, such as production and sale of programmes and refreshments on the night, sale of advertising space in programmes and so on. Pupils may raise these in the discussion, and you will have to make a professional judgement about how realistic their models can be. If some realistic figures are provided, pupils could use a spreadsheet to model income and expenditure to determine the cost of putting on the production. At the very least, they will need a notional figure of the overall cost of mounting the production, in order that they can establish a cost per potential seat sold and so make decisions about ticket prices. If there are no costs identified, then even one ticket sold would result in a profit.

[2a] As the notion of selling equal numbers of different types of ticket does not apply to school productions this could be rather confusing. Using the model, pupils are able to type "m" or "f" on to the dance floor and see the figures and calculations change.

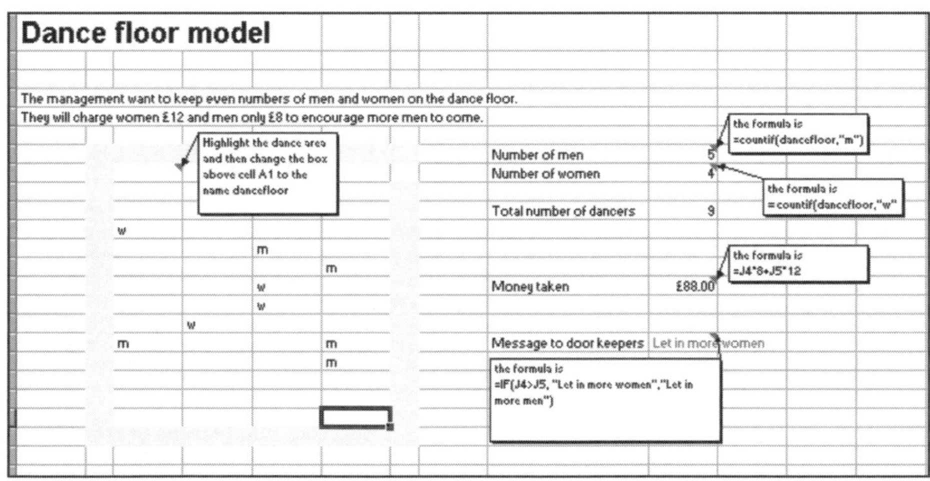

Pupil Resource 4

A connection can obviously be made with the sale of different types of seats for the production, so that specific seats can be reserved and the income updated. The model uses COUNTIF and IF statements and these will need careful explanation. If pupils are unlikely to be able to construct a similar model for themselves later it seems of little use to work through this model. You will need to decide whether this is appropriate for some or all of the pupils in the group. This context is returned to later in Lesson 4

[2b]/[3a]/[5a] You will need to determine how many seats the hall can accommodate. The exemplars in the unit are based on 220 tickets, but you could work with a different number if you wish.

The demands of this task, and its importance to the project as a whole suggests that it might be better if pupils at least began work on it in class, so that support can be given. The exemplar spreadsheets provided as possible solutions illustrate the demands of the task. It seems unrealistic to expect that most will be able to develop a model of the level of sophistication of the exemplars without considerable support. For example, these are suggested as possible model solutions that pupils might produce:

Finance solution 2

Drama production seat booking sheet

a	a	c	c	c	a	c	a	c	a		a	c	a	a	a	c	c	c	c	c
c	a	c	a	a	c	a	a	c	c		c	c	c	a	c	c	a	a	a	c
a	c	c	c	a	a	a	c	c	c		a	c	a	a	c	c	c	c	c	c
a	a	a	c	a	a	a	c	c	a		c	a	c	a	a	c	c	a	a	a
c	c	c	a	c	a	c	a	a	c		c	c	a	c	a	c	a	c	c	a
a	a	a	c	c	c	a	c	a	a		c	c	c	a	a	c	c	c	c	a
a	c	a	c	a	a	a	a	c	c		c	c	a	a	a	c	c	c	a	c
a	c	a	a	a	c	c	c	c	c		c	c	c	a	a	a	c	c	c	a
c	c	c	c	a	c	a	a	a	c		c	a	c	c	c	a	c	c	c	c
a	a	a	c	a	c	a	a	a	a		c	c	c	a	a	a	c	c	c	a
c	c	c	c	c	c	c	c	c	c		c	c	c	c	c	c	c	c	c	c

Number of adult seats sold	91
Number of concession seats sold	129

Cost of adult seats	£3.50	Total seats sold	220
Cost of concession seats	£2.00	Total seats unsold	0

the formula is =220-P21

Total money taken to date	£576.50
Overall Profit	£241.50

Teacher Resource 8

This model uses **=COUNTIF(Auditorium,"a")** or **=COUNTIF(Auditorium,"c")** to count the tickets sold and calculate the income.

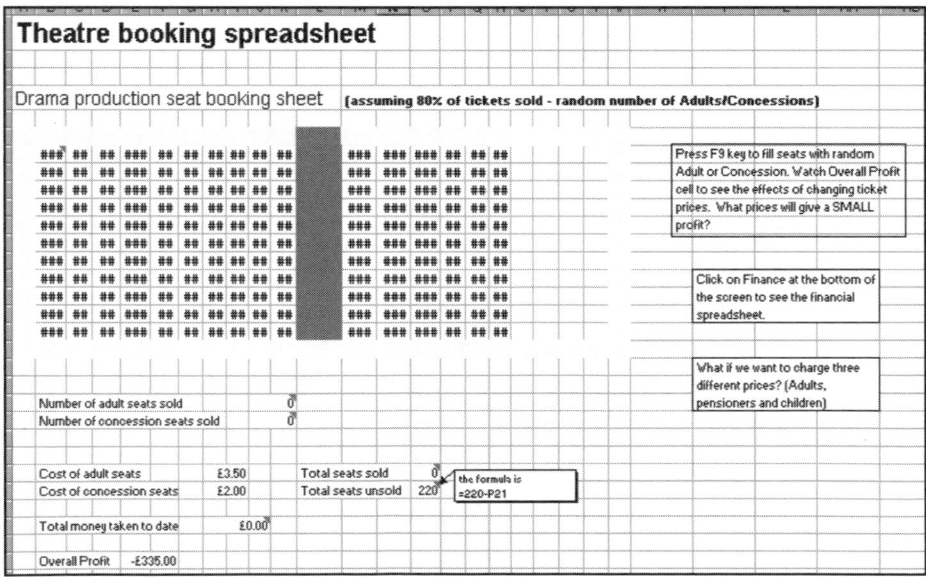

Theatre booking spreadsheet

Drama production seat booking sheet **(assuming 80% of tickets sold - random number of Adults/Concessions)**

###	##	##	###	##	##	##	##	##	##		###	###	###	##	##	##
###	##	##	###	##	##	##	##	##	##		###	###	###	##	##	##
###	##	##	###	##	##	##	##	##	##		###	###	###	##	##	##
###	##	##	###	##	##	##	##	##	##		###	###	###	##	##	##
###	##	##	###	##	##	##	##	##	##		###	###	###	##	##	##
###	##	##	###	##	##	##	##	##	##		###	###	###	##	##	##
###	##	##	###	##	##	##	##	##	##		###	###	###	##	##	##
###	##	##	###	##	##	##	##	##	##		###	###	###	##	##	##
###	##	##	###	##	##	##	##	##	##		###	###	###	##	##	##
###	##	##	###	##	##	##	##	##	##		###	###	###	##	##	##
###	##	##	###	##	##	##	##	##	##		###	###	###	##	##	##

Press F9 key to fill seats with random Adult or Concession. Watch Overall Profit cell to see the effects of changing ticket prices. What prices will give a SMALL profit?

Click on Finance at the bottom of the screen to see the financial spreadsheet.

What if we want to charge three different prices? (Adults, pensioners and children)

Number of adult seats sold	0
Number of concession seats sold	0

Cost of adult seats	£3.50	Total seats sold	0
Cost of concession seats	£2.00	Total seats unsold	220

the formula is =220-P21

Total money taken to date	£0.00
Overall Profit	-£335.00

Teacher Resource 6

This second model uses the formula: **=IF(RANDBETWEEN(0,1)=1,"a","c").**

Both solutions are dynamically linked to finance models on a separate worksheet. Both models have errors in cells O25 and O26 relating to the comments inserted.

An additional difficulty with the second model is that some cells appear at first to represent two seats (columns B to G) and some only one (columns H to K). A closer look at the model shows that data in columns B to G are copied to columns M to R, thus achieving the 80 per cent sales level. This is potentially very confusing for pupils trying to work out how such a model operates. The model can be explored by inserting "a" for adult or "c" for concession into the cells and then seeing the results. In this model the function key, F9, is supposed to generate random numbers, but this function does not appear to be set up properly.

These resources are intended for use by the teacher, rather than pupils directly, but even so they will need careful checking and revising and time given to work through the possible solutions. The expectation that pupils will create models like this is not a reasonable expectation, unless they are given substantial support. An exemplar solution is essential for pupils even though they may have access to it only temporarily.

Although Teacher Resources 7 and 8 are more straightforward, you will need to allow plenty of time for working through these resources if you are to use them to suggest solutions for the tasks.

[4a] As in Unit 8.4, it is questionable whether it is necessary to use RANDBETWEEN to generate numbers to test the model. Pupils could generate their own numbers based on realistic estimates of the numbers involved.

For example, for every ten Year 6 pupils attending with concessionary tickets there are likely to be 15 adult tickets sold, with another 10 concessionary tickets sold to younger siblings or grandparents. This would give a ratio of 15 full price tickets to 20 concessions, and pupils could work with a range of numbers fairly close to this approximation to test their models instead of using RANDBETWEEN.

[7a] One concern expressed about this activity in Unit 7.3 also applies here: that logos such as Becta's will not be familiar to pupils. An additional factor here is that some of the designs, the clip art frog and photo of the cow are not logos at all. A selection of real logos would be better. It will be important to stress to pupils that the comparison should be made between coloured and monochrome images, rather than images which are being projected, because the use of colour is the key difference here. The pupil resource makes reference to file size as a factor in the selection of images as logos, and this is something that the teacher will need to prepare and research if it is to be discussed.

[8a] Pupils' solutions are going to be used and tested in this lesson. The starter refers to the review of the models following this feedback. There are significant organisational issues which are not addressed explicitly:

- Have the models already been used by Year 10?
- Have arrangements been made for Year 10 pupils to attend for a part of this lesson?
- If Year 10 pupils are attending to use the models during the lesson then some time must be allowed for this and it should be written into the lesson plan.

Whatever approach is adopted, careful preparation is needed.

[9a] The comparison between the iMac and Barbie magazine covers is interesting, and has the potential to challenge pupils' assumptions and stereotypical thinking. The lesson notes identify ways in which the magazine covers both follow certain conventions, despite being aimed at very different audiences. One of the factors identified in the PowerPoint display for the pupils is that the "human face" on the cover boosts the sale of the magazine. The lesson notes are more honest and attribute this to the "female face", implicitly acknowledging the audience. This is a useful discussion point for pupils. Given the amount of discussion in this starter, ten minutes seems an inadequate time allocation.

[**10a**] Although not a difficult concept, the use of mail-merge is a technique which needs to be followed through in stages. The PowerPoint presentation (Teacher resource 13) comprises twelve slides. It would not be good teaching practice to show it to pupils and expect them to recall and implement the steps involved. The difficulties of using PowerPoint resources online or as printed handouts has been discussed as various points in this book. If pupils are to use mail-merge it is important that they are taught the process or that good paper-based support materials are provided for them to use independently.

[**11a**] The notes suggest three possible PowerPoint presentations for pupils to evaluate before beginning to create their own. These are:

http://edweb.camcnty.gov.uk/camgrid/heads/ColinHurdDfES.ppt
http://wsgfl.westsussex.gov.uk/grid+/Keystage2/DT/casestudies/londonmeed/Presentation.ppt
http://www.teachingideas.co.uk/ict/files/multimediapresentations.ppt

The first is a presentation about various school improvement issues intended for showing to Headteachers, and as such, is not particularly relevant to the pupils. The second could not be found on the Internet at the time of writing. The third is a presentation intended for pupils in Key Stage 2. It illustrates some of the more lively features of PowerPoint such as text animation effects and sound effects. Although it is an attractive presentation, it could be argued that these are not the aspects of the application that pupils will need to be encouraged to use. Also, some of the effects used, such as text animation letter by letter are not considered good practice in presentations.

Rather than using these examples, it might be preferable to put together a brief PowerPoint example yourself illustrating the features you want pupils to use. Alternatively, you could use good examples of pupils' own work in PowerPoint from Unit 7.1, from this unit or from work in other subjects.

[**12a**] Although not stated explicitly, it seems likely that it is the presentation, rather than the pupil's solution, which is being evaluated.

[**12b**] Once you have asked pupils to write a script for a presentation, it is likely that they will create a document that they will then read to their audience. Perhaps it would be better at this stage to try to establish better practice by asking them to make notes which they can use to structure what they have to say about their solutions.

Units mapped to National Curriculum for ICT

National Curriculum reference	Year 7 units	Year 8 units	Year 9 case studies
Finding things out **1) Pupils should be taught:**			
a) to be systematic in considering the information they need and to discuss how it will be used	7.1 7.2	8.1 8.2 8.3	9.1 9.2a 9.2b 9.3
b) how to obtain information well matched to purpose by selecting appropriate sources, using and refining search methods and questioning the plausibility and value of the information found	7.1 7.2 7.5	8.1 8.3	(9.2a) (9.2b) (9.3)
c) how to collect, enter, analyse and evaluate quantitative and qualitative information, checking its accuracy	(7.5)	8.4	9.2a 9.2b

Developing ideas and making things happen **2) Pupils should be taught:**			
a) to develop and explore information, solve problems and derive new information for particular purposes	7.4 7.5	8.1 8.4 8.5	9.2a 9.2b 9.3
b) how to use ICT to measure, record, respond to and control events by planning, testing and modifying sequences of instructions	7.6	8.5	9.1
c) how to use ICT to test predictions and discover patterns and relationships, by exploring, evaluating and developing models and changing their rules and values	7.4 7.6	8.4 8.5	9.1 (9.2a) (9.2b) 9.3
d) to recognise where groups of instructions need repeating and to automate frequently used processes by constructing efficient procedures that are fit for the purpose	7.4 7.6	8.4 8.5	9.1 9.3

Exchanging and sharing information **3) Pupils should be taught:**			
a) how to interpret information and to reorganise and present it in a variety of forms that are fit for the purpose	7.3 7.4	8.1 8.2	9.1 9.2a 9.2b 9.3
b) to use a range of ICT tools efficiently to draft, bring together and refine information and create good-quality presentations in a form that is sensitive to the needs of particular audiences and suits the information content	7.3	8.1 8.2	9.1 9.2a 9.2b 9.3
c) how to use ICT, including email, to share and exchange information effectively		8.1 8.2	9.2a 9.2b (9.3)

Reviewing, modifying and evaluating work as it progresses **4) Pupils should be taught to:**			
a) reflect critically on their own and others' uses of ICT to help them develop and improve their ideas and the quality of their work	7.1 7.3 7.4 7.6	8.1 8.2	9.1 9.2a 9.2b 9.3
b) share their views and experiences of ICT, considering the range of its uses and talking about its significance to individuals, communities and society	7.2 7.6	8.1 8.2	9.1 9.2a 9.2b 9.3
c) discuss how they might use ICT in future work and how they would judge its effectiveness, using relevant technical terms		8.2	
d) be independent and discriminating when using ICT	7.1 7.2 7.3	8.2	9.1 9.2a 9.2b 9.3

Breadth of study **5) During the key stage, pupils should be taught the knowledge, skills and understanding through:**	
a) working with a range of information to consider its characteristics, structure and organisation	All aspects of the Breadth of Study requirements are addressed throughout the three years of the strategy.
b) working with others to explore a variety of information sources and ICT tools in a variety of contexts	
c) designing information systems and evaluating and suggesting improvements to existing systems	
d) comparing their use of ICT with its use in the wider world	

Note: Units shown in brackets indicate partial coverage of the National Curriculum.